OCCUPATIONAL SOCIAL WORK

OCCUPATIONAL SOCIAL WORK

Bradley Googins, Ph.D.
Boston University
School of Social Work

Joline Godfrey, M.S.W.
Polaroid Corporation

Prentice-Hall, Inc., Englewood Cliffs, New Jersey 07632

Library of Congress Cataloging-in-Publication Data

Googins, Bradley
   Occupational social work.

   Bibliography: p.
   Includes index.
   1. Welfare work in industry.   2. Welfare work
in industry--United States.   3. Employee assistance
programs.   4. Employee assistance programs--
United States.   I. Godfrey, Joline.   II. Title.
HD7261.G66   1987   362.8'5   86–25514
ISBN   0–13–629445–6

Printed in the United States of America

10   9   8   7   6   5   4   3   2   1

ISBN   0-13-629445-6   01

Prentice-Hall International, Inc., *London*
Prentice-Hall of Australia Pty. Limited, *Sydney*
Editora Prentice-Hall do Brasil, Ltda., *Rio de Janeiro*
Prentice-Hall Canada Inc., *Toronto*
Prentice-Hall Hispanoamericana, S.A., *Mexico*
Prentice-Hall of India Private Limited, *New Delhi*
Prentice-Hall of Japan, Inc., *Tokyo*
Prentice-Hall of Southeast Asia Pte. Ltd., *Singapore*

CONTENTS

FOREWORD

Most textbooks induce sleep with circumspect accounts of the accepted wisdom in a given field. That is, they offer information so bland and unimaginative that students tune-out (and turn on rock videos for a little relief). This occurs because the purpose of most textbooks is to present a batch of theoretical information and useless facts that students can memorize and feedback at exam time. Hold your hats, this book is different.

First, it is about *real problems*. What could be more real (and important) than helping people to deal with the personal problems created in society and in the family that are brought into the workplace (like alcoholism, drug addiction, chronic depression and alienation)? And what could be more real (and important) than helping people to cope with the personal problems that result from the interaction between their tasks and their personalities? Dealing with those levels of real issues is the primary task of the occupational social worker, according to Bradley Googins and Joline Godfrey, the authors of this remarkable text.

Second, the book is not a narrow, provincial or conservative view of the profession. Instead, it seeks to enlarge the scope of social work by including not just the psychological issues that have been the traditional focus of the field, but setting the individual employee in the broader context of the organization and society. The authors show that an effective social worker can improve not only the employee's quality of life, but can have impact on the performance of the organization in which the individual works, and on the community in which the individual lives. Moreover, the social worker can change the organization, making it both more humane and more effective.

Thus, third, this lively book is about *change*. In the authors' view, the occupational social worker is not a "life adjustment counselor" who seeks to get workers to conform to intolerable working conditions, but a change agent whose goal it is to have healthy people working in healthy organizations. In short, the authors recognize that you can't have effective, motivated, committed and loyal workers in organizations that are run like sweatshops, prisons or boot camps.

Moreover, the authors know of what they write. Googins is a respected member of academia who grounds everything in these pages in sound scholarship. Godfrey is a successful business executive (in addition to being a trained social worker). She has put into practice everything that is prescribed in these pages, having done so both in the context of a very large, established corporation (Polaroid), and in a small, growing business that she herself created (Odysseum).

What I find so exciting about this book, then, is not just that it reflects the state-of-the-art in the fields of social work, occupational psychology, and business management, but that it creates the prospect that the occupational social worker can have real impact on real problems. The authors urge social workers to get out of their offices, and into the workplaces of their clients. In short, they treat occupational social work as a serious profession. And that's the way it should be treated. Read this book and you will want to get right to work helping people and organizations to perform more efficiently, effectively, productively, and humanely. In my experience, society needs tens of thousands of the kind of occupational social workers that Googins and Godfrey seek to train. May I urge you, then, to follow the authors' advice and get on with the challenge at hand!

James O'Toole

Professor of Management
School of Management
University of Southern California

ACKNOWLEDGMENTS

A book such as this which reflects the early stages of development of a field is subject to the cruelest fate of all: the passing of time. Since the early drafts, and indeed since the manuscript has been completed, the field of occupational social work has continued to grow and evolve in a manner unimagined just a few years ago. But such are the inherent dangers of trying to capture the essence of a quickly changing field.

Precisely because of these rapidly changing forces, we tried to draw on those in occupational social work who are on the front lines and consequently have the best feel for the currents and directions of occupational social work. We especially would like to thank Ruth Antoniades, Peggy Berry, Bruce Davidson, Dawn Harlor, Jim Lakis, Joan Lancourt, David Mercer, Jonathan Milton and Jim Wells among others who generally gave of their time while we picked their brains and examined their practice roles. Ellin Reisner deserves a special place for her enthusiastic support, creative ideas, and countless hours of interviewing. Dr. Paul Kurzman was also most generous in offering to read the drafts.

Writing this book has helped us to clarify the goals of the occupational social worker: to achieve balance in the provision of equality, liberty, justice, and excellence at work for workers, shareholders, host communities and consumers. Our analysis of these goals and desire to achieve them have been influenced by many people, including our families, who first showed us the powerful, positive influence work can be in the life process. Polaroid Corporation provided a laboratory setting in which ideas and theories could be tested. For the patience and tolerance of Leo Miller, John Harlor, Gerald Sudbey, I.M. Booth and the late Bill Rebelsky, we are grateful. We also thank Jim O'Toole, Bob Schrank, Barbara Toffler, and Chuck Powers for their support and guidance.

At Boston University support on all levels was extraordinary. Dean Hubie Jones could not have been more supportive, and on more than one occasion provided the time, resources and encouragement without which an undertaking such as this never finds the light of day. Clerical assistance of Mary Gill, Susan Bahrawy and research assistants Serena Shapiro and Kathleen Jordan have our eternal gratitude for their countless hours. In Sherborn, Ridgely and Nicholas were often resentful of lost hours together, but always supportive.

Finally, despite all this help, support, encouragement and caring, the two of us stand alone with the book. We hope it is useful and enjoyable, despite its limitations, and will be a contribution to the exciting world of occupational social work.

Bradley Googins
Joline Godfrey

Boston, Massachusetts

CHAPTER ONE
OCCUPATIONAL SOCIAL WORK
An Overview

INTRODUCTION

Over the past decade, a new set of innovations has evolved throughout
public and private institutions and unions in the form of human services in
the workplace. The programs in themselves are not new, nor do they address issues and problems unrecognized: alcoholism, drug abuse, stress,
marital problems, retirement, relocation, emotional illness, and change. It is
the *setting* in which these problems are recognized and dealt with that is
revolutionary. The line between the production goals of the corporation
and the human and social needs of the employee has traditionally been a
demarcation well defined and rigorously maintained. The concerns of work
and the problems of individual employees and their families, it has been
felt, are best viewed as separate worlds—a bit like our national thinking
about separation of church and state. The proliferation of human service
programs and the emergence of the social work profession in this setting
signals not only a softening of the distinctions between these two worlds but
an acknowledgment of a false dichotomy. Work and family, or the personal
and social lives of employees, do not constitute separate and unrelated
spheres. The changing demographics of the larger society (single parents,
dual career families, "baby boomers" entering the work place) along with
cultural and value shifts of the past twenty years have presaged new needs
and behaviors for workers. These developments have stimulated new responses in the workplace and on behalf of workers.

The Rise of Occupational Social Work

Until a few years ago, the concept and practice of occupational social work were virtually ignored by all but a handful of social workers. Although there is a history of social intervention in the workplace (antecedents of modern day social work practice in industrial settings could be found over a century ago), only within the past decade has any systematic practice emerged. In this brief period, a new client population has been identified, a field of practice has developed, and a new group of practitioners has taken its place as a specialty within the profession.

The rise of occupational social work, particularly in the past two to three years, is unprecedented. Seven years ago less than fifty practitioners could be identified. Today this number has swelled into the thousands. But it is not just this dramatic influx of practitioners that is notable; cultural and environmental shifts at work have been equally dramatic over the past decade, constituting imperatives for change that have brought the social work profession into new frontiers. Opportunities unimaginable a decade ago are opening up prospects for new and creative forms of practice. Social workers now counsel employees on a wide range of personal, family, and social problems; present policy positions on community relations to corporate executives; mediate disputes; develop and conduct stress management programs; and assist corporations on issues such as layoffs and retirement. These and other interventions stand as a monument to the responsiveness of the social work profession and its ability to identify and tackle new problem areas and population groups whose needs have previously been ignored or underserved.

The social work profession has strategically positioned itself to meet the growing range of human problems that affect the American work force. Employee assistance programs abound; traditional community health and human service agencies have begun to work with local businesses and industries; personnel and human resource departments, as a matter of course, examine the human factor within the work environment. Social workers have forged their way in assuming roles in training, social corporate responsibility, labor counseling, and health promotion and prevention, creating innovative programs and meeting the psychosocial needs of the work world.

All of this has not evolved without conflict and opposition. The introduction of social workers into the mainstream of a mixed capitalist system has raised considerable concern within the profession itself. For some, the social change goals embedded in the social work profession cannot coexist within the framework of American work organizations. For others, the dangers of being co-opted by the perceived values and goals of business and industry negate potential gains. Still other practitioners view the movement into the work world as a retreat from the public sector, embattled by the new federalism. In each of these perspectives, a distinct clash of values exists, pitting those who define workers and the workplace as an underserved and ignored population against those who fear that the embrace of such a field of practice runs contrary to the values of the profession itself. Although this conflict is as old as Porter Lee's early debate within the profession on cause versus function (1932), it has again surfaced as the occupational social work movement becomes a significant force.

DEFINITION

Exactly what constitutes the nature and boundaries of occupational social work continues to be elusive. Whereas the population seems easily identified, the client is difficult to determine. Though counseling troubled employees is closely akin to other social work roles, assisting a corporation in defining its social responsibility is not. While conducting employee assistance programs is a typical activity, developing a program on ethics for a company is not. The wide range of roles, functions, and programs that has developed continues to expand the scope of the field and contribute to the absence of a program typology, legitimate boundaries, and a definition encompassing the dimensions of the field.

In coming to a definition, consideration must be given to why and to what end social workers would operate in the world of work. On the most basic level, the work world is an arena for practice in which human and social needs arise. From this perspective occupational social work is no different from similar activities in schools, hospitals, neighborhoods, and numerous other settings. What differentiates the work arena is the novelty of this practice, its apparent clash with traditional social work values, and the relative ignorance of the profession of the milieu, i.e., work organizations and culture.

One way to understand the nature of human services at work is to question why the workplace would value human services. Unless there were some intrinsic value in having social workers provide services at the work site, businesses, industries, and unions would not find it in their self-interest to sanction these activities. Vinet and Jones (1981, pp. 22–23), in their survey of occupational social workers, reported two major factors which these social workers cited as key sanctions in work organizations. First were social problems already identified by:

> precipating events (violence, strikes, high turnover, high costs of recruitment, and low productivity) that may have been symptoms of problems that enhanced receptivity to social service programs;
>
> the top management conclusion that company survival during a recession rested on a manager's ability to motivate workers toward greater productivity;
>
> a key company leader's improved functioning as a result of counseling for personal, psychological, or alcohol-related problems;

legal or social mandates for services;

ignoring social conditions which lead to greater outside interference, more regulations, and increased "costs";

negotiating benefits for social services with unions.

Second was a valuing of employees in the corporate philosophy and culture.

These factors provide a background for understanding the role and function of human services in the workplace. While they do not specify what social workers can do, they do give information as to what the organization needs and why. In many instances, social work attempts to meet client needs by discerning the client's perceived problems and needs within a prescribed value framework. In the workplace, "starting where the client is" encompasses an understanding and acceptance of the organizational and the individual employee's needs. A systems perspective in the mode of family therapy is perhaps the most cogent analogy. This defines the needs of the system (organization and employee) as the starting points of social work practice in the workplace.

Throughout this book the term "field" is used to indicate practice parameters. Defining the activities as a field of practice, as in the field of occupational social work, implies a specialization or an area of interest. This terminology is often applied in professional circles such as law and medicine. In the instance of workplace practice it can only be used in the loosest of terms. This is not a clearly identifiable field, only a rapidly evolving practice that in time may well take on the more comprehensive characteristics of a field. At the present time the state of development is very rudimentary. What *it* is, is far from circumscribed, again complicating definition.

Even the label attached to practitioners who operate in this sphere is up in the air. The term *industrial social work* is avoided in this text for two reasons. First, *industrial* is a term derived from the European practice of social work in industry, which has limited relevance to today's work organizations. In addition, the move toward a postindustrial economy is well underway, and the use of the phrase "industrial social work" is fast becoming an anachronism. Second, social workers are not the sole practitioners found in workplace human service positions. While social work is the only profession to articulate a field of practice, many other professionals, quasi-professionals, and paraprofessionals occupy similar positions in companies. Because the field is in the process of becoming, no universally accepted standards have yet been adopted, and no profession or group, social work included, can lay claim either to a developed professional body of expertise or to the market itself. This is not the case in Europe, which will be described in a later chapter, where industrial social work has developed into a more defined and universally accepted practice. For these reasons, we have relied on the broader term *human services in the workplace*, although the specific practice by social workers will be referred to as *occupational social work*.

Finally, for the purpose of reference, if not argument, a concrete definition of occupational social work is proposed: ...*a field of practice in which social workers attend to the human and social needs of the work community by designing and executing appropriate interventions to insure healthier individuals and environments.*

Predecessors of current activities—welfare capitalism, the social betterment movement, and occupational alcoholism—have all left their imprints and contributed to the present state of human services in the workplace. The 1980s represent another stage of development for the American workplace in its attempt to balance employee needs and production goals. The emergence of human services for employees is part of a larger complex of forces concerned with the new values of the work force, a changed demographic, increased competition from abroad, and diminution of the welfare function played by government. All of these factors have become prominent at the work site over the past decade and continue to reshape and redefine the nature and function of work, workers, and work organizations. The rise of human services, consequently, is in part defined and shaped by these collateral factors, all of which have either forced or persuaded the work organization to incorporate human services as an integral part of its institutional system. What was once relegated to public and voluntary agencies now is being assimilated into corporations and unions in the form of entitlements thought to establish healthy and productive employees and environments.

MAJOR ACTIVITIES

As suggested earlier, human service activities that have developed over the decade under the *rubric* of occupational social work are difficult to codify, in large part due to the differences that exist among these activities. These differences are reflected by settings (unions versus corporate), functions (counseling versus policy development), and the level of intervention (macro versus micro). Nevertheless, it is possible to describe some of the type of activities that have evolved. Below is a sampler of occupational social work interventions. This is not an attempt to provide an exhaustive typology, but rather to point to the variation in programmatic functions that fall under the heading of occupational social work.

Counseling Programs

Counseling programs dominate occupational social work much as they do the social work profession itself. Early counseling programs tended to be singly focused and issue-oriented, often alcohol-related. "It seems that in the initial stage, social services are provided in the workplace to deal with one or two specific problems such as alcoholism or drug abuse. Management…may think that the solution is to employ a counselor to deal with these particular problems" (Ozawa, 1980).

In fact, counseling as a primary method of initial organizational entry has proved highly functional to relationship building and contract setting between the service provider and the workplace. Potential consumers of the services (employees), buyers of the services (management and/or unions), and social work professionals have an opportunity to establish norms, expectations, credibility, and respect around identified issues (e.g., alcoholism, retirement counseling, stress). While a comprehensive survey of social services offered by Fortune 500 companies has yet to be conducted, many existing programs have had their beginnings in single-issue service programs. As these programs have taken hold, broader, more comprehensive counseling programs have evolved. It should be emphasized that this form of workplace social service, i.e., counseling around a single problem area, is often a critical phase in the introduction of the social worker and the work setting to one another. The next stage of growth is a result of both the social character of the profession and the needs of the workplace.

Multiservice Programs

The 1979 Report on the Conference on Social Work Practice in Labor and Industrial Settings noted that

> …companies want the professional who is comfortable and sophisticated in advocating for their workers in the broader community. In addition to clinical skills they want a professional person who can represent their interests in a system-sensitive way in a society upon which they are dependent— for political sanction, customers, and a work force. Trade unions, likewise, want a helping professional who can document membership needs and be firmly committed to being an agent of change. Being a skillful service provider is always necessary, but rarely sufficient (Akabas et al., 1979, p. 34).

This statement is borne out in the multiservice programs that have evolved in companies like Digital Equipment Corporation, New England Telephone Company, Polaroid, Western Electric, and Northern States Power Company. The range of services offered by these companies, as well as by some unions, implies opportunities for both micro and macro interventions. With idiosyncratic variations, these companies offer under one umbrella a constellation of services including but not limited to:

COUNSELING

Group and individual
Referral and follow-up

Outreach
Crisis intervention

PROGRAM DEVELOPMENT
Substance abuse
Stress
Divorce/separation, education and support
Retirement counseling
Health promotion

CONSULTATION TO MANAGEMENT AND/OR UNIONS

Employee concerns and needs
Organizational and group dynamics
Policy input
Environmental sensing

RESEARCH

Demographics of service users
Comparative treatment effectiveness
Recidivism
Employee/system attitudes
Work and the family
Stress factors, support, and prevention
Effects of rapid change at the workplace

TRAINING AND EDUCATION

Management training
Substance abuse
Stress awareness
Communication

Social and Community Change Programs

Another group of program activities distinct from the multiservice program can be classified under social and community change. Included here are affirmative action, community relations, and corporate social responsibility programs. Social workers in these arenas often have a macro perspective on problem solving and on the introduction of change within the organization and between the organization and the larger community.

Affirmative action   The affirmative action department may be on the cutting edge of social change strategies, significantly impacting the work experiences of affected groups in the organization, (i.e., those designated as legally protected categories) or handling administrative responsibilities in a style that is either aggressive or protective of the status quo. Social workers employed in this area are involved in diverse roles, including administrative training, recruiting, policy development, research, and advocacy. Activities run the gamut from implementing affirmative action policies to monitoring and analyzing recruitment and hiring practices to involving the corporation in the legislative process around appropriate issues at state and national levels.

James O'Toole, chairman of the 1973 *Work in America* report and the author of the more recent *Making America Work*, states, "Diversity is the single most important factor in the American workforce" (1981). Daniel Yankelovich (1981) tells us that a generation ago a typical worker was a man working full-time to provide complete support for his wife and children. Today fewer than one of five people conforms to this standard. Given this radical change in workplace demographics and a 51 percent unemployment rate among minority youth, it is clear that affirmative action has an important role to play in helping American business recognize its organizational makeup, understanding the implications of those changed demographics, and building an organization more amenable to the diversity of people, values, and experience in today's workplace.

Community relations   Many companies today see themselves as citizens of the communities in which they operate. As host, labor pool, and neighbor, the community likewise has an abiding interest in the corporation. Therefore, as guest, neighbor, and force in the community, the corporation has much to gain from building a relationship of mutual respect with the community. Where once business decisions may have been made from purely economic or technological vantage points, increasingly they are made within a multidimensional context of factors: social, political, ethical, cultural, economic, and technological.

John W. Morrison, chairman and chief executive officer of Northwest National Bank in Minneapolis, stated it simply: "No business, no institution has an inherent right to exist. If a business is not perceived as responding responsibly to the needs and wants of its many constituents, it will surely have problems. Society either won't permit it or will put constraints on it in the form of laws and regulations, hampering it from performing its primary mission efficiently." (Corporate Brochure, 1983)

This function of relating the community to work organizations and vice versa has only recently been carried out by social workers at companies such as Digital Equipment Corporation and Equitable Life. Since the community has traditionally been the province of social workers, the field of community relations is well suited for social workers. Activities include assessing plant-community problems, developing programs that help the organization better understand the community, and working with minority communities to introduce new manufacturing operations within their borders.

Corporate social responsibility   A growing awareness of the interdependence between corporations and the larger society has spawned social corporate responsibility departments in many large companies. While only a few social workers have moved into these positions, the nature of the role fits the training and value orientation of the profession.

There is great diversity in this area within the corporate world, ranging from lip service to active leadership. In the city of St. Paul, Minneapolis, for example, a community ethic developed at the turn of the century which implies: "If you are to be a corporate citizen here you will also participate in the growth and responsible development of the community." Social responsibility as a business norm exhibits itself through corporate giving, consultation with city planners, and involvement with community organizations. Activities in this area include establishing and maintaining corporate giving programs; working with local communities on joint partnerships in housing, schools, employment training, and economic development; and assisting the corporation in involving its members in civic and community groups.

It should be acknowledged that the above-mentioned programs, like all programs with stated goals of human service or social responsibility, have potential to pacify constituents and maintain the status quo or to function as true agents of change in the continuing quest for conditions of human dignity and just community values. How that choice gets made is not simply a matter of what a corporate management thinks it wants, but is also determined by the ethics, values, commitment, and style of the individual directly responsible for a particular program. Social change does not necessarily begin with outside management; sometimes it starts with individuals from within.

Each of these examples represents new roles for social workers. Roles often eschewed because of the inherent tensions between the social change orientation of social work and the nature of large work organizations are increasingly synergistic as the complexities of our environment demand increasingly sophisticated responses.

Personnel/Human Resources

Another arena for social workers lies in human resource departments. The complexity of managing a work force with a mix of values, needs, and expectations, in environments (both natural and corporate) of finite resources and decreasing opportunities, has given rise to more sophisticated human resource management systems. Social workers are filling roles not imaginable ten years ago in this area. A list of job titles in which social workers are represented illustrates: organizational development specialist, benefits and compensation administrator (perhaps to be called entitlements manager in the future), project manager, educational specialist, trainer, communications specialist, personnel administrator, and relocation specialist. A common reaction to this list is "but those aren't social work jobs." In a traditional sense that is true. But the field of personnel/human resources has been forced to change from a world of hiring, firing, and administering benefit programs to one of creating and shaping and monitoring the work environment. Motivation, interpersonal relations, process, and healthy and productive work forces and environments are now the concern of human resource management.

To the workplace and these multitudinous roles social workers bring core social work concepts and skills:

a psychosocial understanding of individuals in relation to the environment
relationship building and contract establishment
use of the self as a tool
an ability to listen with the "third ear" (i.e. well developed diagnostic and assessment skills)
process problem solving

The social worker as human resource specialist represents a hybrid of social worker and personnel specialist, who is beginning to affect the direction and contours of the work environment.

MAJOR ISSUES CONFRONTING OCCUPATIONAL SOCIAL WORK

As social workers assume positions within the workplace and as the workplace comes to understand social work skills and knowledge, new applications of social work are emerging. In retrospect, what has occurred over the past several years has been more serendipitous than rationally planned and executed. The ideas and energy of a handful of innovative practitioners, rather than any rationally conceived plan by the profession, are primarily responsible for what has come to be titled "occupational social work." Likewise, the activities and roles generated in these early stages did not evolve from any carefully designed model, nor have they been universally accepted by the social work community. As isolated programs have become identified as a field, a number of issues have come to the fore, evoking responses within the profession ranging from mild questioning to outright denunciation of the occupational application as antithetical to the nature of social work. A few of the more persistent issues are briefly noted here; they will be examined in more depth in later chapters.

"Is this an appropriate setting for social workers?" A profession that grew up identifying with the poor and beleaguered has been at times indignant about offering aid to people who actually have jobs. Some social workers conversant with Marxist philosophy were hesitant to support a system — the workplace — they saw as essentially exploitive. Others simply felt that the profession had more immediate obligations to populations that were without the support of work. Strangely enough, many social workers did work with employed individuals or families in the context of settlement houses or private practice. Little attention, however, was paid to the working dimensions of their lives; it was assumed that family and social relationships were the only appropriate realms of practice.

Thus, for social work educators, writers, and practitioners, the proper realm of social work has been the family and the community. Schools, courts, hospitals, and street corners were milieus that were sanctioned. The milieu of work was not. As recently as the late 1970s student interns placed in work settings reported hostility from peers and professors. The persistence of some social work professionals who pioneered in the work setting, the growing sophistication of certain faculty members in schools of social work, and a developing body of knowledge that encompasses the nature of work, culture, and human development are finally changing this bias. Work-focused social work is becoming legitimate.

Social workers entering America's corporations in the roles of alcoholism counselors or clinicians, under the auspices of a labor union or management, set down their tools in a new environment. In these roles other questions have arisen:

To whom does allegiance belong? The client? The employer? The profession?

What are the limits of intervention?

What treatment methods are available and effective?

What responsibility do social workers have for advocacy and systems change?

Social workers have labored hard to develop relationships and establish contracts that would answer these questions in ways not offensive to their moral intuition on the meaning of responsibility in occupational social work. Over time, as work cultures have grown more familiar, these workers have developed relationships of respect and credibility that have allowed them to thoughtfully negotiate answers to the questions above. The answers vary from community to community, from hospital to hospital, etc.

In many companies the early contracts to provide clinical or single-issue services are evolving into more generic roles. As described earlier, social workers now work in affirmative action, human resources management, and labor and community relations. With the expansion of occupational social work, increasingly complex issues emerge and some of the old questions still beg debate.

What is an occupational social work identity?

In the face of competing claims and organizational pressure, how does one maintain the integrity of professional ethics?

How are client, role, and task identified in this system?

What are the skills needed to be an effective occupational social worker?

Where does the professional look for continuing education and development?

It is to the credit of the profession that the issues have become complex and increasingly sophisticated. Forums for professional debate are proliferating, a body of knowledge is growing, and an understanding of the worker and the workplace is emerging.

But there is one more area awaiting public debate: personal economics and job security. As public sector funding continues to decline, many social workers are looking to the private sector to fulfill their own work and economic needs. American corporations increasingly value and reward human resource skills, an attractive experience that few social workers in the public sector have realized. Thus, while the profession continues to wrestle with its ambivalence in moving into the workplace, individual professionals are drawn to the business world for economic security, job satisfaction, and recognition.

Unfortunately, a desire for economic and job security is insufficient to assure professional effectiveness in the workplace. Only a passion for learning about the meanings of work in people's lives, the ability to enter a foreign culture, and adequate training will insure the highest levels of professionalism. Just as the educational system has developed expectations for social workers in schools or as the study of gerontology has promoted quality work with the aged, it is time now to be concerned with curriculum development and standard setting for occupational social work.

The American workplace is experiencing radical cultural, technological, social, and economic changes. As social work becomes more conscious of its resistance and ambivalence to change in its own profession, it will be more proficient at responding to the diverse issues of its clients.

Clearly, the more deeply the profession enters the world of work, the more difficult the issues become and the more likely it is that conflicts will intensify. Effecting change in any organizational context is difficult; within work organizations, value dilemmas become all the more problematic. In the past decade, we have just begun to raise the most basic issues of social workers operating in work settings. The issues that emerge in the coming years will be determined in large part by how much further the profession steps into this practice arena.

THE NEW PRACTITIONER

As debate intensifies over the nature and appropriateness of social work within the workplace, many of the issues raised relate to basic questions: are social workers whose primary practice is within work settings in fact *doing* social work, or are they moving into a different profession? Do these social workers share the ideology and change orientation espoused by the profession and contained in the National Association of Social Work code of ethics? There are no answers to these questions because no systematic survey or occupational analysis has been carried out. Yet a certain suspicion exists that the goals and values of the profession are compromised.

Much of the uneasiness is derived from the profit-making nature of most work organizations. This is problematic for a profession whose public mandate and arena of practice have kept it separate and ideologically distant from the workplace. However, the value dilemmas confronting the occupational social worker are in reality no different from those facing social workers in public settings: Where does service end and advocacy begin? How does the practitioner balance professional ideals and institutional constraints and realities? Because the social worker at oil company Y reports to a board whose primary goal is maximum profits, it is assumed that all activities in the corporation, such as an employee counseling service, are directly related to that end. However, when we examine the social worker employed by a state department of mental health, we tend to oversimplify the goals of the common good while forgetting political and organizational realities.

Let's take as an example two practitioners, each of whom has a case load—one of oil company employees, the other of mental health patients within a state hospital. At company Y an employee seeking assistance for a marital problem incidentally details a practice of demanding excessive overtime of employees, who feel forced into quietly accepting, fearful of losing their jobs if they don't comply. Further investigation by the occupational social worker indicates the practice is widespread, yet subtle enough to be hidden and denied without a thorough expose. The social worker can ignore this exploitation or can risk his or her own position by bringing it to light and challenging the practice.

Now let's look at the social worker at the mental health facility. Physical conditions have deteriorated, due to lack of state appropriations, to the point where many of the professional staff fear for patient safety. To mount an effective campaign might require exposing the conditions, challenging the superintendent, and admonishing the state legislature. This action would also jeopardize the social worker's job and require an advocacy stand beyond the duties spelled out in the job description.

In both of these situations the need for institutional versus, or in addition to, individual change is clear. What might be labeled exploitation at company Y would be called negligence at the state hospital. While many social workers would be quick to find fault with the company Y case as an example of maximizing profit at the expense of employees, the state hospital case is equally, although not as obviously, problematic. Each practitioner faces institutional abuses which call for change.

The social work practitioner in the private sector has much in common with public sector social workers. In the Vinet and Jones (1981) survey of occupational social workers in the state of Washington, the majority viewed their roles as having particular relevance for resolution of immediate problems and did not see themselves as broad social reformers. This view, for better or worse, parallels that of social workers in most settings. The same survey, however, reported that work-based social workers felt criticized by their peers as being co-opted by and selling out to business and labor.

Perhaps these judgments and accusations are the cost of pioneering. Certainly the practitioner in these work settings is both an explorer and an entrepreneur. The workplace represents a gigantic and complex arena into which the social worker has tentatively moved, unsure of what kinds of needs exist and what degree of receptiveness awaits. Compared to other social work settings, the sense of isolation is acute, not unlike that felt by a missionary who has traveled into uncharted territory without support of colleagues. The workplace, while not hostile, is cautious, unsure what this person is here for or how best to use him or her.

The practitioner in the workplace has been challenged by the professional peer group and cautiously received by the client group. The development of program models or roles might best be characterized as muddling through a series of incremental steps, achieved primarily by sensing the immediate needs of the environment and creating mechanisms to meet them. As the remaining chapters point out, this process is both frustrating and challenging. For the adventurous and those who work well independently and with minimal structure, these positions offer an unparalleled challenge. For those who need established program boundaries and directives, the experience would be more frustrating. Regardless, these first developmental years have brought into existence a field of practice as diverse and innovative as any within the social work profession. While the tip of the iceberg has been exposed, it is the undiscovered and the potential that mark the future of human services in the workplace.

LOOKING AHEAD

While the first decade of occupational social work has been eventful, sparked by new program models, rapid growth, and the emergence of a new field of practice, the real challenges and the greatest potential lie ahead. The first decade has closed with occupational social work still very much in its infancy, familiarizing itself with a new environment and taking some initial steps into a relatively unknown new world.

In attempting to presage the future it is important to examine the social context that surrounds the development of occupational social work. There are several indicators to help guide this exploration.

1. *The economy.* It is somewhat curious that occupational social work experienced its initial growth in the early 80's during an economic downturn that many labeled a severe recession. With almost no exceptions, these programs were

not cut or eliminated when the economy worsened. The viability and usefulness of programs set up to deal with problems of alcoholism, drug abuse, and emotional and marital difficulties are demonstrated by their survival, and even modest growth, in bad times.

2. *The privatization of social services.* The advent of the new federalism brought an increased set of expectations of the private sector. Among these expectations is the notion of corporations becoming more involved and providing a greater share of resources and services. Regardless of what political shifts occur over the next several years, this movement toward the private sector has become a direction likely to persist for some time. The privatization of social services will increasingly draw social workers into the private sphere as both consultants and providers. If the federal social legislation of the 1960s and early 1970s laid the groundwork for government-sponsored growth in those decades, the new federalism doctrine lays the base and provides the incentive for privately based social services.

3. *Changing demographics.* The world of work is undergoing the most dramatic change since the Industrial Revolution. Fueled by the civil rights and equal opportunity movements and by changing economic conditions, work forces have changed, reflecting dramatic increases in women, single parents, and men whose organizational mobility is increasingly defined and influenced by working wives. In addition, other cultural influences are accompanying employees into the work site. Today's employee (and even more so tomorrow's) is finding a different balance between work and family, is looking for greater satisfaction and degree of decision making on the job; and is increasingly aware of geopolitical tensions in the larger environment, such as nuclear arms and economic survival.

4. *Issues in productivity.* Related to changing demographics is the quest for a renewed productivity. Challenges from overseas and the failure of short-term, profit-oriented management have confronted American business and industry with a major conundrum. To some extent, the issue of increased productivity lies within human perspective and not merely in technological failures or weaknesses. Occupational social work, growing out of a rich tradition in treatment of human behavior, understanding of group and community dynamics, and sensitivity to culture and environment, comes at a propitious time when new answers and structural change are being sought to move the American work scene into a new era of opportunity and productivity.

These factors contribute heavily toward assessing a positive role for social workers in the world of work. The challenge for occupational social work is to have a vision that goes beyond a micro counseling program and is positioned to meet the needs of this new client system. Ozawa (1980) projects four stages of social services: (1) single service orientation, (2) comprehensive services, (3) organizational intervention, and (4) community building. The first decade focused on stage one, with the beginnings of stage two just recently occurring (Akabas, 1978; Fine, 1982; Kurzman and Akabas, 1981).

Most activities in stages two, three, and four are macro-level activities requiring intervention and change in large systems. This has not been the dominant mode of social work practice, which has tended to follow a medical model, i.e., individually oriented practice. If, however, social work is to have a significant and lasting impact at the workplace, it will be in the area of organizational and institutional change. During the early 1960s, when work organizations were struggling with unparalleled growth and large-scale social change, social workers were unwilling and unable to respond to this need, and organizational developers moved into the vacuum. Even today the occupational social work community, flushed with the victory of establishing countless counseling programs, is primarily treatment-oriented, and a rush of treatment along medical lines could well freeze occupational social work into a traditional micro mode.

What, then, are the challenges that lie ahead? Consider the following possibilities.

Social work in its totality is relatively unknown to those in the world of work. On one hand are traditional stereotypes of social work and social workers. On the other hand, the activities of the first decade of occupational social work have served to inform and demonstrate the knowledge and skills of the profession. These programs and the efforts of individual social workers with unions, corporations, and other work organizations have initiated the crucial task of transmitting what social work is and how it can be useful in work organizations. The particular skills used in solving social problems are very much in demand, but they must be tried and tested in practice. This has begun to happen in areas as diverse as social corporate responsibility programs, training departments, corporate foundations, and human resource management departments. What has begun on an individual basis must now be organized purposely and deliberately by the profession itself. The multiple problems that workers and work organizations face are often compatible with the values and skills of social workers and within the interests of social problem solvers. For example, the following problems are currently faced by many industries, businesses, and labor unions:

    implications of demographic shifts
    balancing work and family roles
    preparing employees (and organizations) for the changes of retirement
    creating incentives for a better work environment
    terminations
    worker entitlement and responsibility
    better and more efficient use of health benefits
    health cost containment
    coping with individual and organizational stress

These are areas to which work organizations are increasingly turning their attention and in which social workers could have significant input and influence. There is now a gap between the human problems in work environments and the perceptions by organizational decision makers of the abilities and appropriateness of occupational social workers to alleviate those problems. Unless this gap is closed by entrepreneurial social workers and by continued communication of social work activities as has appeared recently in *The Wall Street Journal, The New York Times*, and *Business Week*, the potential of this field will be limited. However, if the growth witnessed in the first decade continues in the next, the profession will have to struggle just to keep pace with ongoing developments.

The challenge of institutionalizing the range of social services within work settings lies at a critical juncture. Because there is a rapidly growing awareness and consensus that a number of problems can and must be dealt with in the workplace, the question arises: who can and should provide these services? Social work is at a distinct advantage, both because of its ecosystem framework and because it has gradually assumed visibility and credence through its counseling and employee assistance roles. Attempts to move into new areas hinge upon the trust and competence established by this first generation of occupational social workers.

In the midst of this rosy picture, a few caveats would not be out of place. Many of the value conflicts discussed earlier will intensify over time. Visions of social reform and structural change, so intimate a part of the profession, will be confronted daily by the goals of the client system. While these conflicts are not substantively different from those of social work practice in the public arena, practitioners will have to look to the time-tested principles of beginning where the client is and building alliances so that ideals of social justice in the workplace can take root. Practitioners will be forced to develop patience that will allow this process, which needs time and the purposive and skilled efforts of the occupational social worker, to develop and take hold. Finally, these vanguard professionals will need the courage to test their own assumptions about what is "right."

In summary, the decade ahead can be seen as either an opportunity or a threat. The lessons of the early welfare capitalists discussed in the next chapter cannot be lost. The needs of working men and women are only now coming to the consciousness of the social work community, and the methods of meeting these needs are both ill defined and fraught with value conflicts. How the profession addresses these issues is yet to be settled. On one hand, there is the danger of xenophobia, by which the profession, because of traditional value dissonance with the world of work, refuses to embrace this environment and client population. On the other hand, there is the danger of a rush to treatment by which all problems become medicalized and treatment is confused with intervention.

By avoiding either extreme, social workers are in a position of almost limitless challenge. The world of work represents a core social institution whose members are faced with a variety of human and social problems. While its borders and doors have been closed to the social work profession in the past, the ground-breaking work of occupational social work has provided a model and a glimpse of future possibilities. The remainder of this book will explore in detail various aspects of this social work practice, its potential, and its challenges.

CHAPTER TWO
OCCUPATIONAL SOCIAL WORK
History, Development, and Definition

Occupational social work has historical and developmental roots in earlier programs and policies. This chapter examines the influences that have shaped the field and that account for the practice itself. It discusses historical precedents that have set the table for occupational social work; explains policy context by describing and analyzing the occupational social welfare system, a largely invisible one in which occupational social work is one element; and examines definitions of and assumptions about occupational social work.

At first glance the delivery of social services in the workplace seems a recent phenomena, primarily the result of the industrial social work movement of the 1970s. While employee assistance programs and affirmative action initiatives are new forms of social work practice, the attempts to meet the social and individual needs of employees have a history which predates the profession of social work itself.

HISTORICAL PERSPECTIVE

American Welfare Capitalism

The transformation of America from a largely agrarian society to an industrialized nation in the nineteenth century brought with it a new work experience. The rise of the factory, the urbanization of the population, and a flood of immigrants (largely rural peasants) converged in a new industrialization, representing an avenue into a new world of limitless horizons. In the short span of a generation, the country began moving from a society of farmers to an industrial complex, creating, in effect, a place of work different and separate from the home. This metamorphosis did not occur without great cultural and social changes. The early industrialists needed a healthy, orderly, behaved, and loyal work force; the uneducated immigrant was unsocialized to any norms of the workplace, often adjusting only marginally to an urban existence of squalor, sprawl, and density.

These conditions led early industrialists to involve themselves in the socialization of their employees. The impingement of social problems on the American business community became apparent from the social unrest of labor. Between 1880 and 1900, almost 23,000 strikes took place at over 117,000 businesses (Hanger; 1904). The combination of a labor force unsocialized to the working world and the constant threat of restless workers and visions of a workers' revolt led to the active involvement of industrialists in what has been termed "welfare capitalism."

From roughly the beginning of the post-Civil War industralization movement through the Great Depression, American business and industry have sponsored a host of programs aimed at creating a working and community environment that would insure healthy and productive employees while ameliorating the potentially disruptive conditions mentioned above. During this period, housing was build for employees and their families, schools were established, churches were constructed, medical care was provided, pension funds were introduced, recreation centers were established, magazines were published, and profit sharing and stock ownership were introduced. Just about every problem discussed under today's social welfare programs was addressed by industrialists in this early form of welfare capitalism. Alcoholism is a case in point demonstrating the extent of this welfare system.

Welfare Capitalism and the Treatment of Alcoholism

Early American capitalists struggled long and hard with men whose rowdy drinking and carousing carried into the factories and undermined values that owners relied on to maintain a loyal, virtuous, and, above all, hard-working labor force. Consumption of alcohol was an activity that interfered with the goals of an industrial society and the pragmatism of economic efficiency. In contrast to today's widespread strictures against drinking on the job, earlier industrialized work sites were often the locus of drinking, in many cases condoned and paid for by companies in recognition of immigrants' drinking practices (Sinclair, 1962) or as a reward, as was the practice on ships. It was not until the influence of the temperance movement that drinking on the job virtually disappeared from the American workplace. The moral crusades of the temperance movement, cries for industrial efficiency espoused by the Taylorists, and liabilities under the newly enacted Workman's Compensation laws combined to create new policies in which alcohol and employee drinking were banned from the workplace.

Though responses by companies to the problem of alcohol were sporadic and idiosyncratic, they were far from isolated. Company newsletters were used for not-so-subtle education campaigns. Sears and Roebuck, for example, exhorted its employees to substitute the virtues of diligence and thrift for the evils of drinking and smoking (Emmet, and Jevek 1950). Henry Ford employed harsher methods, hiring a corps of investigators who made home visits every six months to examine many aspects of employees' lives, from English language proficiency to amounts of life insurance. He also required an assessment of habits, including the degree of alcohol consumption (Brandeis, 1976).

In an increasingly organized approach to intervention, the rise of company doctors and nurses became important in combatting the alcohol problem. Often doctors were held with great suspicion by workers and not without reason, since they often determined whether the company would pay for an illness: their power was considerable. This was particularly true for alcoholism. A manager of Proctor and Gamble, for instance, declared that his company would pay disability benefits only in the case of bona fide sickness. He then defined real sickness as a willful act of the employee and specifically excluded illness "as a result of going out and getting drunk" (Brandeis, 1976, p. 98).

Alcoholism is just one example. What developed during this period was an attempt to harness the raw and—as generally perceived—crude habits and life-styles of employees to the needs of an efficient industrial machine. What evolved to meet this need was a forerunner of modern day occupational social work. Rooted in blatant sexism, this effort was initially aimed at the large number of female factory employees. "It is of great interest to note that much of the industrial movement was 'womaned' since men still clung to the dominant value of being close to the land. Consequently it became very difficult to attract the non-immigrant male population to this new industrial worksetting." (Brandeis, 1976, p. 148).

Probably the first industrial social worker was Mrs. Aggie Dunn, hired in 1875 as "social secretary" for the H. J. Heinz Company of Pittsburgh. For the next fifty years, "Mother" Aggie Dunn interviewed, hired, counseled, and generally watched over her twelve-hundred girl brood at the pickle-packing firm (Miller and Coghill, 1964, p. 35).

From these early gender-bound functions, industrial social workers (then called social secretaries or welfare workers) broadened their practice to encompass entire work groups, bridging communication gaps between employers and employees and assessing the needs of the environment.

...an early and key instruction to welfare workers was simply to establish contact. This could be done by following the foundryman's advice, "Meet them while at work: meet them out of hours." And meet them social workers did sometimes through an ambitious schedule. Clara Kenyon of the Olympia Mills of Columbia South Carolina took as her first task the meeting with every employee at her home; the expedition required her to visit 500 houses. Regular contact was built into the instructions. Edgar Adams, general superintendent of the Cleveland Hardware Company, instructed his welfare worker to visit each employee within a week after the employee began work, and at least one year after thereafter (Brandeis, 1976, p. 112).

As the function of social secretary faded, welfare capitalism flourished to become a more organized movement by the first several decades of the twentieth century. Its aim was to block the formation of unions by developing appealing company-sponsored services that would, in effect, persuade wavering employees that unions were not really necessary. Though the strategy ultimately faded and failed, its impact on the future was cemented. The social welfare tradition embraced by the early capitalists was incorporated several decades later into a new discipline, the personnel specialist (Sloane, 1983, p. 10). Consequently, responsibility for employee welfare, work satisfaction, and environmental fit encompassed by the first industrial social workers was passed on to personnel departments and more recently to human resource departments. What began as socializing, then union-curbing and paternalistic, became in later decades negotiated rights and expected benefits.

The pall that hangs over the historical roots of occupational social work as a result of social welfare capitalism should not be overlooked or underestimated. The ultimate failure of welfare capitalism lay in its inherent paternalism and its lack of respect for worker autonomy. Because social workers participated in this movement, they have inherited its negative associations. Even the prototype of the activist social worker, Jane Addams, was at times allied with this movement, praising the National Cash Register Company for its welfare program and using her influence to promote similar programs in other industries (Roger, 1978). This association engendered animosity between unions and social workers, particularly since many early social workers were wives of industrial capitalists. For all the activism of social workers in the social reform movement early in this century, there was a dark side of social work which naively colluded with industrialists to diffuse and weaken the forces of unionism. While modern-day occupational social work can be traced to a different ideological base, it cannot entirely disassociate itself from these roots. These beginnings also serve as a caveat to modern practitioners of the delicate balance between serving the human needs of working people and meeting the production and profit goals of any work organization. The dilemma is on going and serves to keep the practice honest and to intensify awareness of the dynamics operating within the American workplace.

The Human Relations Movement

The second building block for human services in the workplace was the human relations movement. This ideology was promoted in the 1930s and 1940s primarily as an antidote to the mechanistic and faceless Taylorism, which emphasized individual competitive performance measured by time and motion studies (Taylor, 1911). The human relations school of thought attended to how individuals felt, viewing this as an important part of workplace behavior and performance.

> The ideology embedded in the Human Relations movement suggested a shift in orientation and strategy. The easily taught simple techniques of Taylorism had not solved the problem of securing voluntary employee cooperation, which still loomed large as ever. The well-known Hawthorne Studies (Roethlisberger and Dickson, 1939) made this evident and provided some new guidelines for solving this problem. The studies suggested—and the Human Relations movement came to espouse—that performance was a result of how employees felt they were targeted, and how they felt about their work, their co-workers and their supervisors. As one analyst has suggested: it "reduced social and organization issues to personal troubles" (Brawn, 1978, p. 367; Trice, 1984, p. 248).

The human relations movement paved the way for human services at the workplace and provided an alternative to the "work or be fired" ideology. It sought to satisfy security needs through fringe benefits that protected the employee from sickness, accidents, old age, loss of job, and other external threats. In addition it encouraged management to adopt a more humane world view, supporting and working with groups of employees to meet needs for belonging, dignity, and even participation in problem solving and decision making. While many have charged this movement with the same manipulations and paternalism of welfare capitalism, it is nevertheless integral to most personnel practices today.

Human services at the workplace have evolved directly out of the human relations ideology. Values, assumptions, and goals of human service programs in work organizations are both compatible with and dependent upon that ideology. In particular, human services at the work site are strategies to mold concern and caring and to meet social needs, with a concomitant increase in productivity. Bartell (1976) saw the human relations movement as a response by business and industry to a host of environmental pressures:

> a broad social movement emphasizing the social responsibility of industry and desire by industry to prevent government from legislating such responsibility;
>
> development of psychological theory stressing higher human needs and the importance of being fulfilled (job satisfaction or a sense of purpose);
>
> growth of labor unions;

increased size of organizations and resultant bureaucratization with greater spans of control (with the resulting problems of maintaining control);

improved education of workers and higher worker expectation;

specialization of workers and greater costs of training;

emergence of a specialized group in industry whose role was to negotiate between labor and management (Bartell refers to this group as a "prime consumer of human relations ideology");

belief in an industry maxim that "a happy worker is a more productive worker," with a corresponding investment of money in studies to that effect;

institution of industrial relations schools in major universities, often subsidized by industry

The compatibility of social services in the workplace with the human relations movement is evident in light of these factors. Closing the gap between work and the outside environment produces a work environment where the individual interacts with other individuals in a human dimension and the nonwork worlds of employees become less and less distinguishable from the work worlds. The two-world myth (Kanter, 1977) becomes most improbable in the ideology of the human relations movement. This development set the stage for the legitimacy and function of occupational social work.

Occupational Alcoholism and Employee Assistance Programs

The third significant development leading to social services in the workplace is the development of the occupational alcoholism program (OAP) and the employee assistance program (EAP). These programs have become significant only in the past five to seven years. Nevertheless they have served as a phalanx and a ground breaker for both the social work profession and the introduction of program models and services. Prior to this movement occupational social work was limited to a handful of idiosyncratic programs in a few industries and schools of social work. With the advent of the OAP/EAP, human services at the workplace were able to gather momentum and establish a legitimacy of their own.

The first OAPs were formed in the 1940s. As business and industry strengthened institutionally, new mechanisms for dealing with alcoholic employees emerged, and a unique set of interventions was tailored to the needs and dynamics of the workplace. The primary goal of these programs was to assist alcoholic employees by identifying the alcoholism and getting them into treatment and self-help groups such as Alcoholics Anonymous.

The emergence of EAPs in the 1970s represented a new strategy and an expanded version of OAPs. The EAP introduced a so-called broad brush or expanded scope which reconceptualized the OAP into a program in which job performance criteria legitimated other emotional, personal, and behavioral-medical problems as part of staff responsibility. These two program types will be discussed in greater detail in the next chapter. Suffice it to say for now that the EAP placed alcohol abuse in a broader context, and the perceived negative drawbacks of the OAP (alcohol stigma and unrealistic supervisory functions) were countered by the EAP through programmatic and ideological shift. Though arguments over these two models still exist (Roman, 1981), the majority of programs have been influenced by the National Institute of Alcohol Abuse and Alcoholism strategy and have adapted the EAP model.[*]

Federal initiatives of the early 1970s, aided by occupational program specialists within the privately funded National Council on Alcoholism, were the catalyst for rapid adoption of the EAP model, which shows every indication of strengthening. A professional organization, the Association of Labor and Management Administrators and Consultants on Alcoholism (ALMACA), was begun with NIAAA assistance. Today it underscores the field's growth, serving the vast majority of EAPs with a network of four thousand members.

THE OCCUPATIONAL SOCIAL WELFARE PERSPECTIVE

The predecessors of occupational social work can be traced to the needs of work imperatives, i.e., an orderly work force. An understanding of this context is aided by examination of the little-discussed and little-analyzed system of occupational social welfare.

Although the common perception of the welfare system relates to public programs and services, the fact is that the largest and most extensive welfare system is located in the world of work. The system of benefits and services which we refer to as the *occupational welfare system* stands alongside both the public and the private voluntary systems as a quasi-silent partner in meeting the social and human needs of our society. This curious amalgam of profit-making capitalism and an array of social benefits constitutes a unique and critical part of the social welfare system.

The almost universal lack of acknowledgment of the occupational social welfare system, in light of its status as a genuine partner with the public sector, is indicative of both cultural social biases and a failure to grasp the pluralistic nature of our society and its complex social welfare system.

The occupational social welfare system is defined as a system of benefits and services directed at social and health needs of workers, provided in and by the occupational setting. These benefits and services are distinguished from those provided by either the public or the private voluntary sector in that entitlement is a function of employment in the work organiza-

---

[*]For the purpose of clarity we will continue to refer to all work-based programs for alcoholics as EAPs, keeping in mind the absence of any universal program type.

tion or membership in the union (Weiner, 1971). The practice has been referred to as *American welfare capitalism* (Brandeis, 1976) or *occupational welfare structure* (Titmuss, 1968), among other terms. In essence, the system provides health and social services above and beyond wages or salary. Some benefits come from legislation in the public sector; others result from the policy of a particular company or union. Regardless of their origin, all are sponsored and financed by the work organization, thus constituting a separate occupational welfare system. Consequently, for those Americans who work, a package of benefits and services is available which is theirs only as a consequence of their work role. Not surprisingly, the extent and nature of this system differs within and between work organizations. The system is not based on equity or arranged within a framework of just rewards. Instead it is created from a complex of negotiated settlements, demands of enlightened self-interest, and publicly mandated policies. This unevenness presents problems, which must be examined in light of the larger social welfare system and within the broader context of how society cares for its members. But at this point let us turn to the nature and functions of the occupational welfare system.

Occupational social welfare is nearly as old as the beginning of industrialization. The welfare capitalism movement described earlier was defined as "anything for the comfort and improvement, intellectual or social, of the employees, over and above wages paid, which is not a necessity of the industry, nor required by law" (U.S. Bureau of Labor Statistics, 1919, p. 8). This movement, initially modest in scale, met a host of workers' needs, particularly at large industrial sites. Housing, day care, education, recreation, pension, profit sharing, and medical care were well developed in many companies by the early part of the twentieth century. The ultimate form of this early welfare capitalism resulted in company towns, which were built, financed, and serviced by the employer for employees and their families. Literally everything in the town, from stores to libraries to worker housing, was provided by the company. While this began on a small scale, it soon reached dramatic proportions. By 1916, at least 1,000 firms had provided housing for over 600,000 employees and their families; this constituted almost three percent of the population of the United States (Brandeis, 1976, p. 38). This surpasses any public housing program ever undertaken by the public welfare system.

What was remarkable about the occupational welfare system in this early period was its size and autonomy. All these services and benefits were available before the onset of major public sector programs, and in an era when government was very much in the background. By the 1920s the primary institution for meeting social needs was the workplace. While the private volunteer sector was very much part of the picture, it was the occupational sector which stood in the forefront. Almost all needs that the public sector addressed in subsequent decades can be traced back to the efforts of the early capitalists.

Driving Forces

There is nothing inherent in either the American economic system or human nature to account for the development of a welfare system within the workplace. Nevertheless, there are several forces that account for the rise of this system and its place within our society. These are the demands of an industrialized nation, the rise of unions, and the functions of fringe benefits.

Demands of an Industrialized Nation   The cultural values that underlie the founding of America and the establishment of its political and economic system are independence and self-sufficiency. These values formed an essentially residual social welfare system which argued for social policies that would meet human needs on an emergency basis, only when other mechanisms such as the family and the economic sector had failed. Formulated and conceptualized in an agrarian society, these values and policies were woefully inadequate in the context of industrialization, immigration, and urbanization.

Providing for the welfare of individuals was an essential part of the American experience. From the earliest incidents of almsgiving to the organized efforts of the late nineteenth-century charity organizations, America has had deep cultural commitment and proclivity toward eliminating human misery and eradicating pauperism. This altruistic bent, entwined with American ideals, constitutes an essential part of the American character. But as the institution of work moved people from the farm and the home and as industrial technology and specialization led to the emergence of occupations, professions, and worksites, residual concepts of charity were inadequate to meet the social needs of workers. The private/voluntary sector was intended to meet emergency needs and was inadequate in the face of a growing need for institutionalization of services that could assist the family in carrying out the social demands of society. For example, education, once adequately handled at home by the flickering light of the fireplace, now required greater sophistication to respond to the needs of the workplace. The family, in terms of both time and resources, was unable to meet these needs alone.

Before government assumed some responsibility for meeting these needs, industry carried the load. In 1929, for example, of the 147 textile mills in North Carolina not located where children could attend established schools, 129 mills voluntarily subsidized education to some degree (Brandeis, 1976, p. 34). In later years when the government assumed responsibility for institutionalizing social welfare needs such as education, the occupational system worked alongside the public system, both instigating services and providing them on a more institutionalized basis.

As long as the dominant philosophy of social welfare services remains residual, the occupational welfare system will stand firm. The complexity of an industrialized society (and especially that of the postindustrial society) requires a myriad of institutional services if the economy is to be peopled by healthy, productive, trained individuals. The occupational arena itself depends on a finely tuned and productive labor pool. If the public social system does not or will not meet these needs, industry and business will, by necessity, have to provide ongoing services and programs.

Unions   Organized labor unions play a critical role in the occupational welfare system. Deriving their mandate in part from their roots in guilds and benevolent associations, unions forged a role of protection and advocacy for the economic health and welfare interest of their constituents. In the course of this development, unions argued and negotiated for, as well as sponsored, many of the programs and services of this welfare system. This inner-directed movement continues to characterize the occupational welfare system.

Ironically, a primary goal of early welfare capitalism was to stop unions from forming in factories. It was hoped that company benefits would be effective deterrents, winning over the hearts and minds of laborers who might envision a better world through unions. As a matter of record, the great birth of unions on a widespread basis occurred during the 1930s, when the last vestiges of welfare capitalism were receding and glaring failures of the system were fast appearing and causing its unraveling. As unions gained favor, the issues of wages, working conditions, and job security were at the top of the agenda. But soon to follow were vacations, health insurance, pensions, and a host of other benefits.

The dialectics of labor-management relationships became an integral part of work institutions. Although no more than 30 percent of the work force has ever been unionized, organized labor set the stage for the adversary nature of the employer-employee relationship, assumed leadership, and broke ground for social welfare benefits through which all employees ultimately gained. The very nature of independent entities, i.e., the union arguing for and protecting membership priorities and management equally and forcefully making the case for maximum profit and productivity, instituted a conventional process of bargaining, negotiating, and defining workplace policies. It was within this adversarial process of self-seeking that the occupational welfare system took form. The system emerged as the result of the give-and-take between labor and management.

Fringe benefits   The third factor driving the occupational social welfare system is commonly called fringe benefits, those perquisites and benefits that employees receive in addition to financial renumeration of salary or wages. Systems of fringe benefits vary both within and between industries or work institutions and can include such contemporary items as tuition remittance, transportation, day care, and personal leave days, along with the more traditional pension benefits, social security, health insurance, vacation time, and sick days. The fringe benefit package is a mainstay of the occupational social welfare system, providing employees with benefits and services designed to meet their social and health needs.

The origin of these benefits can be traced to the late nineteenth century, but a real growth spurt came during the wage and price freeze of World War II, when unions claimed nonsalary items for their membership. This proved to be a gold mine for unions and management, and it legitimized the scope of the occupational welfare system. In effect, all employees have two systems of renumeration for their labor. One provides a monetary payment; the other assures nonfinancial benefits. This dual system recognizes the need and establishes the basis for employees to enter the market economy to purchase goods and services through direct financial payments. It also addresses various health and social concerns of employees and their families through an economy of scale that employers can realize by sheer numbers.

The status of fringe benefits has been widely debated and is aptly summarized by the title of Donna Allan's book, *Fringe Benefits: Wages or Social Obligation.* "In the modest name of 'fringe benefits' a whole system of social benefits has been developing in private industry, reported in the press in bits and pieces and known more by its extent than by its nature and significance" (Allan, 1968, p. 3). This statement marks the beginning of the expansion of fringe benefits during the 1970s to the point where many companies are "yelling 'uncle.'" The growth of services in the public sector during the 1960s was followed closely by this growth of occupational benefits. As the 1980s progress both public and private sectors are feeling the effects of a changing economy, and in the occupational area fringe benefits are receiving the bulk of the scrutiny. When General Motors found that it spent more for its health insurance benefits than for the steel that went into its cars, it became concerned.

Obviously, the issue of fringe benefits is complex. It is not the purpose of this chapter to examine it exhaustively, but merely to point to its importance in the occupational social welfare system. Fringe benefits form the crux of this system and as such contribute to the delicate balance between public, private, and occupational sectors in meeting the social needs of individuals and families.

Parameters of the System

The occupational welfare system exists primarily as a functional interchange between employees and employers. Employers need a system to insure a productive work force whose social needs are met to the extent that production is not substantially hampered. In this sense, today's employers are not substantially different from their predecessors, the American capitalists, in their intent to provide basic benefits. Employees, on the other hand, tend to view this same system as either an extension of benefits and due compensation for their labors or, in the case of organized labor, as bargained benefits for maintaining organizational loyalty and support. Benefits, which have developed on a parallel with public sector social programs in the 1960s and 1970s, have become as important to employees as salary and wages. They have, in fact, become a major determinant for employees and their families in considering specific jobs, companies, and industries.

The mutual needs of employees and employers have in large part accounted for the existence of this occupational welfare system, but it is by no means a simple system explained by a mutual exchange theory. The complexities of labor-management relations within the American economic system and in the context of a democratic society suggest some of the broader parameters. Add to these the variants of union and nonunion work sites, regional differences, and historical and cultural variations between and within companies. What particular benefits and services a family receives will depend to some degree on the company, union membership, one's occupational group(s), employee's area of the country, and whether the employee is paid a salary or hourly wages. All of these variations are accidents of a welfare system that has been created and maintained not by coercive mandates or by a centralized, organized umbrella agency, but by principles of self-sufficiency. There is little pretense of achieving equality among recipients, of insuring that a base of services is a right of all employees. Historically just the opposite has been exposed and promulgated: each company, operating in an essentially competitive environment, provides particulars of its occupational welfare system primarily through the principles of programmatic competition. What services must be provided to remain competitive, in terms of both expense, which relates to profit margins, and attractiveness, which relates to recruiting and maintaining employees, are the determinants. Several years ago, for example, a large electronics firm conducted a feasibility survey on provision of child care for its employees. After several months of investigation, its board of directors decided against the plan. Employees, after receiving word of this decision, created such a clamor that the decision was reversed. Provision of this benefit came about primarily because of a high level of competition among electronics firms for highly skilled engineers and through the pressure of the employees themselves. Thus, the unique dimensions of a particular occupational welfare system change over time as the forces of the marketplace come into play. These same forces account for markedly different benefits among companies and even among industries. What is happening in one airline, for example, directly affects another airline. An industry as a whole often has an occupational welfare system more similar among its members than between it and other industries. What is unique to this welfare system is not only its location within the world of work, but also its role in providing welfare benefits to the majority of Americans. Contrary to popular belief, most citizens depend on this system rather than the public system for their welfare. So stigmatized is public relief or welfare that any intimation that benefits and services provided in the workplace are part of a public welfare system evokes denials and denunciation. But this system plays a vital role in the overall national welfare scheme.

Take, for example, retirement provisions. Every society must deal with its members who can no longer take part in the production process because of illness, disability, or obsolescence. Regardless of the reason, in a fundamentally moral society some provision will be made. Prior to the 1930s and passage of the Social Security Act, the concept of retirement was practically nonexistent. Life expectancy was considerably lower and those who worked did so until health gave out. Care for those unable to work was seen as a family responsibility, and the extended family provided for the retiree until death. With increased industrialization, the obsolescence of the extended family, increased life expectancy, and establishment of mandatory retirement age in many businesses, the need to make provisions for those moving out of the workplace came to be perceived as a social responsibility. Although relatively few are able to provide for retirement years through private means, the vast majority of workers depend on a combination of Social Security and pension plans, two of the occupational welfare system's major benefit programs. To take part in these, an individual must be attached to a place of employment. It is through an occupational role that an individual can receive such benefits.

That these welfare benefits are work-related is at the crux of the occupational welfare system. Through a contributory system a portion of employee wages is deducted and is supplemented by the employer. To view this as welfare may seem to be stretching a point, since the individual worker actually contributes to the Social Security fund. Nevertheless, as others have pointed out, the general acceptance of Social Security as an insurance plan is tied into the American ethos of work and self-reliance (Romanushyn, 1971). By conceptualizing the program under a private notion of insurance, the stigma of welfare is avoided. Although many aspects of the system do resemble private insurance, most workers receive far in excess of what they put in, reinforcing the argument that this benefit is part of a welfare system.

Pensions, although a newer development and far less widespread, constitute a second benefit for the retired population. These have a distinct private emphasis, unlike Social Security. Both employer and employee contribute to the system, which is managed by private banks, insurance companies, and professional money managers. Unions have similar funds. Benefits are paid out based on contributions, years of participation, and actuarial tables. Public sector involvement is of a purely regulatory nature, insuring that employee rights are protected against unreasonable vesting qualifications and unfair terminations immediately prior to vesting eligibility, and providing contingencies for work organizations that go out of business.

Both of these benefits are aimed at providing for and protecting the retiree. But, to benefit, one has to be in a workplace and meet minimum requirements. Otherwise, provisions for retirement fall to either an individual's private resources or the largess of the voluntary sector. If companies and unions were concerned solely with wages and issues of productivity, those separated from the workplace would be forced to rely on themselves and their families or to have the public sector assume total responsibility. Thus, either by design, philosophical compatibility, or historical evolution, the occupational welfare system is the locus from which the vast majority of retirement needs are met through an institutional benefits system.

This example demonstrates the close relationship between the occupational and public welfare systems. Social Security, while conceived and enacted within the public sector, is essentially conditioned and financed by the private sector. If you don't work, you won't receive benefits. If you do work, your employer matches your contribution, a benefit which is decidedly part of the occupational system. Obviously this relationship has implications for the broader issues of society's responsibility for the social, economic, and health needs of its members. Why, for example, should the private sector determine retirement benefits? The construction worker retiring at 65 may well have a Social Security monthly benefit which barely covers basic needs. It is unlikely that this worker has a pension, given the type of work. Also, Social Security benefits are tied to the amount paid into the system, which is simply a factor of how much was earned. The lower the wage, the lower the Social Security benefit. Conversely, the insurance executive retiring at 65 receives maximum Social Security benefits and additional pension benefits, providing in retirement about the same income he received while working. This situation is an accident of level of income, corporate decisions on pension plans, and eligibility rules within a work organization. Consequently, in our society, provisions for those whose productive work life is at an end are left to the idiosyncracies of his or her set of work and wage variables; for many this means moving from self-sufficiency to poverty. Social Security was enacted not as a pension plan, but as an insurance plan to supplement other income, and provides only a small base through which some basic necessities can be met. By relying on the occupational welfare system to provide for needs of the retirement years, our society reflects a system of reward based on class and political representation rather than standard and equal norms and retirement benefits.

The parameters of the occupational welfare system are drawn around the majority. The sixty million people who do not work by reason of age, unemployment, pursuit of education, or disability are by definition excluded. Those within the system receive some basic benefits and services, but are subject to the vagaries of particular company policies as well as to their position in the organizational hierarchy. This is not intended to be an equitable system, but rather one built on pragmatic principles of rewards and negotiated benefits. To understand the occupational welfare system fully is to understand the nature of an economy, labor and management relationships, and tax codes that view nonsalary benefits in a very different light than salary.

ELEMENTS OF THE OCCUPATIONAL
SOCIAL WELFARE SYSTEM

Unlike the public welfare system, which has discrete programs and benefits, the occupational social welfare system has few set programs and many variations. Although large companies must remain competitive in the extent and variety of benefits, tremendous discrepancies remain both between and within companies. For example, Jim B., a machinist at the nonunion Dixon Press, may be in an occupational social welfare system in which his retirement is covered by Social Security, his health by a company group health plan (for which he must pay half), and his safety and security by unemployment and workers' compensation. Burt J., a vice-president of marketing in the same company, enjoys the same benefits, plus a company pension, full health insurance coverage, life insurance, and a company car. Next door Joyce S., a machinist at the Trenton Tool and Die Company, a union shop, is covered by the same benefits as Jim, plus full health insurance, a union pension, a family dental plan, and supplemental union benefits in case of layoff.

The variations among these examples indicate the unevenness of the system. While every person who enters the work force joins the occupational social welfare system, benefits and services vary. Nevertheless, the system can be understood by examining those elements that are relatively common to employees and those which are either new or traditionally found only in selected areas.

Core Services and Benefits

The primary concerns of the occupational social welfare system center around illness, accidents, and past earned income. Consequently the system is characterized as essentially fiscal in nature (Weiner, p. 14). Companies and unions through fringe benefit packages expend enormous amounts of money on health and disability insurance and pensions. While this is considered nonsalary for bookkeeping and tax purposes, money is paid out through third-party mechanisms and insurance plans for the direct benefit of such employees.

Such services, paid for by the occupational sector, cover the health and retirement needs of millions of Americans. Some employees have maximal coverage, through a Master Medical Blue Cross/Blue Shield plan, for example, while others are covered by a minimal plan that does not reimburse for many health problems. Some companies pay the total cost, while others pay a portion with the employee paying the remainder.

Pension and retirement funds also vary. Large companies, public agencies, and occupations where unions are dominant are much more likely to provide retirement benefits than smaller, nonunion organizations. Pension plans, annuities, and retirement benefits themselves exhibit the most variation among core benefits in the occupational social welfare system. The complexities of eligibility, vesting rights, contributory formulas, and transfer rights give each plan unique characteristics. It was this very complexity that created a climate of abuse in which few employees actually realized retirement benefits due to fine-print clauses and manipulations whereby employees would be laid off or fired just before retirement eligibility. It was not until government regulations were instituted through the Employee Retirement Income Security Act in 1974 that some of these abuses were remediated.

A final set of core benefits centers around the protection and security of the worker and his or her family. While these are usually associated with public benefits and are regulated and administered by governmental agencies, they can be conceptualized and integrated in the occupational welfare system from which they emanate and by which they are financed. They include protection from job loss—unemployment compensation; protection from injury on the job—Workman's Compensation; and security from disability—provisions under the Social Security Act. These occupationally based and financed benefits wrap a protective cloak around employees and their families, providing limited assistance when needs arise due to economic or health adversities and giving credence to the phrase "from womb to tomb."

Supplemental Benefits and Services

The explosion of fringe benefits over the past two decades has been phenomenal. The parallel system of benefits and services that arose alongside the more traditional wage and salary categories not only transformed how employees were remunerated for their labors, but in effect opened up a private social welfare system for those who worked. While the origins of and motivations for such benefits and services have shifted over time, the trends have continued and, particularly during World War II, set the stage for the institutionalization of the system. Because there is no standardization among work organizations, this panoply of benefits is not and has not been viewed as an organized, coherent, purposeful system. Instead it has resembled more of a consumer marketplace, where a benefit or service emerges in one place and, depending on its popularity, may catch on and spread to other companies. Over time some of these have found their way into union contracts instituting a degree of stabilization. These *supplemental benefits and services* are almost too numerous to categorize. Below are a few of the more common.

Expanded health benefits: Unions and other interest groups have pushed for and received a broad range of health benefits beyond the standard health insurance coverage discussed above. Examples include prescription drugs, hearing aids, visual aids, dental insurance, annual physicals, and mental health treatment.

Child care: Many companies have established or contracted for child care programs or subsidies for their employees. These services are offered in a variety of forms, some on-site, others contracted through community-based programs. The increase in two-career families and single parents has hastened the development of these programs.

Profit sharing: Sharing of profits through a company plan has increased in popularity. This has been particularly true over the past several years, as foreign competition has forced companies to enter new arrangements of buy-backs and employee profit sharing. In some instances such a plan substitutes for a pension or retirement system, while in others it supplements such a system.

Educational scholarships and loans: The cherished value of education is often reflected through benefits of the occupational social welfare system. Many companies establish scholarship and loan funds for children of employees who matriculate at the nation's colleges and universities.

Tuition remittance: Many companies also provide full or partial tuition for employees who take courses and/or pursue degrees.

Sabbaticals: Once an exclusive benefit of academia, the concept of creating a set period of time (usually three to six months) to rejuvenate or take a brief respite has become increasingly popular.

Supplemental unemployment income: This is primarily a union benefit whereby laid-off employees can supplement unemployment compensation with union funds, enabling them to live on a sum that closely approximates their salary when working.

Employee services: Employee assistance and counseling programs, which have mushroomed dramatically during the past five years, serve employees and families who are experiencing substance abuse, mental health, legal, and/or financial problems. Preretirement counseling attempts to prepare employees for the transition into life after work.

Credit unions, buying clubs, and recreation programs: These are additional aspects of the expanding occupational social welfare system.

These supplemental benefits and services represent some of the major ones in today's occupational social welfare system. They augment core benefits and as such are constantly in flux, changing or expanding their scope and eligibility. As there is no uniform system, individual companies and unions initiate a benefit or service which often is picked up by others either through the collective bargaining process or through replication because of the reputed success of a particular experiment. In sum, these supplemental benefits and services provide a unique and exciting dimension of the occupational social welfare system. It is within the context of this system that the more recent practice of occupational social work is to be understood.

OCCUPATIONAL SOCIAL WORK PRACTICE

The notion of social work practice in the workplace is consistent with the social work orientation toward other settings and populations. Predating the current involvement with the workplace are significant practice specializations such as gerontology, oncology, families and children, schools, prisons, and neighborhoods.

Why then did it take so long for social workers to become involved in the arena where the majority of adults derive much of their identity and in which personal and social needs are met? "A majority of Americans spend a good part of the day there, derive most of their income from it, and build their social lives around it" (Johnson and Tropman, 1979, p. 215). Several factors can be cited to shed light on this paradox.

The Two-Separate-Worlds Theory

The individual's network of family and social relations and the world of work have traditionally been viewed even by social work as separate and unrelated. Despite the fact that each is concerned with and impacted by human behavior and a wide range of social problems, the boundaries of each have been firm and exclusionary of the other. Kanter (1977) argues that the idea that work life and family life constitute separate and nonoverlapping worlds with their own behaviors, functions, rules, and domains is a myth. Despite the widespread observation that everyone brings their home life into work and vice versa, at least to some degree, the work world and most institutions operate as if work lives and family lives were parallel systems with few links.

A similar situation exists, at least on the level of perception, between the worlds of work and social work. Social workers have been absent from the work world since they have not seen it as an appropriate or legitimate locus for practice and because those within it have not seen social workers as having a legitimate stake or skills that would be useful. While common interests are in fact present, it is only recently that the barriers have begun to break down to allow mutual movement and recognition of those interests.

Untested Assumptions

The two-separate-worlds view that has permeated the profession emerged in part from the perception that the workplace constitutes an environment inimical to social work values and practice. Consequently the work environment is assumed to be neither open nor conducive to those concerned with social and individual needs. Many social workers would assume in the workplace the absence of a humanistic culture, the preeminence of technology and profit, and an inherent contradiction between profit making and justice or equity.

For their part, corporate leaders have been unconvinced of the value and propriety of social workers in their companies or unions and are in some cases jaundiced about the human relations, organizational development, and social service movements of the past five decades. Thus the tension between social work and the workplace reflects each domain's perception of the other and is aggravated by perceived value conflicts, stereotypes, and distancing by the social work profession.

Image

Related to the first two factors is an image problem which besets social work. This image has significant negative tones, which impede the movement of social services in the workplace.

> ...to be quite blunt, social workers have an image problem with industry. Social workers are perceived to be fuzzy thinking do-gooders who see industry as interested only in profits and as exploiting its employees. Whether this is true, this is the perception of many businessmen who know social workers through serving on boards of social agencies and by the services we deliver (Fleming, 1979, p. 185).

Another not-so-incidental aspect of the image issue is related to the predominance of females in the profession. Not unlike most in the helping professions, the majority of social workers are female, with the usual connotations of soft, caring, warm qualities running flat against the "hard" culture of the male-dominated work world. The remnants of the friendly visitor–welfare mother era are very much alive in today's society and difficult to shake within the work force. Fortunately, changing images of women generally and their greater involvement in the workplace are altering that image.

The negative image of the social worker has presented a formidable barrier to opening avenues into the workplace and to demonstrating the transferability and usefulness of social work practice in the private sector. Ironically, a long-standing system of social benefits and services—the occupational social welfare system—does not use social workers. For a profession whose primary clientele has been the poor, oppressed, and disadvantaged, acceptance by the work world has been and continues to be hindered by images of oppression and exploitation. This is all complicated by a lack of clarity within the profession on what image should be projected.

The Unknown

Another barrier to social workers in work settings is an ignorance of both the realities and the needs of this environment. The workplace is a setting in which social work has not had a significant impact or presence. It represents an unexplored galaxy, one of the last arenas for breaking new ground. This unknown space has a mysterious language, a variant culture, and an orientation to products and services rather than people. While the frontier has been crossed by a few courageous pioneers, the vast recesses have yet to be explored or even contacted. As with all unknowns, there are fears, both spoken and unspoken, some relating to unresolved value conflicts and others to the viability of such a journey. Nevertheless, as the characteristics of this environment become better known and the needs understood, much of this "black box" may be conducive to widespread exploration.

OCCUPATIONAL SOCIAL WORK—TOWARD A DEFINITION

The terms *occupational* or *industrial social work* are perhaps the best known and most widely used phrases representing the activities of social workers in work settings. Their origins are tied primarily to the welfare movement of the late nineteenth century (Popple, 1981). The inadequacy of the term *industrial* is manifested in light of changing economic and demographic realities. America's work force has moved dramatically from the predominant industrial base of the last century to the high tech and service economy of what many futurists have coined the "postindustrial" or "information" society. Consequently, social workers attempting to serve a new client population start off somewhat out of sync by identifying their roles with terminology from another era. For this reason we prefer the term *human services in the workplace* or *occupational social work*, encompassing the broad parameters and changing realities of the client population. While this may seem like mere semantic distinction, professional image, focus, direction, and definition are influenced by the choice of terms.

Rather than begin with conceptual definitions, it might be best to describe the phenomenon we wish to define. Over the past decade, various human services activities have developed in the workplace—employee assistance programs, fringe benefits, employee benefit packages, and occupational, industrial and social services. There are no common models, program designs, or universal service areas. Instead, what has emerged is a series of activities tied to the dual goals of increased productivity and healthier work environments. "Their aim is to increase productivity, improve the stability of the workforce, enhance the general well being of workers in industry and large, nonprofit organizations, and strengthen the relationship of workers with their unions and their employers" (Ozawa, 1980, p. 464).

The phenomenon of social workers in the workplace has resulted from changes in the workplace; a reconceptualization of social work mandates; an acceptance of business, industry, and unions as legitimate arenas for social work intervention; and most importantly, an evolving, somewhat serendipitous series of events that have developed what many are calling a field. Thus, occupational social work has become a professional specialization in which a range of services can be described. Perhaps the first attempt to define this phenomenon was in 1979 by the Council on Social Work Education:

> Social Work in industrial settings...encompasses a host of services delivered to workers and members directly at the workplace through management and trade union auspices, or contracted by such an auspice to an outside consultation or community facility...industrial social work also includes services to management and union leadership with regard to affirmative action, supervisory training, organizational development and human resource utilization of social work expertise to serve the needs of workers/union members and to participate in the formation and carrying out of the industrial social welfare goals.... These host settings provide an opportunity to intervene in multiple environmental systems.

Kurzman and Akabas (1981) tackled the definitional issue by describing a population of interest and unit of attention.

> The authors define the population of interest as workers and the auspices as trade unions and employing organizations. The unit of attention encompasses the points of interaction where service delivery or policy positions adopted by these institutions affect the availability of services and the enactment of social welfare programs and policies. In essence it constitutes the social welfare agenda of society as it intersects with the interests, needs and responsibilities of work institutions and clients in their role as workers (p. 52).

We will repeat our proposed definition of occupational social work as stated in Chapter 1: *a field of practice in which social workers attend to the human and social needs of the work community by designing and executing appropriate interventions to insure healthier individuals and environments.* This definition recognizes that social work practice in the workplace draws upon basic social work professional and practice frameworks within a particular setting—the world of work. This is not to negate the need for particular knowledge and skills to practice in this setting, but recognizes it as an environment in which human and social problems exist, much as in the family or community. Consequently the social worker can bring into this environment the core of the profession's knowledge and skills, to which must be added the unique characteristics, behaviors, and needs of work institutions.

Much has been made of the field of occupational social work within the profession over the past several years. To a great extent this attention has been the result of the novelty of the setting and value conflict: how can the values of social work be reconciled with the values and goals of profit-making institutions? Despite this perceived obstacle, the profession is armed to meet individual and social needs within work organizations. To be distracted by a side issue is to lose sight of the basic mandate of services and intervention to a population in need, a mandate no different from that for other settings or population groups served by social workers.

Having emphasized the commonality of this practice with all of social work, we note that occupational social work does constitute practice in a unique setting. To what extent do social workers or other human service professionals have a mandate there? If such a mandate does exist, what is it? To support our definition of human services in the workplace, we will outline our assumptions underlying the practice and legitimacy of those services.

1. The workplace is a community in which human needs and problems are present. It is also part of a larger community, the government-business-social nexus that constitutes the world in which each of us lives.

2. The current structure, culture, and design of today's work organization does not adequately address or meet the needs of a population moving inexorably into a new age.

3. Social work is in a position to meet some of these needs in light of its professional mandate and the unique training and skills of its practitioners.

Workplace as community Despite attempts to segment the workplace and dichotomize it from the social mainstream, work constitutes one of the central institutions of our society. The workplace is a functional community in which employees may also be spouses, children, lovers, parents, and friends or enemies. Those within the boundaries of work experience the same range of feelings, problems, and emotional highs and lows as outside the company doors.

This functional community constitutes a major unit of the larger social system, with its own set of rules, norms, behaviors, and cultural values. For the employee entering this system—both in a time dimension, i.e., being at the workplace for a certain time each day, and in recognizing and accepting cultural and organizational roles, norms, and expectations—there exists a duality in terms of life needs. On one side exists the world of work, a world complete within itself. Here there is a job to be done, an economic contract by which employee and employer agree to both conditions and outcomes. This work world is driven primarily by a task orientation. The other side is the nonwork system, in which the employee operates with other role conditions or contractual agreements. In this arena a task orientation tends not to predominate, and process and affective needs are more primary.

The work-nonwork dichotomy, while real in some fashion (physical separateness, distinct rule makers, etc.) is in reality less distinct. Consequently, work and work issues enter the home and family, while home and family are also brought into the work sphere. By recognizing this simple phenomenon, one's perspective on the workplace transcends the traditional narrow concept of work as a purely economic domain. It is instead a vibrant, dynamic, functional community of individual social beings and multiple social groups that together form an interrelated whole, in turn related to the larger society. Because each individual brings personal habits, issues, and problems into the work world, it is inescapably a place in which human problems, emotions, and needs exist.

While this seems a simple observation, recognition and acceptance of it by service providers and corporate managers is by no means universal. The dichotomy of work and nonwork has been perpetuated to further the productive and economic goals of the work organization. However, shifting demographic characteristics and societal changes over the past decade have broken down the dichotomy and turned more attention to the human issues brought to the workplace.

Thus, our first assumption underlying the practice of human services in the workplace begins with recognition of the work environment as a social system, influenced by economic goals and individual and societal needs. While the primary purpose and nature of the system is economic, the presence of the human dimension, particularly its interrelation with the broader social environment, constitutes a legitimate focus of attention. As corporations are compelled to address these issues, occupational social workers and other human service professionals face an opportunity that, if missed, will mean having ignored basic professional responsibilities.

Current organizational structures, cultures, and designs are inadequate to meet their social needs.   Our second assumption relates to the capacity of the workplace to carry out services to meet its social needs. Recognizing that needs or problems exist is not the same as doing something about them. Consequently a case needs to be made that current organizational responses often are not effective.

Social workers moving into union or business settings may become enthused with the novelty of the setting and practice issues. However, it should be clear that the issues and problems (alcoholism, stress, retirement, etc.) are not new to the work organization: they are as old as the organization itself. What is new is effective intervention and the definition or recognition of the problem. One has only to recall the welfare capitalism movement to be reminded of the long-standing struggle employers have waged with these issues.

The desire to deal with issues of the human side of the enterprise may not be matched by the organization's resources. For example, an organization may recognize drug abuse as a problem and desire to assist abusers in seeking treatment; it is unlikely that it would have appropriate personnel or expertise. Problem resolution in the past generally meant either firing employees whose drug abuse blatantly impacted job performance or ignoring the problem. The personnel department may have collaborated with legal counsel, perhaps even the medical department. However, as the societal definition of the problem has moved from crime to illness and treatment has changed from punishment to cure, new resources have been required.

Many companies are just now positioning themselves to handle the expectations that have emerged over the past few years. Some companies are obvious leaders. Counseling employees about personal and family problems, attempting to meet special needs of handicapped employees, and setting up preretirement programs are examples of needs now handled, though not always optimally, by work organizations. For many organizations, units such as personnel, employee relations, and organizational development would be logical places to look for assistance with such issues. However, these units have been operating under different auspices and mandates and do not respond in the same ways a helping professional might recommend. For example, personnel units or human resource departments are usually structured and staffed along compensation, recruitment, benefit, and policy lines. Their preparation for moving into areas such as those mentioned is often limited. Organizational constraints in the mainstream of American business and industry are impediments to addressing and meeting the human needs of their employees. Social workers being hired for the first time to work in these environments can expect to face many obstacles in placing human needs on the company agenda and in gaining significant support for achieving change. There is a legitimate role for social workers to assist work institutions in responding to the range of problems besetting the contemporary workplace, as well as treating individual problems themselves.

Social work is able to meet human needs in the workplace by virtue of professional mandate and unique training and skills. Our third assumption in establishing human services in the workplace is that social work has the knowledge and skills to apply to the needs and problems of work organizations. While this has not been self-evident to either work organizations or the social work profession, the pioneering work carried out by individual practitioners, several schools of social work, and entrepreneurial social workers over the past decade has demonstrated a useful role for the profession.

Two factors can be cited to account for the premise that social work can play a central role in meeting human and social needs in the workplace: developmental direction and conceptual compatibility.

Developmental direction. As the workplace became open to dealing with alcoholism, and as occupational alcoholism, employee assistance, stress management, and other programs were established, the development of human service personnel has taken place. Signs of "professionalization" and the rise of an occupation have become visible. Over the past several years, the Association of Labor Management Administrators and Consultants in Alcoholism (ALMACA) and the Occupational Program Consultants Association (OPCA) have emerged as primary movers. Certification standards are being developed, professional curricula are being taught, and the issue of credentialing has surfaced.

Social work, on the other hand, has been the primary discipline to actively pursue professionalization in the industrial and occupational social work movement. Unlike other human service professions such as psychology, psychiatry, vocational rehabilitation, and nursing, social work has formed national initiatives and convened a task force out of its national office and has a group of recognized leaders associated with workplace practice. By carving out a niche, social workers have provided initial leadership in developing programs, staffing existing employee assistance and related programs, and offering training in a number of schools of social work. The profession has staked a claim in the occupational welfare system and is effectively and convincingly developing an identifiable presence and body of knowledge.

Conceptual compatibility.   In addition to having established a programmatic presence in the workplace, social work has the advantage of a conceptual framework compatible with the nature of the workplace and the needs existing within it. The concept of person in situation and a systems approach to problem solving is fundamental to social work practice and is particularly appropriate for workplace practice.

The systems approach to problem solving is a genuine advantage to practice in work organizations for several reasons. First, the workplace is a complex system in which any intervention requires a broad conceptual and practice approach. To utilize a single method (e.g., counseling) or to zero in on one problem (e.g., alcoholism) is to intervene in only a partial manner or to respond only to symptoms. Such activities are not to be negated, but it should be recognized that problems exist within a context, and treatment and resolution require both macro and micro solutions. Consequently, the broader systems approach of social work theory is well suited to the work environment.

A second advantage of the systems approach relates to the complexity of the interface between human vagaries and production at work. The workplace has traditionally dealt with its social aspects either through broad approaches such as organizational development (or, more recently, quality of working life) or by regulations, rule setting, or disciplinary strategies. The humanization of the workplace, as concretized through such services as child care, programs for stress management, health/fitness, and preretirement, etc., demonstrates a recognition of the interrelatedness of human dimensions and economics. Social work introduces a framework that can assist both the practitioner and the client—in this case the workplace itself—

to grapple with the proper balance between the demands and needs of the organization and those of the employee, the family, and the larger community.

In summary, these three assumptions underlie the rationale, legitimacy, and presence of social work in work organizations. While each of these can be challenged and tested, they represent a basis for occupational social work practice.

CHAPTER THREE
A SOCIAL WORK PERSPECTIVE ON WORK

WORK: HOW IT CAME TO BE AND WHAT IT HAS TO DO WITH SOCIAL WORK

It is no accident that social work has come to the world of work reluctantly. The scope of work is so large, sprawling, and multifaceted that one could argue that a profession experienced in and skilled at working with "person in environment" is not adequate to the task. Work is history, religion, culture, politics, and society as well as personal, individual, and systemic. Social work, busy improving the lot of the individual at the bottom of the social strata, has scarcely had time to attend to this other domain, which with the Industrial Revolution became a discrete notion, almost with a life of its own. In spite of the historical ties of social work to the world of work described earlier, work was a sphere that seemed to be taking care of itself. If social workers could get families and individuals healthy and secure and then work toward social justice, they would have their life work cut out for them. Workers were at least eating; they were not perceived to need the services of social workers. The aims of this chapter are threefold:

    1.   To illustrate the evolution of work, from its roots in the philosophical and religious ferment of the Reformation through the ideas and people that triggered the Industrial Revolution to the present century. We look at how work has gone from a background assumption of life, that is, life is work, to a discrete foreground concept demanding the involvement of social work.

2.   To stretch the social work conceptualization of work beyond the psychological to include more fully the social, that is, to develop a true psychosocial understanding.

3.   Having brought work to the foreground, to suggest a way to approach its broad dynamic, to acknowledge the currents and complications of work in what has quickly become the postindustrial age.

This last aim is meant to be debated, experimented with, and modified as continuing learning and discovery dictate. But to enlighten the present and move us into the future, let us turn to the roots of thinking about work.

AN INHERITANCE OF IDEAS

Work has probably been a discrete but unnamed idea since the earliest hunting and gathering societies first distinguished between rest and nonrest. And when the Great Pyramid of Giza was built about 2500 B.C., a highly sophisticated, systematic, and rational system of work organization demonstrated a keen understanding of logistics, the division of labor, and technological innovation. The Western conception of work has evolved largely from the ideas and influences of such people as Thomas More, Desiderius Erasmus, Martin Luther, and John Calvin in the sixteenth and seventeenth centuries and in the eighteenth and nineteenth century from the likes of Jean-Jacques Rousseau, Adam Smith, Thomas Jefferson, members of the Lunar Society, Karl Marx, and Sigmund Freud.

More, Erasmus, Luther, and Calvin did not write about work per se, but their ideas about God and state and the nature of humankind profoundly affected the development of thought that culminated in the Industrial Revolution and ultimately in our views about work today. Their key roles during the Reformation helped shape a world that would look more specifically at work. They questioned the assumptions of their age and challenged with their words and actions the values of their times.

"Ringers" of the Renaissance

These brief profiles are of men we might call "ringers" today: individuals whose powerful ideas and life examples helped set the Western stage for the movers and shakers of the eighteenth and nineteenth centuries. Again, they were not concerned with work per se; their lives were devoted to the proper roles of church and state, the meaning of human life, and their visions of a "right" world. But modern debates and philosophies about work have been affected in no small part by the legacy of their influence on church, state, and humankind.

Thomas More was a lawyer and politician. Born in England in 1478, the son of a judge, he served as a page to Cardinal Morton, then pursued an education at Oxford and later studied law in London. More was by virtue of his birth and education a solid, respectable member of the English middle class. In 1523 he was the speaker of the Commons and from 1529–1532 lord chancellor of England. But position for its own sake was not important to More. A man of deep Christian belief, acutely sensitive to the human condition, he came to believe that the form of social civilization need not be attributed to the whim of God or the curse of original sin—the prevailing concepts of the time, with roots in Greek, Hebrew, and Roman history—but rather could be found in the social structures built by humans. His classic work, *Utopia*, was an attempt to provide an alternative, to conjure up a vision; he described a classless, moneyless society in which price is determined by the needs of the parties involved to maintain their given status. In More's utopia everyone worked, fought, and studied. There was no division of labor. His ideas about the ideal social structures in which humans might live peaceably added a challenging voice to his time. His vision affected other thinkers of his era, including the Dutchman, Erasmus.

Desiderius Erasmus, born in Holland in 1466, was an Augustinian monk of the Renaissance. A meeting with Thomas More in 1499 was pivotal to the beliefs that Erasmus developed and propagated. For Erasmus, More and his colleagues demonstrated that argument and worship need not be mechanical and superstitious, but that Christianity could be an expression of broad and tolerant virtues, of a wholeness of body and spirit.

In Italy, Erasmus encouraged a movement of tolerance and humanism. In contrast to the position of the medieval church (and in concert with More's thinking), humanism did not view nature as temptation or the flesh as evil and did not support the doctrine of original sin. Instead the humanist turned to the "pagan" classics of Greece and Rome to support the argument of original goodness—the Greek belief that the soul and the body are one and that the actions of the body naturally and fittingly express the humanity of the soul. The primacy of religion in the late fifteenth century was such that humanists did not see themselves as antireligious, but as mere protestors against abuses of religion, against the social structures created by humans. Christian virtue and the complete universal person were the thematic armor of the humanists as they criticized the corruptions of the Church. Erasmus was a radical. He gave a voice to the discontent of his age. He articulated dissatisfaction with the place and prerogatives of churchmen, whose excess of pomp and superstition led to seeds of inquiry and rebellion against such emptiness. With his writing Erasmus helped to loosen the grip the Church held on the minds of its people.

This challenge to the Church, with its inherent questioning of blind obedience to a corrupt structure, was another element in the emerging consciousness of individual autonomy and human worth, the idea that as human minds are unbound from authoritarian institutions, they are free to form their own futures. Erasmus wanted citizens to question their religious institution. In the 1980s he would be called a "New Age" thinker, pushing toward the future.

Martin Luther, an Augustinian monk and contemporary of Erasmus, also sought to bring a new consciousness to his age. Erasmus attempted in his satires on the Church to prompt a reexamination of religious doctrine without polarizing opinion so greatly as to preclude the ongoing debate between the Church and its critics. Luthur, however, had no similar concern for the cause of moderation. Disgusted by his observations of the immoral life of priests and cardinals and their corruption of church rites, Luther posted his *Ninety-Five Theses* which led to an acknowledged break with the Church of Rome in 1520. Luther attacked the entire theology and structure of the Church by teaching salvation dependent upon an individual's own faith and contrition, abolishing the need for sacraments and a hierarchy to administer them. Erasmus had hoped to make humanism a movement of universal peace across Europe. Unfortunately, Luther's attempts at religious reform could not have succeeded without political support which undermined the cause of such peace. By 1525 his universal Christian ideal became a German nationalist ideal. Eventually he invoked the secular arm of the German princes to enforce his doctrine. The result of Luther's influence was a division between the inner life of the spirit, which was free, and the outer life of the person, which was subjugated to authority. The zeal of Luther, which shifted from religious ideals to nationalism, was the foundation for a new identity, a new way to see oneself in the context of institutions, and was instrumental in the development of a secular authority, coincidentally setting the stage for loyalties to the authority of work institutions.

Influenced by his elders, Erasmus and Luther, John Calvin believed that humankind was helpless before an omnipotent God and predestined for either damnation or salvation. By the mid-sixteenth century Calvin had renounced Catholicism and settled in Switzerland to write a detailed system of morals, polity, and dogma. Both Luther and Calvin touched chords of discontent in Europe by offering alternatives to the traditional church. In this environment, Calvin was prevailed upon to apply his laws in Geneva. There he established two bodies of government—the ministry and the consistory. The ministry was an army of Protestant preachers, trained in Calvin's doctrine to promote a regimen of early rising, hard work, good morals, good reading, thrift, and abstinence. The consistory handled questions of morality. Its decisions were enforced by civil officials, thus turning moral questions into questions of law, subject to the state. Calvin's intent was to make an institution fit for worship of God and to build a system that would make humans fit to worship God. Indeed, these were the very qualities that later industrialists would seek to reinforce and reward. In a sense we might think of Calvin as the first training manager for industry!

The importance of these men lies not in their views on work but in their contributions to a new set of values, values that would slowly infect and affect the work-worker-workplace complex as we know it today. These were men apart. To some degree their individual efforts were national and variable, their tactics differed, and their visions of a new age were not consistent. But their observations on life and the questions they raised were all part of the movement called the Reformation. The European mind gained a new ethos, a new world view, a series of novel political, social, and economic ideas that challenged the power of the Church and left a void to be filled.

The Industrial Revolution and Revolutionaries

It is a giant leap from the Reformation to the eighteenth century Industrial Revolution, but we are attempting less to teach history than to understand our legacies. Though the Industrial Revolution is often depicted as a discrete event, it was actually a convergence of history, ideas, organizations, and inventions, both social and technical. While Luther and Calvin were reconstructing relationships between people and the Church, Copernicus and Galileo were hypothesizing new laws of the mechanics of the skies. No longer accepted as constants, both man and nature were vulnerable to inquiry, and inquire led to more inquiry. In the 1600s groups of scientists met to discuss their work. Galileo belonged to the Academy of the Lynx-eyed, a group of science enthusiasts in Rome. Descartes, Fermat, Pascal, and others were meeting at about the same time in Paris. In London the Royal Society was founded in 1660 and opened with a lecture on astronomy by Christopher Wren. The Reformation and the ideas of the scientific revolution were leading toward what became the Industrial Revolution.

Like the men of the Reformation described above, the luminaries of the Industrial Revolution were a new breed. Their education was different and their wealth was different. Dissatisfied with the impractical education of the universities, they were educated in schools that stressed knowledge in medicine, logic, modern language and science, electricity, and chemistry. They founded small, informal scientific societies, which were alive with new ideas.

The expansion of credit and a general stimulus to investment created conditions in which wealth could be created from industries which this new breed was creating and inventing. They were in some respects the first entrepreneurs—people who invented from a sense of natural curiosity in an age that would invest in them.

Organization and invention were driving forces of the Industrial Revolution. Through the mid-1700s most work, with the exception of processes that dealt in raw materials, such as coal mining and glass making, was done in the home. Weavers, for example, were delivered thread after it had been shorn from the sheep, cleaned, combed, and spun. The home weaver was his or her own boss, selling finished cloth back to a wool merchant. As population and demand grew, however, this routine became too large, complex, and costly for wool merchants to tend. Thus this and other finished goods businesses, such as cotton, nails, needles, gloves, and hats, eventually were "rationalized," that is, operations were brought under one roof to enable control of materials, tools, and time. In this way the cottage worker shifted

from an independent business person to wage earner, and factory organization was instituted. By 1820 the transformation from home to factory had in
large part occurred in the manufacturing arena. "Organization" had facilitated the shift. The use of water power, then steam, then coal to run the new
machines being invented further enhanced the development of the factory.
Then financing processes changed. Historically, since the Church had re-
garded all forms of lending (except to government) as usury, inventors had
had difficulty securing funds to develop their inventions. The expansion of
credit and investment enabled a collaboration between factory owners and
inventors, resulting in ever-more-mechanized factories.

The men most intimately involved in these developments were people
of varying attitudes and bent. To break through traditions of the past, to
innovate, is a feat generally accomplished by nonconformists. So it was with
the business people and technicians of this era. It is difficult to categorize
this group neatly; two sketches will illustrate.

Josiah Wedgewood (1730–1795) founded Wedgewood Potteries. Es-
teemed for his improvement in temperature control and measurement in
the firing of pottery, and later a pioneer in the development of canals and
roads to transport his goods, Wedgewood is also remembered for his obsession with control and efficiency of people and working conditions. The
humanistic notion of people as ends in themselves, rather than means to an
end, apparently had not impressed itself upon Wedgewood. Josiah
Wedgewood had a wooden leg, and the tale is told that when he noticed a
piece of poor pottery on a workman's bench, he would smash it with his leg
and chalk on the bench, "This will not do for Joseph Wedgewood."

Later, Robert Owen (1771–1858) stood in contrast to Wedgewood.
Owen, the son of a saddle maker, was by the age of twenty-one in charge of
a factory of five hundred people. With a firsthand knowledge of factory
conditions—squalid surroundings and long hours for adults and children
alike—Owen wrote *A New View of Society*. He message was simple. He maintained that the human character is formed in early childhood, completely by
environment. Thus, his book became an appeal for factory reform in particular and social reform in general. A man of his word, he made his factory
in New Lanark, Scotland, a model that the industrialists in America later
copied. He provided workers with better housing, food, and clothing, in-
sisted on education for their children, and instituted new standards of clean-
liness and safety in his factories.

From Life Roles to Assigned Roles

Invention, organization, and the ideas of people like Wedgewood and
Owen merged with the forces of growing urbanism and alterations in the
authoritarian power of the church. A world of life roles dictated by the
necessities of survival, family, and church was metamorphosing to a world in
which roles were assigned by virtue of market need and efficiency.

Work as described by the first economist   In 1776 Adam Smith, in *An Inquiry into the Nature and Causes of the Wealth of Nations*, defined work as an activity requiring the worker to give up tranquility, freedom, and happiness. "Wages," he maintained, "are the reward the laborer receives for this sacrifice." Generally pronouncements such as this are interpreted as proof that Smith subjected workers to cold, harsh, and manipulative economic forces. Smith's real contribution, however, was introducing science and a historical method into the study of economics. By doing so he provided a previously nonexistent means of ordering people's material lives, offering another means of controlling the world of matter. He replaced the tyranny of chance with analytical tools to control economic activities. This was also a means of organizing the activity called work.

We note here that today's worker, with an increased sense of entitlement, seems no longer willing to strike a bargain such as Smith offered. The growing insistence on some degree of "tranquility, freedom, and happiness" at work as well as enlightened self-interest on the part of some businesses has resulted in policies and work experiments aimed at meeting new and changing needs of workers. The search for balance between rights and responsibility, humanism and exploitation, is setting the stage for a debate of philosophical inquiry and concrete change at work for the coming decades that Smith forecast. One of his positions was that personal self-interest is the best regulator of the well-being of society. Smith had in mind that the long-range effect of an action, not the immediate and obvious one, would be the determiner of well-being. However, the doctrine was misapplied by the educated, the manufacturers, and the owners of newly enclosed land. It is only in our time that expediency has been questioned in light of long-term effects. In spite of Smith's philosophical and scientific contributions, he was short-sighted in treating labor as a commodity rather than an activity. His theory of wealth, which treated labor in terms of supply and demand, provided a rationale for cruel treatment of workers. A second view that left an indelible mark on work organizations of the Industrial Revolution positioned the worker as a "machine of production." Smith conceived the growth of wealth as occurring by division of labor and greater capital investment. Thus, in spite of what he saw as the degrading effects of specialized employment, particularly as practiced at the time, he reasoned that the relative wealth of the masses was compensation.

Work as political philosophy   Karl Marx entered the mainstream as a revolutionary reconceptualizer of work, with its meaning and function his primary emphasis. He saw work as central to human existence and mastery of work as a liberating activity. Thus he said of labor, "real freedom, whose action is, precisely labor... which has...created the subjective and objective conditions for itself...becomes attractive work, the individual's self-realization; which in no way means that it becomes mere fun, mere amusement...really free working...is at the same time the most damned serious-ness, the most intensive exertion." Marx's aim was not to eliminate work but to remove what he saw as the miseries of work through the elimination of capitalism. In *Das Kapital* (1848) he described the misery of the English working class. Work in itself did not cause misery; rather, capitalism and the class system made the terribleness of work inevitable.

In the end, Marx was not concerned primarily with work; rather, he was seeking a just world. Capitalistic control of the means of production, and subsequently the nature of work, was simply a manifestation of injustice to him. Nevertheless, his focus on that particular manifestation sparked a debate on the nature of work now well over a century old.

Psychology and work   Over eighty years later, as economic depression and massive unemployment struck industrialized nations, Freud wrote *Civilization and its Discontents*. In that era of despair, Freud asked what people demand of life and wish to achieve in it. He asserted that "they strive after happiness; they want to become happy and remain so" (p. 23). In exploring circumstances that result in happiness, he made his now-famous case for Eros and Ananke—love and necessity. These two great powers, he main-tained, were responsible for the development of civilization and were the enablers of community living. Placing work in the context of Ananke, he stated, "No other technique for the conduct of life attaches the individual so firmly to reality as laying emphasis on work; for work at least gives a secure place in a portion of reality in the human community" (p. 27). While "love and work" is a phrase every Freudian neophyte glibly utters, less often noted is another statement in the same paragraph: "The great majority of people only work under the stress of necessity and the *natural* human aversion to work raises more difficult social problems" (p. 27). Freud thus articulated an enduring paradox: the importance of work, yet a natural aversion to it. Moreover, he framed work as a manifestation of psychological conflict, an element to be considered in the building of a "good life." Like Smith and Marx, Freud was not investigating work per se, but his primary interest seemed to be unavoidably affected by the nature, practice, and meaning of work.

Modern Views on Work

Population growth, invention, capital, urban settlement, and educa-tion combined to fuel the Industrial Revolution, and the ideas of people like those described prompted a consciousness of the institution of work. The study of work has become almost an obsession, as evidenced by the number of books about work and the workplace on the best-seller list since 1980. However, work continues to be a changing, elusive subject.

Twentieth-century concepts of work   In 1956, as the world was settling down after World War II and the Korean War, sociologist William Whyte described *The Organization Man*: "the ones of our middle class who have left home, spiritually as well as physically, to take the vows of organization life…the mind and soul of our great self-perpetuating institutions" (p. 3). But just fourteen years later, futurist Alvin Toffler stated, "The old loyalty felt by the organization [person] appears to be going up in smoke. In its place we are watching the rise of professional loyalty" (1970, p. 146). He further quoted John Gardner, who declared that "the loyalty of the professional is to the profession and not to the organization that may house him [her] at any given moment." Both the organization person and the professional exist in Western business today. From either perspective, work is an organizer of life, not inherently good or bad.

Charlie Chaplin in the classic movie *Modern Times*, caricatured the assembly line as dehumanizing. Yet a factory worker may claim, "I like working on the assembly line; my mind is free to think of other things while my hands do work automatically." Studs Terkel introduced his book, *Working*, by saying, "This book, being about work, is by its very nature about violence — to the spirit as well as the body…. It is about a search, too, for daily meaning as well as daily bread, for astonishment rather than torpor, for a sort of life rather than a Monday through Friday sort of dying" (1972, p. xiii). Terkel interviewed well over a hundred people about what they do all day and how they feel about it. Terkel's depiction of working reality is loving, authentic, and intuitively sensitive. Yet it is not the whole story. Tracey Kidder, in *Soul of a New Machine* (1981), records the thoughts of a man working with a group developing a new computer. "The reason why I work is because I win…. I'm sitting here burning myself up and doing it because I like it. You wouldn't have to pay me very much to do this." Kidder observes, "He likes not having to punch a time clock. But he knows that his freedom from company clocks doesn't stem from corporate altruism. 'They don't want us to know how many hours we work. If we did, they'd have to pay us a lot more…. But…I don't work for money'" (p. 191).

James O'Toole, chairman of *Work in America* and the more recent *Vanguard Management*, sums it up perhaps most adroitly: "Diversity is the single most important fact about the work force. Indeed, by aggregating the countless studies of worker attitudes, values, and satisfactions that were conducted in the 70's, one arrives at a singularly significant conclusion: Workers are not alike; they have different needs, interests, and motivations. Moreover, these characteristics constantly change throughout the career of each worker.

So here we are in the 1980s, out of the Industrial Revolution, into the postindustrial era, and heading for the third millenium. The term *postindustrial* indicates in some part the changing nature of work. As *industrial* referred to the shift from an agrarian to a manufacturing society, postindustrial indicates a shift from manufacturing to information and service. This is not to say that manufacturing is obsolete but that it is being done differently. Bob Schrank, in *Ten Thousand Working Days*, uses the microprocessor to illustrate the difference between the industrial and postindustrial eras.

> The microprocessor is affecting the workplace the way the fractional horsepower motor affected housework appliances and small tools. The secret of all housework machinery is the cheap, universal, fractional horsepower motor. It runs the refrigerator, vacuum cleaner, dishwasher, clotheswasher, dryer, blender, air-conditioner, food processor, mixer, malted milk machine, electric can opener, rotisserie, meat slicer, hand drill and on and on. The fractional horsepower motor was critical in liberating women from a big part of housework. It is one of those inventions that periodically come along and change our whole way of life.
>
> The microprocessor has the same kind of unlimited application. It is already being installed in many household machines, telling the fractional horsepower motor what to do. We can begin to see how the microprocessor may change our lives. In the office, the microprocessor provides the brains for word processors, electronic typewriters, copiers, and telephone answering machines. In manufacturing, the microprocessor is being used to monitor and control continuous process plants, assembly operations, warehousing systems, and robots that perform such tasks as painting and welding. There are thousands of applications still waiting. As we continue to look for ways to survive in the fiercely competitive international marketplace, we will turn more and more to microprocessors to run the machines to do the work.
>
> Some experts have said that the microprocessor is just another tool and therefore should be treated like a screwdriver or a hammer. That argument is usually made in response to a growing concern that people have about "what this thing might do to our jobs." The important distinction to be made here is that hand and power tools are primarily extensions of muscle power. In contrast, the microprocessor goes beyond muscle—it is the first to replace brain power. When I worked in engineering, I had to learn to use a slide rule. That required some knowledge of mathematics, logarithms, and so forth. The slide rule was an extension of the user's brain as the hammer is a weighted extension of the arm. The slide rule is now obsolete (I have a couple if someone is collecting). It has been replaced by a hand-held calculator run by a microprocessor. To get an answer, all I need to do is push some buttons, yet I may not have the slightest idea how the calculator arrived at them—nor do I need to. The brain power is in the machine (1978, p. 43).

Sweat and human calculation were integral to the Industrial Age. Integrating and managing information, ideas, and people are synonymous with the postindustrial era. No wonder work has been a frustrating topic of study for social workers and others. It is an elusive force, changing like a chameleon with shifts in technology, economic systems, and social values. Social work as a profession must view work as a dynamic but primary institution of significance on a par with the family and community. The experience, quality, or absence of work affects the individual, the family, and the community in profound and lasting ways. The nature of work defines social relationships, frames political argument, and touches the core of human identity.

SOCIAL WORKERS AND WORK

Skilled social workers develop a composite understanding of an individual by collecting information on her or him alone, as a member of a group, and within a family, with each profile contributing different facets and perspectives of the whole person. So it must be with work. There is no linear history of work, no simple economic or psychological explanation, no clear ideological interpretation, no cultural or ecological view sufficient in itself. Only a composite can begin to provide an intangible essence of work, and at that we find the picture is not clear, but diffuse and elusive. The supposed boundaries of work, leisure, and personal life have become blurred. A company credo at Honeywell Corporation issued in 1980 included the following statement of principal: "Work life and personal life have interacting needs that will be recognized." Here was one of America's largest institutions of work acknowledging the ambiguous overlap of work with an individual's social life. This overlap complicates attempts at a scholarly understanding of work. Indeed, as civilization has evolved, what actually constitutes work has become more often a matter of world view, that is, "in the eye of the beholder." Yet, this relativistic view of work is inadequate, and professionals in many disciplines are organizing ideas and theories to facilitate the study of work.

Thus we call for a more organized approach to the subject than previously available to social work scholars, for a conceptual framework useful to the social work practitioner. Such a framework must be multidimensional. Further, to be synergistic with social work practice, it must eschew a myopic view of work and compel the practitioner to look at it from many angles. From the inception of the Industrial Revolution, new or emerging disciplines have helped to sculpt the landscape of what we now study as work. Increasingly, fields such as literature, history, theology, economics, sociology, and anthropology are enriching our experience and understanding of work for clients or client systems; we are building a wider range of insights and interventions than would be possible with a narrow ideological perspective. Obviously, the social worker in the work setting cannot and should not be an expert in all disciplines. But psychological precepts may constitute an "ethnocentrism" for social work. One need only review any social work practice text: if work is referred to at all, it is in the context of self identity. By incorporating contributions from other perspectives, a broader social work construct of work can be articulated.

To better illustrate what we mean, let us look at some specific contributions to the work experience from other disciplines.

Work: Views Through Other Disciplines

History One method of illuminating the concept of work is to review its history. It must be remembered, however, that history is not dispassionate, but a recording of facts as the historian perceives them. History is concerned with time, place, and events. A psychosocial history helps answer various questions: How did the individual get to this point? What are the contributions of the past to the present? How have the cumulative events and forces of the past affected the nature of work? Do we appreciate the power and strength of traditions, such as those associated with apprenticeship, with roots in the medieval guilds of the Dark Ages?

History is rarely documented in a value-free manner. But specific events can stand as chronological signposts, which contribute insight to what has happened or what may come. The development of irrigation systems in the river systems of the Nile, for example, has been connected by Karl Willfogel to the increased specialization of work. He suggests that the use of large labor forces necessitated an organizational hierarchy. Large groupings of people in a single area and increased food supply have supported the emergence of specialists: potters, weavers, metalworkers, scribes, lawyers, and physicians.

The *Encyclopedia Brittanica* (1984) states, "The history of civilization is bound up with changes in the means by which the activities necessary to society's survival (work) have been analyzed or organized. As the number of human beings on Earth has grown, they have become increasingly dependent upon each other."....This article describes the various methods by which work has been organized from prehistory to the present day (vol. 19, 933).

History provides a framework for a chronological evaluation of work, shedding light on current events and forces. It is useful in several ways: it is an aid to understanding the "grand scheme" of things, and it places industries, groups, regions, and individuals in contexts. Modes of practice and policy are often derived from an understanding of history and subsequent context.

Anthropology Anthropology, meanwhile, attempts to understand work in the context of specific cultures. In the mid 1970s, social work curricula began to emphasize the importance of ethnicity to social work practice. In an era of racial tension in many cities, the power and destructiveness of white, middle-class ethnocentrism was becoming painfully apparent. Efforts of social work schools raised our awareness of the importance of ethnic heritage in practice with clients and communities and contributed to the defusion of tension and to educational improvement for subsequent generations of social work students. But mere awareness of ethnicity is insufficient for the social worker who practices in a pluralistic society and workplace. An anthropological understanding of work enlarges the practitioner's view of work, worker, and workplace.

To an anthropologist, work is not a matter of time, place, and events; rather needs, relationships, environment, and ceremony are more telling symbols. The tasks and agreements that contribute to the maintenance of society or culture illuminate for the ethnographer the meaning and function of work in that community. It does not take great imagination to understand that work in a small Italian village, where the relationship of people to food is still quite direct, is different from work in midtown Manhattan. Anthropologists tell us that prehistoric people engaged in activities necessary to their societies' survival. This was their work. We imagine that their tasks involved supplying their most basic need: food. These food gatherers and hunters organized their lives around finding and procuring food. Whether their lives were consumed by this work is not clear. Delineation of work and leisure is culturally determined. However, we can surmise that in the earliest human groups it was necessary for all to contribute to the task of food gathering and that their social structures, relationships, and customs were integrated to support that goal. Technological simplicity also implies minimal work specialization. Such societies are not typically characterized by extensive division of labor, except perhaps by age and sex. Such an integration of task accomplishment infers ways of working that are tied more closely to seasonal and ceremonial cycles of the culture than the hierarchical imperatives. Thus hunting and gathering societies were necessarily cooperative in relation to capturing animals, gathering edible plants, and distributing food. When agriculture was introduced, "work" became more complex, with production of surplus, development of tools and weapons, increased specialization, and more differentiated roles. Of what relevance is this to the modern social worker? Anthropology reminds us not to make assumptions about work and its meaning solely from the data of our own experience. Rather, we are urged to examine, observe, and value work in the contexts of both the micro- and macroculture of a particular work group. As we will discuss in more detail in Chapter 4, the culture of work varies within and between industries, over time and among regions. The hazy distinction between even the cultural concepts of work and leisure may pose serious practice questions. Let's consider this description of a computer technician: He "owns his small computing system and after a long day in the lab, he will go home and tinker with it.... He says that what he does at work serves as recreation for him. At work he deals with hardware; when he's home, he focuses on software—reading programming manuals and creating new software for his own computer" (Kidder, p. 195).

The question can be raised whether some careers have not come full circle. That is, are some computer mavens more like their agricultural ancestors in the integration of work and leisure in that there is less segmentation of the 9-5 work, after 5 leisure syndrome?

Sociology   "The sociological imagination," wrote C. Wright Mills, "enables its possessor to understand the larger historical scene in terms of its meaning for the inner life and the external career of a variety of individuals.... The first fruit of this imagination...is the idea that the individual can understand his own experience and gauge his own fate only by locating him within his period...and only become aware of others in his circumstances"

(1959, p. 5). The sociological connections of individuals and society are directly applicable to a social work understanding of work. The work of the individual at a specific point in time cannot be fully understood apart from structures of work, societal forces, and the experiences of other workers and nonworkers.

The effects of social structures—roles and organizations— on variables such as occupation and group identification compel the "sociologically imaginative" outlook that Mills advocates. Three particular books stress the importance of a deep awareness of social structure and their effects on roles of the individual.

White Collar is the now-classic account of a "type" of employee that emerged after World War I. In the introduction to this study, author C. Wright Mills maintained that "by examining white-collar life, it is possible to learn something about what is becoming more typically 'American'…. What must be grasped is the picture of society as a great salesroom, an enormous file, an incorporated brain, a new universe of management and manipulation. By understanding these diverse white collar worlds, one can also understand better the shape and meaning of modern society as a whole, as well as the simple hopes and complex anxieties that grip all the people who are sweating it out in the middle of the 20th century" (1956, p. 353).

Mills described bureaucrats, professionals, salespeople, and clerical workers. He outlined dynamics of status, success, and power as they affect these groups. His was a picture of a bland and impotent "middle class." "Since they have no public position, their private positions as individuals determine in what direction each of them goes…. So now they waver. They hesitate, confused, vacillating in their opinion, unfocused, and discontinuous in their actions…. They may be politically irritable, but they have no political passion. They are a chorus, too afraid to grumble, too hysterical in their applause."

A more contemporary examination of another "collar" is Louise Kapp Howe's *Pink Collar Worker*. Though not a trained sociologist, Howe examined five traditionally female occupations: beautician, saleswoman, waitress, clerical worker, and homemaker. She analyzed who they were, what exactly they did in their work, where they did it, when they worked, and why. This study illuminated the contributions of such workers. But, equally important, it raised questions of structure, national policy, and assumptions that shape the meaning and experience of work for millions of women.

Sociologist Mirra Komarovsky based her book *Blue Collar Marriage* on a series of case studies of working class families. Though her focus was marriage, it was the blue-collar milieu that framed the study, pointing out again how roles and structures of work insinuate themselves on the experience of individuals and families.

These three studies each examined a different slice of the Western work experience. White-, pink-, blue-, and "no-collar" workers are of course dynamic groups, each existing in certain periods of time, surrounded by laws, policies, traditions, and beliefs that make absolute description illusory. Only if society never changed could we count on sociological description to be stable and reliable. Caution must be used in categorizing people based on the apparent color of their work collars. Nevertheless, categories are useful for organizing possibilities and for posing questions to investigate. This is the value of a sociological perspective to the social worker.

Social Work and Synthesis

We have attempted to heighten the reader's consciousness of the criticality of a multidisciplinary understanding of work and working. By drawing on history, anthropology, and sociology, we hope to have illustrated the relative weakness of a purely psychological or political focus on work. The disservice done to client systems by emphasizing these two perspectives alone certainly must violate tenets of social work ethics. It is beyond the scope of this chapter to provide a comprehensive study of all related disciplines and their contributions to the study of work. Certainly theology, macroeconomics, and philosophy are additional fields that would need to be included in such an undertaking. We have merely pointed out that an understanding of work is at best what Mason and Mitroff (1981) call "a messy problem," a multidimensional, dynamic entity.

We propose the following argument for a broad conceptualization of work within the practice of social work:

> The person in the social environment is the business of social work. Work is an aspect of the environment of fundamental importance to person and community. The complex nature of work compels a multidisciplinary awareness of the phenomenon that both transcends and subsumes psychology or ideology. Social work practice then achieves a more complete understanding of the person within the social environment. Ultimately, this perspective should lead to sounder, more responsible practice, particularly in the work setting.

Ultimately we are suggesting that social work as a discipline accept the burden of the needed synthesis. A psychosocial approach to work with individuals was once considered radical. Its efficacy, however, became its most compelling argument. In light of this tradition, it would seem not such a huge leap to integrate the cultural-historical with the psychosocial. Legitimizing such a framework would enhance both skills and understanding and would be the first step toward a coherent and functional social work view of work.

Why are we so insistent upon a framework for work? Why do we insist that social work curricula pay attention to work as a developmental and social force? We do so because ironically, as alluded to earlier, just when some social workers began to label themselves "industrial" social workers, the world changed. Journalists began referring to the "postindustrial era."

The Industrial Revolution had apparently waned; working America was notably different. This is "our" time; the postindustrial age will demand the attention of social workers in every specialty. From questions and problems of this era will emerge research and arenas of practice for social work far into the next century. Change will be the central theme.

POSTINDUSTRIAL WORK AND SOCIAL WORK

The form and substance of this so-called postindustrial age are still emerging. People who work sense that something is different. The old "givens" of work are no longer reliable, but as yet there are few new givens.

As management guru Peter Drucker put it, "You don't have to worry about workers under 25, they have great mobility. And for the ones over 55, it's a problem of waiting for retirement money. But the workers between 25 and 55 who are married with small children and a mortgage—that's where the problem is. And this is where I think the social turbulence of the next 20 years will be" (Cook, 1982, p. 163).

Caught in a kind of technological time warp, the children of auto workers in Detroit can't depend on retiring from the auto industry as their parents did—either the plant will be closed or they will have to compete with robots for jobs. Entry level jobs requiring only basic skills of manual dexterity and simple direction following are rapidly disappearing. Noncomplex work is more quickly and efficiently done by automation. It is more likely that today's first job will be in a fast-food establishment or somehow connected with processing information than on an assembly line. The assembly line, for decades a symbol of the worst aspects of work—boring, repetitive, and authoritative—is fast becoming an anacronism. Training alone is not the answer. Though education is increasingly geared to the use and application of the computer, change is occurring so fast that training is often obsolete before it has been completed.

"In the current system," Dr. James O'Toole tells us, "general, basic, liberal education is provided to the children of the privileged, who then are able to pursue advanced, specialized education in preparation for good jobs. In contrast, narrow vocational education is given to the children of the disadvantaged who then enter the kinds of jobs that technology is eliminating" (1983, p. 16).

"The only hope for the disadvantaged," he continues, "is to learn to read, write and compute so they can acquire the skills needed for the jobs of the future." Soon "there will only be work for those who have the skills of speaking, listening, observing and measuring and the confidence to use their minds to analyze and solve problems" (1983, p. 16). Success will come to those who have "learned how to learn; the unthinking jobs will all be done by machines" (1983, p. 16).

What has all this to do with the practice of social work? Perhaps as much as anything, the term *postindustrial* marks an awareness of change. Transcending both politics and economics is the fact that for millions of the employed and unemployed in America, the world indeed is being transformed.

James Cook described it this way: "The U.S. is profoundly changing the way it uses [people] and materials, capital and manufacturing processes. We are undergoing what economists (and social workers) call a structural change, touched off by a spurt of energy prices but stemming from an even more fundamental cause" (1982, pp. 163–164). Those fundamental causes he refers to as "downsizing."

> Take the downsizing of American automobiles. It began with the need to save gasoline. It is ending with a saving of everything—rubber, steel, glass, and above all labor. Though few people realized it at the time, Congress, in legislating fuel-consumption standards for American cars, committed itself to a radically different industrial structure. You downsized the American car to save gas, and you wound up downsizing not only the U.S. auto industry itself but a substantial part of the industrial base that supported it (1982, pp. 163–164).

Now that improved technology makes "less is better" feasible, it is also economically preferable, and "autos," Cook points out, "are only the beginning" (1982, pp. 163–164). Downsizing cannot be done without pain—lots of pain. Thought of in this sense, the current industrial depression has virtually nothing to do with "Reagonomics," "Volckeronomics," or "Carternomics." Nor will it yield readily to politicians' simplistic cures. If not politicians, who does have a cure for the pain of structural transition? Social work has done much to help understand and facilitate structural change in families and communities. Perhaps application of those skills to the transformation of the nature of work is possible. Workers whose skills have become or are nearly obsolete, those facing potential layoff, even those with new job opportunities are feeling bewildered, off-balance, frightened of the pace and effects of change in their lives. A Fortune 500 executive, in a speech to officers of his company, said, "The single greatest constant we will need to learn to manage...is change." He went on to list four issues in flux which are affecting the nature of work:

> The search for balance between a drive for greater employment security and worker entitlements on the one hand and the need for more self-responsible employees, able to function effectively in an ambiguous environment, on the other.
> How to make the technological transitions necessary to compete successfully in world markets with the skills of existing work forces.
> In an increasingly diverse work force, rules and policies once workable are now dysfunctional; developing new policies, which meet the needs of all

work "stakeholders," is now the charge.
   The dynamics of change themselves.

Another corporate executive, writing about a similar theme to his company's employees stated,

> For the past several years, we have experienced some difficult times. This has also been a period of learning and accomplishment.... As we have had to adapt to conditions for which our normal personnel policies and procedures were not intended, we have remained consistently proud of our employee programs and you our employees. However, as we look forward and try to picture the human system that will complement these emerging technological and organizational strategies, it is our belief that we have an opportunity and an obligation to change our personnel practices in a positive direction, while remaining unalterably committed to the principle [upon which this company was founded].

CONCLUSION

We have attempted to describe the environment into which the brave social worker ventures. For a profession whose tenets include "knowing the environment," an understanding of postindustrial work is imperative. It is fundamental that social workers be able to comprehend work through the eyes of the clients they serve—individuals, labor, management, and the community—to most effectively "be where the client is." It is equally important that we have conceptually enabling theories and constructs on work that act as tools of integration.

   In 1968, Helen Harris Perlman devoted a full chapter of the book *Persona* to a discussion of work. That was a foreshadowing of a social work consciousness of the fundamental importance of work. Concluding that chapter, she wrote, "The spillover of the problems or pleasures of work into other life roles, its effect upon marriage and parenthood, its effect upon the growing child's idea of the values and opportunities in the workaday world—these and other considerations are grist for the thought, observation, and helping actions of all those concerned with human fulfillment" (1968, p. 84). Based on that perspective, we maintain that research questions and arenas of practice emerge naturally from a social work conceptualization of work.

CHAPTER FOUR
WORK THROUGH THE EYES OF THE OCCUPATIONAL SOCIAL WORKER

In Chapter 3 we addressed what every social worker should know about work, tracing its emergence as a separate and distinct institution and emphasizing that an understanding of work must go beyond psychological precepts and ideological politics to the insights of history, sociology, and anthropology. In this chapter we move closer to the heart of occupational social work practice by looking at the individual in the context of work and introducing a framework for understanding the workplace itself. To do this we rely on three elements: the workplace milieu, functions of work, and stakeholders in the work complex.

Milieu, integral to social workers' understanding of "person in environment," is most commonly that of family or community in social work education. "Functions of work" and "stakeholders in the work complex" are two additions we propose for the occupational social worker's analytical categories. Social workers are trained to observe intrapsychic dynamics, interpersonal relationships, and idiosyncratic situations and events; work functions and stakeholders are suggested as supplemental aids to the specialist.

PERSON IN CONTEXT OF WORK

During the time Freud was developing his methods for unraveling conflicts in the human psyche, society held the family as a unit of fundamental importance. Particularly in the middle-class families he knew, roles were rigidly established, and status, respectability, security, and values were derived from them. The family was a compulsory organization. As Robert Frost put it, "Home is the place where, when you have to go there, they have to take you in." For the family of the early 1900s, it was necessary to "look after the old, the young, and the sick.... They were chained to one another and could not get away." Small wonder that Freud unleashed a search of family history and dynamics to untangle the conflicts and behavior of men and women. So much family data was available that the skilled clinician was rich in material with which to work.

The contemporary family is, however, a more voluntary unit. The context in which people are defined and shaped is more complex. Peter Drucker, in observing family changes, remarked, "All the talk about alienation in our society greatly underrates the ability of human beings to form communities. We're building voluntary communities. The power of the nuclear family is augmented now by social peer groups, mentors, and support systems" (Cook, p. 163).

Such shifts bring work into a sharper light—as a surrogate family augmenting the nuclear family, and as a vehicle for projection and displacement from the nuclear family. Work, in the life of today's citizen, holds a meaning that may be as significant as the family was in Freud's era. Take, for example, John DeLorean's remark to Gail Sheehy in *Passages*: "My dad was a factory worker. He had very few interests. He was an alcoholic. No person has had the influence on my life that Bunkie Knudsen (General Motors general manager) did" (p. 67). We do not want to minimize the impact of his father on John DeLorean's life; his need for Knudsen's guidance may well be explained by the lack of a relationship with his father. The point is to emphasize the malleability of people well beyond early development. Erikson points out,

> Nothing less is at stake than the development and maintenance in children of a positive identification with those who know things and how to do things. Again and again in interviews with especially gifted and inspired people one is told spontaneously and with a special glow that one teacher can be credited with having kindled the flame of hidden talent. Against this stands the overwhelming evidence of vast neglect.

We know from our social work therapy the value of the "reconstructive emotional experience." It should not surprise us, then, that what Erikson reports about school children is also true for adults at work. Indeed, in *The Life Cycle Completed* (1982), he states, "To adulthood we have assigned the critical antithesis of generativity vs. self-absorption and stagnation. Generativity encompasses procreativity, productivity and creativity, and thus generation of new beings as well as of new products and new ideas including a kind of self generation concerned with further identity development" (p. 67). We have observed that a closely knit work group, the guidance of a wise and patient manager, or the tyranny of an obsessive supervisor can affect profoundly the view of reality that an individual may develop in the workplace.

In his early writing, Erikson describes work as a sense of industry which develops in early school-age children. In describing the formation of identity, he states, "With the oncoming latency period the advancing child forgets, or quietly sublimates...the drives which have made him dream and play. He now learns to win recognition by producing things. He develops perseverance and adjusts himself to the inorganic laws of the tool world and can become an eager and absorbed unit of a productive situation" (p. 24). Later, Erikson alludes to the influences of factors outside the child's primary environment: "The ego, if understood as a central and partially unconscious organizing agency, must at *any* given stage of life deal with a changing self which demands to be synthesized with abandoned and anticipated selves" (p. 211).

We are profoundly shaped by family and social relationships—the familiar arenas of social work practice. Likewise we are touched and affected by developmental tasks of mastery that develop with adult notions of work. It is with this less familiar arena that we are concerned here.

WORK AND PERSON—ORGANIZING CONCEPTS FOR STUDY

To understand family forces in the developmental process, social workers observe milieu, intrapsychic dynamics, interpersonal relationships, and idiosyncratic situations and events. These categories enable us to analyze and synthesize individual cases. When used as a framework over time with many people, they also contribute to an understanding of family and social systems. These categories are also fundamental to our study of the workplace, as they illuminate forces, patterns, and dynamics not otherwise apparent. It is presumed that social workers are, at a minimum, knowledgeable in these categories. For the occupational social worker, there are two more categories we believe must be added to the repertoire of practice knowledge: functions of work and workplace stakeholders. Underlying these additional categories is the necessity for a more intimate understanding of the milieu of work, as distinguished from those of family and community. This section will discuss those three concepts in preparation for occupational casework examples.

Workplace Milieu

Milieu generally refers to the environment in which a person exists. The social environments of family and community are usually seen as the dominant areas of influence in an individual's life. Indeed, since the time of Jane Addams, social workers have developed "eagle's eye" views of their client's milieu. Every settlement house worker knows the neighborhood police officers, which storekeepers are sharp observers of community life, city council members, and latent community controversies. Every caseworker knows the family history, its relationships, and its place in the community.

Knowledge of milieu guides assessment of an individual client's symptoms or pathology, and suggests interventions that may be successful. It also provides the worker with a medium for reality testing unavailable to the clinician who studies an individual in isolation, apart from his or her significant environment. To attempt to treat employees in isolation from their environments is to construct a reality that does not exist.

But just what is the work milieu? There is no single description to "sum up" the work environment. It varies from industry to industry, within each industry, and even within a particular company. There may be similarities that are recognizable from company to company, but specific work environments are as idiosyncratic as individual families. There are, however, five elements that can be used to analyze a specific milieu: setting, task, organization, population, and culture.

Setting Setting is multifaceted. It may be an office complex or a factory; a region, such as a coal mine or an oil field; the home (particularly with the advent of personal computers connecting to a central worksite); a hospital or school; a store; or a vehicle, such as a plane, a train, or someday even a space station.

Setting distinctly influences the nature of the work milieu. The limits and customs of liberty, autonomy, cooperation, participation, respect, authority, and communication are affected, though not wholly determined, by setting. An anecdote will illustrate. One company in a western city has been in existence for roughly a century. For many years it had occupied a sprawling group of old warehouses. A relatively small company, it had an air of informality and a familial feel. In the 1970s the company experienced a surge of success and, feeling that it was time to look the part of the successful company, the owners built a new, multistoried facility. After occupying the new complex for a time, one of the owners was asked by an architect how he liked the new building. Somewhat ruefully, the owner replied that it had insinuated an air of formality into the company, which he regretted. And in the placement of officers on the top floors of the building, with lower level employees on floors below, there was greater isolation and separateness between managers and employees and more emphasis on hierarchy. The architect suggested that buildings could be designed in which such results were not inevitable. Intrigued, the owner challenged the architect to produce a facility that would encourage the informality and collegiality that once had made his company special. Two years after moving into its new headquarters, the company moved again— this time to a group of modern buildings that set a tone for collaboration, communication, and relationships, in line with the company's heritage. Walking around this complex, one has the feeling of being on a small college campus, rather than in a more traditional hierarchical workplace. In this case, the setting dramatically altered the work milieu.

Task   In the work milieu, many functions and disciplines converge to achieve one or more tasks—producing material goods, providing information, or furnishing a service. The task orientation binds a work community. While individual needs, goals, and methods may vary within a company, transcending these are the products or services the company provides its buying constituents. Task also has the power to cast various lights on milieu. Some tasks may be particularly uplifting, as in a research lab working feverishly toward a cure for cancer. Others may be onerous, such as the production of chemicals for germ warfare. (What is defined as uplifting or onerous will vary with individual belief systems.) The nature of the task to be accomplished by any particular work institution will, in a general though perhaps subtle way, affect the work milieu.

Task has three elements: the collective task or mission of the whole organization (e.g., to provide farmers with fertilizer); subgroup tasks that contribute to the collective mission (such as production, quality control, or sales); and individual tasks (for example, packaging a specific quantity of fertilizer or overseeing a particular work group). The dynamic interplay of needs and pressures among these elements are affected by the remaining factors of milieu: organization, population, and culture.

Organization   Workplace organization varies widely. Some workplaces are rigidly hierarchical, relying on a chain of command for structure, authority, and task accomplishment. Military installations, insurance, and accounting firms still rely, in large part, on this model to achieve their goals and accomplish their tasks. "Adhocracies" characterize other work organizations, particularly in entrepreneurial firms such as exist in California's "Silicon Valley," along Route 128 in Massachusetts, and in some technical parks in the South. In such work settings, speed and creativity are values key to survival and growth and antithetical to chains of command and hierarchy. Temporary teams, committees, and task forces are more functional in such workplaces than inflexible departments or divisions. Functional, divisional (or product structure) and "matrix" are adjectives that further differentiate work organizations. Referring to kinds of relationships, these terms indicate that power and authority in decision making can be concentrated, dispersed, or shared, respectively, as illustrated in the diagrams in Figure 4-1.

In a divisional organization, each division manager is responsible for all or almost all of the functions involved in providing a product or service. In the traditional functional organization, each manager is responsible for a specified function, such as production, human resources, or finance. In a matrix organization, there are two organizational structures, one arranged by function and the other by project. A vastly simplified description of the

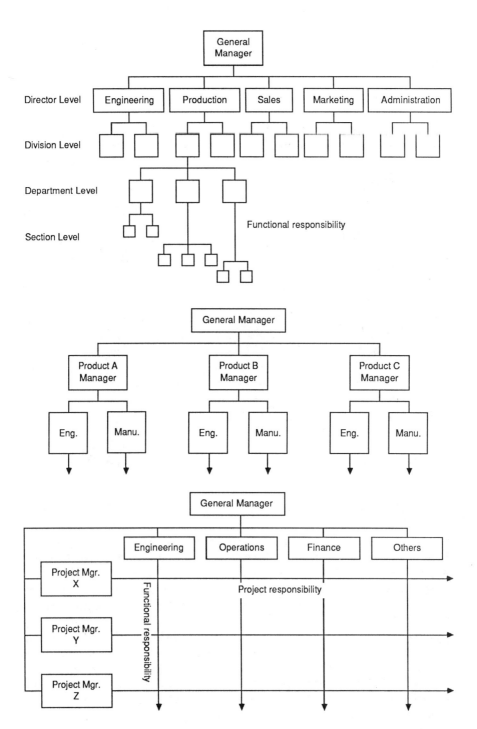

FIGURE 4-1 The traditional management structure; pure product structure; and pure matrix structure.

advantages of each is that divisional organizations foster independence and entrepreneurialism; functional organizations have the potential of great efficiency; and matrix organizations draw on personnel, materials and services from functional units to accomplish specific tasks, theoretically enabling rapid changes and special project accomplishment.

Population Demographics are statistical characteristics of human populations; psychographics, a companion science, are the psychological and sociological distinctions that exist within and between populations that may or may not be demographically similar. Once work populations were relatively homogenous; particular groups, by set or ethnic identification, could be connected with specific types or settings of work. That is no longer true. Today's work is not explained simply. It is female as well as male— twenty years ago there were twenty-three million American women in the work force, whereas by 1984 there were forty-eight million—and includes workers of all ages and races. Persons may be salaried or paid hourly, working part-time, full-time, as consultants, per diem—between 1970 and 1982, there was a 42 percent increase in the number of part-time workers, and they made up 11.6 percent of the total work force. Workers comprise a variety of religions, ethnicities, citizenships, educational levels, marital statuses, family configurations, sexual preferences, and physical abilities. This list suggests myriad composites of today's worker. Each attribute suggests a potentially sensitive theme of which the occupational social worker must be aware. Following are three worker profiles suggesting the complexity of themes brought to and emerging from the work milieu as a result of a diverse population.

Maria is a twenty-three-year-old Mexican-American, hired by a company for a nonexempt (hourly) entry level job. She is a single parent with a high school diploma. Maria is bright, though in spite of her diploma, she is poorly educated. She is the sole supporter of her daughter and tries to send money to relatives in Mexico monthly. The stresses of her life undermine her physical well-being; Maria's susceptibility to illness and her small daughter's needs foster a pattern of work absenteeism, which is affecting how she is perceived by others at work who value the "Protestant work ethic." Whatever Maria's strengths, if she is not viewed as reliable, ambitious, and committed to her work, she will be passed over for raises and promotions.

To the occupational social worker, this situation has significance for both the individual and the organization. What, if any, are the social and psychological obstacles that affect Maria in establishing an intimate primary relationship, which might ease the pressures of single parenting, tight finances, and loneliness? How do her ethnic heritage or her sexual role and identity affect her efforts to be a successful, independent worker in an American company? What are her conflicts, and how are they managed? In what way, if any, is Maria somatizing her conflicts, and what are the implications to her and her daughter? Maria's case is rich in material that stimulates exploration and dilemmas that may be social, psychological, organizational, or ethical in nature.

Other questions surface concerning the work organization. To be understanding of Maria's work and absence patterns may appear humanistic, but to ignore her lapses in attendance and energy may undermine a sense of fairness and reason on which others in the group rely. Balancing flexibility with arbitrary enforcement of policy is a delicate task, which challenges all work organizations. But what is the responsibility of the workplace to a single parent? A number of experimental efforts have been made over the years, e.g., subsidizing private day care facilities and offering day care on the premises, while some have simply ignored the issue. Occupational social workers in community relations, affirmative action, or clinical roles may have varying perspectives on the best answer to this challenge and may collaborate on thoughtful responses.

Even if Maria's work habits were exemplary, her education has likely predetermined her career potential. American business spends considerable money on remedial education of employees who come out of our public schools. This education is primarily in the fundamental skills of speaking and writing English, reading, and arithmetic. The new technologies of postindustrial America are rapidly eliminating lower level jobs which have previously gone to less educated workers. Work observer James O'Toole has stated,

> In the current system, general, basic, liberal educations are provided to the children of the privileged, who then are able to pursue advanced, specialized education in preparation for good jobs. In contrast, narrow vocational education is given to the children of the disadvantaged, who then enter the kinds of jobs that technology is eliminating.... The only hope for the disadvantaged is for them to learn to read, write, and compute so they can then acquire the skills needed for jobs of the future. Soon, there will only be work for those who have the skills of speaking, listening, observing, and measuring and the confidence to use their minds to analyze and solve problems. Those who will succeed in the workforce will be those who have learned how to learn—the unthinking jobs will all be done by machines (p. 67).

We raise this issue again to demonstrate that focus on the individual alone is often insufficient practice when other institutions, policies and social change intrude. The occupational social worker is responsible for understanding and intervening imaginatively, to the benefit of both client and system.

Focusing still on the impact of specific population profiles on the work milieu, let us turn to Adam, a forty-five-year-old white man with a degree in chemical engineering from a midwestern university. He is Catholic, married with two children, and sexually involved with a female coworker. In many ways Adam is experiencing an awakening of emotional strengths he has spent a lifetime denying; he finds himself filled with guilt and conflict.

Though he runs regularly, his blood pressure is elevated. The coworker is pressing him to choose between her and his wife, and his wife is resisting marital counseling. His ability to concentrate and make critical decisions at work is markedly impaired. Having referred others to counseling, he finally seeks out the social worker himself.

From the perspective of an individual, this may be a common tale. But what questions can the workplace environment lead us to explore? What is happening in Adam's career? Does growth seem to have stopped? Are new electronics technologies devaluing his training in chemical engineering? Is he receiving needed reward and acknowledgment at work? How is divorce viewed in a corporation whose top executives are Catholic? From a systems perspective, we are pressed to consider the taboos of this company's culture for coworker involvement. What, if any, are the punishments? Is there a tacit agreement to "look the other way"? Does the social worker in affirmative action see the organization responding differently to men and women in this situation? What is the company's posture on retraining employees over forty for a place in the new technologies? Are there stress management groups in which employees have an outlet for understanding similar conflicts and how they affect health and employment? In these examples, it is easy to see how attention to diverse population facilitates practice shifts from microsphere to macrosphere and vice versa—from individual to system or system to individual. It is this flexibility of perspective and practice that differentiates the medical model employee assistance program from the occupational human service system.

One last example serves to illustrate the multiplexity of responses in a heterogeneous population. *Kir* is a thirty-five-year-old black woman. Though she has a college degree from a small Atlantic Coast college, she has recently started a new career as a plumber. She is engaged and has no children. Breaking into her new field has been difficult—her male coworkers, resisting changes in what they consider valuable traditions, have been surly on occasion or overly helpful in ways that impede her learning. Her boyfriend's ambivalence—his pride in her accomplishment mixed with his notions about women's roles— precipitates mixed messages, which are unsettling their relationship. Recently Kir began to cry for no apparent reason in a meeting with her supervisor. Worried about her ability to succeed, Kir sought the counsel of the social worker in the affirmative action office.

The worker had met with Kir before she decided to pursue her new career. They had spend much time exploring Kir's growing up, the influences that brought her to such a career move, and the potential problems and pleasures of the change. Now they begin dealing with some of the reality issues Kir faces, working to strengthen weakened coping mechanisms and to develop support systems as she straddles the boundaries of the black middle class and the blue-collar working class. The worker also refers Kir and her boyfriend to another therapist to work on the issues they face as a couple.

Still, the worker's exploration is unfinished. How can Kir's supervisor help ease tensions in his group resulting from this break with tradition? Are other women in similar positions facing the same pressures? Would a support group be helpful for them, or would it only accentuate their differences? Are the labor representatives sensitive to the issues so Kir's policy rights are protected, or is this part of the problem?

Culture   Edward Burnett Tylor, an eminent British anthropologist, was among the first to define culture. In 1871, he wrote, "Culture is that complex whole which includes knowledge, belief, art, morals, law, custom and any other capabilities and habits acquired by man as a member of society." Writing for social workers, Carter and Anderson (1974) stated, "Culture refers to the way of life followed by the group, that is, society…that which binds society together and includes its manners and morals, tools and techniques."

In many respects, understanding the culture of work and particular workplaces is a special imperative for social work. In fact, social work is rich with studies that provide insight into client environments: Herbert Gans' study of Boston's Italian West End, William Whyte's description of *Street Corner Society*, and Liebow's *Tally's Corner* shed light on supports and pressures that influence defense systems and coping abilities in the individual.

To date, no similar studies from a social work perspective have been done on the industrial environment. The importance of such work has not been overlooked, however, by anthropologists and management observers. Authors Rosabeth Moss Kanter (1977), Deal and Kennedy (1982), and James O'Toole (1984) have advanced our understanding of companies' diverse and rich cultures which reflect and shape the people who work in them.

In a book published in 1983, Kanter describes the life of a company referred to as "Industrial Supply Corporation" (Indsco). The objective of her study was to "provide a context for illuminating the ways in which organizational structure forms people's sense of themselves and of their possibilities" (p. 3). She carefully describes the culture of the company, using surveys, interviews, meetings, and documents. Implied, but not always stated, as a method was the accumulation of insights through physical presence and observation. Actually being in an environment adds a dimension analogous to the difference between reading psychometric test results and conducting a family therapy session in the home; the ability to absorb information is heightened by the direct experience. Thus, careful study of a culture is dependent on an array of methods.

Kanter reports on the culture of the Indsco setting in detail. First she presents the whole company: how it is structured organizationally, how it compares with other large producers of industrial goods, and how it is seen from the outside. She then moves closer to the innards of the company by describing espoused company values: "Indsco is a moral company— high ethics…Things like cheating on wives don't go over big. High puritan ethics.

Bribe stuff wouldn't happen here—partly because the company is too cheap and partly because there has always been a demand for its products" (p. 30). After referring to an organizational chart—a cultural artifact in itself—she tells us what it's like in this company and how the organization is viewed by its own members. "People like to laugh about it, saying that the organization chart was two miles wide and three feet long, printed on adding machine tape (p. 30). This is amplified by relating company history, and describing attempted and completed changes in the structure and their goals and consequences. Language and procedures are noted to provide insight into what is important, valued, or derided in the Indsco culture. Legends and anecdotal stories contribute further to these insights. In the case of legends, Kanter indicates that these stories correspond to different times in the institutional culture, thus providing knowledge about the nature of change and evolution there. Leadership is referred to as another diagnostic. Both the personalities of individual leaders and the organization's response to them are indicative of styles and behaviors that are sanctioned or discouraged. Expectations about moves, transfers, and status of location speak to additional issues alive in the company.

A description of the physical structure of Indsco sheds light on the reflected self-perception of company employees. Corporate headquarters are described as luxurious and inviting— the building "towered many stories in a major city," a monument to the company's importance. (By contrast, we know of another Fortune 500 company whose employees take a perverse kind of pride in the relative shabbiness of their company buildings—described as a monument to sensibility and equality.) Kanter goes on to describe the hierarchical apportionment of space and offices. "Offices with windows were for higher status managers, and their secretaries were often proud of having drapes. Corner offices were reserved for the top. It was often true that the higher the status of an executive, the less cluttered was his desk" (p. 34).

Notices, cartoons, letters, and announcements posted on bulletin boards issued further telling information. Eating facilities and customs, communication mechanisms, and acceptable styles of dress did not go unnoticed by Kanter as she collected the details of daily living to illuminate the nature of work at Indsco. Culture is not Kanter's theme; she was searching for explanations of behavior and advancement in a large company. Though her conclusions are generic to many large institutions, the idiosyncratic behaviors she observed are critical to our understanding of dynamics in the workplace.

Deal and Kennedy, in *Corporate Cultures*, point out that "each company faces a different reality in the marketplace depending on its products, competitors, technologies, government influences and so on" (p. 13). They maintain that these varying realities will determine, in large part, the inner reality of a particular company—its priorities and its openness to risk and flexibility. However, they point out that values are not standard but a rich complex of basic concepts and beliefs that "form the heart of the corporate culture" (p. 14). Heroes in the Deal and Kennedy model of cultural analysis are those "who personify the culture's values and as such provide tangible role models for employees to follow" (p. 14). While Deal and Kennedy suggest that some companies play a direct and conscious part in raising such people to the foreground, it is perhaps more likely that the vagaries of events, circumstances, and individual personalities are stronger forces than the best attempts of managerial architects in the emergence of both heroes and antiheroes in an institution. Regardless, awareness of heroes, "characters," "villians," and "ordinary folk" will provide clues to the nature of life in a particular workplace.

Deal and Kennedy refer to rites and rituals as "the systemic and programmed routines of day to day life in the company." These may include recreation, employee interrelations, ways of spending time, or company events. Rites and rituals may be trivial and subtle in nature or profound and explicit. Again, it is the complex, rather than the single trait, that tells the tale. Network is described as the "'carrier' of corporate values and heroic mythology" (p. 15). As the primary but informal mechanism for communication, it reinforces a hierarchy of power and behavior.

Deal and Kennedy point out that a company's culture does more than just shape its internal machinations. Indeed, a culture is a sort of fingerprint for the world. Through company products and reports and through coverage by news media and financial analysts, we come to intuitively sense differences between Kodak and Polaroid, IBM and Apple Computer, Delta and United Airlines.

Deal and Kennedy note that having a culture is not equivalent to having a healthy culture. Characteristics they list as potentially damaging for both individuals and the larger corporate body are

> no clear values or beliefs about how to succeed in the business;
>
> many beliefs, but no agreement on which are most important;
>
> destructive or disruptive heroes who build no common understanding about what is important;
>
> disorganized rituals of everyday life. (p. 135–136)

Other symptoms they caution against include an extreme inward focus, eschewing the realities of the larger environment, and short-term focus to the exclusion of a longer range, grander vision. Factors that signal a broad and chronic unhappiness among employees, such as turnover, absenteeism, and what they refer to as rampant emotionalism, should be noted as cries for attention.

O'Toole provides still another perspective on culture that we can use for thoughtful analysis. He exhorts students of corporate culture not to overlook the influences of the broader culture on that of a single company. In making his case, he emphasizes the need for congruence. Thus, efforts in the late 1970s and early 1980s to import Japanese philosophy and culture to American firms could be only partially successful, in that the cultures of Japan and America are fundamentally different. Without resorting to stereotype, O'Toole respects national differences and suggests that those attempting to understand or change culture not be enslaved by those differences, but be cognizant of them.

These writers advocate a more conscious awareness of corporate culture to help understand what makes some companies more "excellent" than others, to increase productivity, to respond to the diverse needs of the work force of the 1980s and 1990s, and to counter global competition. Depending on one's goals, each of these is sufficient reason for studying corporate culture. For the occupational social worker, understanding the culture in which the client population exists is fundamental to understanding the client and the community.

Specifying culture—making it tangible—is more difficult than defining the concept. Drawing from the ideas just cited, we make the following suggestions, intended as guides to the practitioner seeking to understand work and workplace culture.

1. Awareness of the national and local cultures within which a company exists, from which it takes cues, and which it affects is the starting point for any cultural assessment.

2. Understanding the industry the company is a part of— its pressures, markets, values, and traditions—will provide a context for comparison, contrast, and normative characteristics.

3. Study of the corporate mission statement, usually stated both explicitly and implicitly in annual reports and other public records, will inform one as to the intents of the system. In some businesses such a statement may form a detailed charter, subject to minimal interpretation; others may write a few broad goals, with the expectation that they will be interpreted with judgment. In either case a baseline is established for measuring espoused goals against reality.

4. Study of the work population by race, sex, age, home community, ethnic group, and educational level will give insight into the special issues, pressures, and tensions that contribute to the company culture and subcultures.

5. Legends, stories, and folklore about key people— founders, inventors, villains, people who have left the company— will illustrate sources of pride, shame, hope, and projections, and subsequently will illuminate behavior, tradition, and customs. Generally, this information is available from company members with long seniority. People who have invested time in an organization are often pleased to share history and their part in it and should be seen as an important source of information and insight.

6. Dress, office design, and building organization are indicators of formality, rigidity, and flexibility and give yet another view of the culture in which workers coexist. For some employees a tightly structured environment can be supportive, a reassuring reality. For others such a setting can be constricting and frustrating. Lack of clear hierarchy, management by committee, and ambiguity present other double-edged swords. The degrees of structure will have implications for kinds and methods of social work intervention.

7. Identification of the means of communication, formal and informal, that exist to facilitate or retard sharing of goals, news, gossip, or other pertinent company information will shed light on the importance and degree of an open or closed system.

8. Study of the philosophy and methods of internal education and training policies, for indications of attitudes on growth, personal and collective development, and perspective on the future will indicate the value placed on human resources.

Having provided some means for understanding the work milieu, we turn now to the two additional categories that we feel are vital to the occupational social worker's body of knowledge: functions of work and work stakeholders.

Functions of Work

"Functions of work" refers to the roles work itself can assume. Work is not a monolithic notion but a force that can be viewed or used in at least four ways:

as a social microcosm of the larger society;
as a means of personal or collective identification;
as a vehicle for intervention in or maintenance of human behavior systems;
as a diagnostic tool.

Work and the Social Microcosm The future is shaped by the accumulation of decisions and events—those that occurred yesterday, that unfold today, and that wait for us tomorrow. The future does not arrive unheralded. On a daily basis, collective decisions contribute to its coming. Each workplace environment confirms this. In schools, hospitals, high tech companies, or service businesses, individual employees play out their ideas, feelings, beliefs, and needs, and the lone voices become a choir—sometimes discordant, occasionally harmonious. Not surprisingly, the blend affects the lone voice, and occasionally a strong soloist leads the choir. As this occurs interworkplace, so it occurs intraworkplace and interindustry. Never before has the appreciation of the workplace as a social microcosm been so compelling. Suddenly what people in the workplace say, do and think matters.

There is a growing consciousness of and commitment to the concepts of stakeholders, participatory management, and moral responsibility in the offices of middle managers, in board rooms and on the factory floor. The appreciation of human resources in the workplace and the social microcosm was sparked by a panicked response in America to lowered productivity and a loss of national status, self-esteem, and apparent ability. However, the initial hysteria is waning, and there is a growing feeling that productivity, high or low, is a symptom, not the problem. This idea was emphasized in 1982 by the book *In Search of Excellence* by Peters and Waterman. That same year, corporate leaders, journalists, ethicists, and theologians began to speak in terms of "moral obligation, fairness, and cultural values." As company after company struggled with massive layoffs and human pain, the collective work force cried out for self-examination. We know that in therapy, people move when they are in pain. Crisis can be a great precipitator of growth and change; so it was with the workplace. What was happening at work reflected what was happening in America; concerns in the workplace for growth, opportunity, and fairness were political concerns of the society at large.

Work: A Means of Personal and Collective Identification   One of the most frequently articulated functions of work is as a means of *identification*. In response to the question, "who are you?" The typical response is to state one's occupation. Historically, this simple, elegant summing up of oneself has provided a sense of security and sometimes pride. Generations of Italian stonemasons, for example, have given information about their history, family, and community in saying "I am a stonemason." That label alluded to a multidimensionality in the individual, not so predictable in our more fast-paced world, where skill obsolescence is common. An individual educated as a teacher who is working as a security guard has a more complicated task of summing-up to do. Or for one whose job requires few skills, the identification may be demoralizing, damaging to a self-esteem that may have been very high in the context of the family.

Work as a means of self-knowledge or self-identity is also likely to change over the course of the life cycle. For the young person, an occupational label may be a source of confidence, a statement of achievement, a right of entry into the adult world. For an individual in the midstages of life, a label imbued with success may nonetheless foster a feeling of "is this all there is?" A label may not reflect the success one has had—with the advent of retirement, a whole new identity must be forged. Notable, too, is the increasingly frequent response of a surprised chuckle or silence to the banal "who are you?" One professor/author/father/magazine editor/consultant/anthropologist/public speaker answered the question with a teasing "I'm a management guru!" Seventy-year-old Peter Drucker, management consultant/author/professor of Oriental art/novelist, said at one point, "Here I am, fifty-eight, and still don't know what I'm going to do when I grow up." One suspects he might make the same comment today at age seventy-eight. His statement reflects a growing societal reluctance to sum oneself up too simply. Daniel Yankelovich explains this in part by referring to an increasing interest in conceiving self-fullfilment as a process rather than an accumulation of specific achievements, such as job titles. "This process of becoming involves the unfolding of a self whose characteristics and expressions fascinate the one who beholds them—him/herself."

Still another dimension must be added to the complexity of the identifying functions of work. For a time it seemed that an increasingly complicated world would require everyone to specialize in one field or another. Liberal arts schools were under attack for offering "irrelevant" programs. However, now that the pace of change in industry, politics, education, etc, makes the tenure of a specialist somewhat precarious, the question arises, "Will my speciality be obsolete next week? Next year? Can I communicate effectively with specialists in other fields?"

Recognition of this can be seen in companies that are restructuring job titles and responsibilities to make them more inclusive, flexible, or transferable. In many companies, for example, a goal is to broaden the knowledge base and responsibilities of people in skilled crafts to enable them to adapt more easily to rapidly changing technology. The skilled crafts have been organized in a static fashion since the Middle Ages; to change a worker's identity from one of fierce loyalty to a particular craft to that of a multi-skilled expert will have implications both for the individual undergoing the change and for his or her organization.

Work: A means of intervention or maintanance in human behavior and systems. Occasionally a critical job change initially resisted by an employee becomes a source of satisfaction and pride. Jansen was an engineer who enjoyed the isolated aspect of his work. He was free to think, experience, and write for technical journals. His social skills were minimal, however, and family life was passive and somewhat frustrating. As the nature of work changed for Jansen's group, more demands were placed on him to collaborate with the team. His resistance to change was eventually disruptive enough to cause his manager real concern. Determined to expand Jansen's ability, the manager assigned Jansen's work to another member of the group and made him group leader. The manager spent long hours with him discussing leadership styles, delegation, and means of communication. Jansen was also sent to a variety of training programs. Eight months later the manager had a new job, Jansen had replaced him, and his newly earned social skills were positively affecting his family.

Another manager may have simply accepted Jansen's behavior. Without the pressure of change, Jansen might have continued in his engineering work to retirement, perhaps contributing to the corporation on the basis of a work style that was comfortable and functional for him. Or without the interest of the manager, the winds of change might have allowed Jansen to maintain his own style but miss out on new work that developed.

Marx maintained that religion is the opiate of the masses. We suggest that, for many, work is an opiate. It is not unusual for people involved in an exciting project or discovery to devote weeks of twelve-hour days to the effort. In such cases one can often observe people on sharp learning curves, excited about learning, building, and achieving. Twelve-hour days as a long-term style, however, are quite another matter. The worker who regularly requests double shifts, the financial analyst who pours over reports for long hours each night, or the successful vice-president who strategizes with staff long beyond the supper hour may be delaying—until interrupted by a crisis—confrontation with issues that have been successfully repressed, sublimated, or displaced.

Work as a Diagnostic Tool. In therapy, clients act out patterns of relationship that occur in daily lives; the group experience is another context in which unconscious needs, conflicts, and behavior are reenacted. Family therapy is an additional means by which we acquire information about system-wide patterns and the individual. To this list of contexts proffering diagnostic tools, we add work. The work environment is generally all-encompassing; behavior styles, interpersonal relationship, drives, and needs become clearly apparent. Eight hours a day, five days a week, fifty weeks a year is too much time to successfully shield oneself from coworkers. Even in corporate cultures that stress personal distance and formality, individuals show facets of themselves in their responses to that culture. Thus, while the social worker may not have direct access to observing behavior in the family, the work environment is also a laboratory for client behavior.

Sometimes individuals are unwell, and sometimes it is the family that is unwell. Sometimes person and family collude to maintain a system that change might destabilize, for better or worse. So it is with individuals and workplaces. The workplace is not an inherently unhealthy environment. The person is not always inherently healthy (healthy referring there to psychodynamic rather than physical functioning). A practitioner can glean clues to appropriate responses and behaviors by observing an individual in the context of the work milieu. New and old patterns emerge. For example, the work milieu may encourage patterns of dependency that counter the goals of the client and the social worker. Conversely, appropriate independence may be discouraged in the milieu, and an otherwise "healthy" individual may be tagged disruptive or rebellious. Awareness of these dynamics is critical for the practitioner; to assess when and how work can be used as a means of intervention or to understand the positive and negative aspects of maintenance, one must be able to see work as a background for individual pathology and symptoms and a foreground for systemic maladies. The following three cases illustrate:

Case #1. Over a two-month period, referrals to the counseling unit of a large manufacturing plant have increased by approximately 25 percent. Presented problems vary though there is a consistency of symptoms—either heightened anxieties or depression, which share time of onset and vagueness of cause. In the psychosocial assessment, a scan of the environment indicates changes in work organization as a result of "quality-of-work-life" efforts. "I have a different supervisor everyday," "I never know what I'll be doing until I actually get in that day," "I am not working with my old group any longer," and "I don't like moving around so much" were comments frequently heard. In an article in *Social Work,* David Kaplan referred to "disorders of change" and suggested this phenomenon would be increasingly common.

One choice the practitioner has is to treat each client individually, pursuing the roots of the change disorder to either alleviate the anxiety or depression or to help the client adapt, in this case to the so-called quality-of-worklife experiments. An alternative intervention would be to discuss with the quality-of-worklife designers the actual impact of the experiment using the collective data of client symptoms. Interventions at this broader level might include reassessment of the experiment with participation by the affected workers, modifications to the experiment, or a change to voluntary participation in the experiments.

Case #2. No human system remains static for long, and business systems are no different. As times, needs, and management techniques go in and out of vogue, organizational changes occur: for example, a structural shift from centralized to decentralized, a move from matrix management to more clearly defined hierarchies, or a change or redefinition of work group membership.

Ray F. has been a key manager in Celex Corporation's marketing division for seventeen years. She has been referred to a counselor by her manager, who is frustrated with her recalcitrant attitude, temper outbursts, and passive-aggressive blocking of management tasks and goals. Ray, for her part, is bewildered and frightened by the behavior that she feels is uncharacteristic and out of control. Is she experiencing some fundamental ego deterioration? No, she is going through a fairly normal phase of termination anxiety. Her manager has been transferred to a new assignment, the marketing division is being restructured, and Ray is scheduled to join a new multidisciplinary management team. In fact, Ray's own manager, ambivalent over her new assignment and unable to terminate well a group she has lead for over twenty years, has not discussed the new reorganization in any way that gives vent to fears, concerns or losses. To take the micro view of Ray's problems might uncover past losses being triggered by the current crisis. We would, however, overlook the similar but less obvious discomfort of others experiencing the marketing department's demise. And we would miss the opportunity to use the reorganization as a reconstructive experience. Ray may be presented to the social worker as the problem; we know, however, from family therapy that it is often the "healthy" family member who signals trouble and calls for help. Working with this group to better acknowledge and cope with their individual and collective losses could have important implications for their integration into new groups, as well as future change and loss in both personal and work lives.

Case #3. A group of ten engineers is at a four-day retreat to work on a troublesome design problem in a current project. Each day one of the members, Bob J. misses breakfast, asks questions that indicate he has not done the previous night's reading, and engages in lengthy and seemingly irrelevant arguments with members of the group. At other times he lapses into silence, but overall he does not contribute to the group's work. Eager to make the retreat productive, Bob's manager tries to talk with him on several occasions. Having gotten nowhere, the manager visits the counselor when the group returns to the plant. His conversation with the counselor reveals a pattern of behavior that has been getting progressively worse for some months. As the quality of Bob's work and work relationships is being affected and there is no evidence of an environmentally caused problem, the manager determines Bob must seek counseling to explore his behavior or risk a negative job evaluation and a sharply reduced salary increase. Feeling forced into dealing with his behavior, Bob finally sees the counselor. Alcoholism is diagnosed and treatment is begun.

Judgments about intervention depend largely on familiarity with the work milieu, if we are not to confuse symptom with cause, to substitute discipline for treatment, or to encourage solely personal adaptation over organizational change. We have described how the work milieu can be examined through the filters of setting, task, organization, population, and culture. Like family and social relationships, milieu provides a backdrop against which the individual can be understood. Refining understanding is subsequently a matter of observation and inquiry, essential functions for all occupational social work.

Stakeholders in the Work Complex

By "stakeholders," we mean those parties or constituents who hold claims on the operation and nature of the workplace. The work complex includes the following kinds of stakeholders:

> Employees and their families
> Management
> Unions and labor representatives
> Shareholders
> Communities
> Suppliers
> Consumers

Many parties have legitimate, though sometimes conflicting, interests in how the workplace functions. One's assessment of those parties and their claims may be colored by ideological values, but in order for the work mission to be achieved, each party must feel some sense of balance over the long term. Where balance is not perceived, antagonism, self-interest, and adverse relations are inevitable. A description of some of the claims of various stakeholders follows.

Employees and their Families   For those employees who have families, needs tend to converge, so for purposes of description we will explore the employee family together. Employees have the need to work in a safe, just environment. Their interest is generally to maintain the workplace and to improve their lot in it—in terms of financial remuneration, safety, comfort, and the intangibles of relationships and self-esteem. Families have a stake in maintaining the work system as a factor in maintaining the family system. However, their stake is not simply in maintaining the status quo, but also in improving it. How this is viewed or in what terms it is desired is partly the angst of the diverse work force described earlier and partly a function of the great individuality of workers and families themselves.

Management   Management has the same needs as employees and their families and has the additional vested interest of improving the organization's lot, that is, increasing growth and profits. Managers desire this not simply for themselves, but because of the responsibilities they hold for other stakeholders. To fall out of favor with any of the other stakeholders is to risk impairment of the *gestalt*, a consequence for which no management member wants to be held responsible.

Unions or labor representatives   We note unions *or* labor representatives to indicate that organized, dues-collecting unions are not the only form of representation available to employees. Self-representation, ombudsmen company-sponsored representatives are variations of employee advocacy. At stake for these advocates is both the life of the system—without which they would have no context in which to operate—and the protection of their rights to advocate for change as various issues arise. The tension between management and employee advocates has historically been a peculiarly democratic form of check-and-balance system for the protection of both employees and management. Recently, that tension has evolved to a state of greater collaboration. To maintain both the health of employees and the gestalt of the workplace, the "us and them" dynamic has shifted from management and labor to American business and international competition.

Shareholders   For the most part, this group is interested in growth of the system in such a way as to maximize the return on investment. As the motivations of shareholders vary, we will not generalize further.

Communities   A community needs a tax base, employment for its citizens, and good corporate neighbors to contribute to the health of the community. Thus its interest in the workplace is that these benefits exist and are stable. A community may compromise to win certain benefits. For example, though the hope may be for an industry that does not pollute, this value may be sacrificed if the company is labor-intensive and contributes financially to the community.

Suppliers Suppliers are those businesses whose livelihood is based on services or goods provided to other businesses; the maintenance of the business industry being supplied keeps this secondary workplace alive. We saw, for example, in the late 1970s and early 1980s the failure of many suppliers whose existence was dependent on the fortunes of the auto industry.

Consumers Consumers' primary interest in the workplace system is the production of reliable, safe, quality products of value. As companies build reputations that indicate attention to the needs of consumers, e.g., in the care of children and respect for the environment, they gain a psychological benefit in addition to other more tangible ones.

The elements of milieu and constituents of the workplace gestalt are interdependent and interactive. The workplace system is highly complex and irrational; in spite of the best attempts of scholars and managers to tame it, it is a system of fallible humans, competing to meet their needs, both subtle and unconscious and explicit and rational. One set of constituent or stakeholder interests is not inherently better or more important than another, except according to one's value structure.

The stakeholders we have named (and one could list many more) form a gestalt. (The gestalt is, for our discussion here, a particular work and workplace system. A macro social work discussion of stakeholders would view the American work system or global work system as the gestalt.) For the gestalt to operate and thrive, all of the parts must in some manner be attended to with respect and fairness. Healthy work systems accomplish this. Work systems in which the competing needs of constituents are not fairly managed tend either to decline or to operate like disabled families. The challenge to occupational social workers is to understand the functions and disfunctions of competing claims and to help balance the gestalt while respecting the needs of the individual.

WORK: END OR MEANS?

A final point needs to be made. As we have noted, defining and understanding work are value-ridden endeavors. Perhaps nowhere is this demonstrated more clearly than in the differing perspectives of work as a means to an end or as an end in itself. As researchers, humanists, and practitioners, we often identify ourselves with our work and presume others do too. We find it difficult to accept that some people prefer repetitive work and resist increased responsibility to do other things. It is tempting to view such people suspiciously, to seek the roots of their disinterest or recommend quality-of-worklife programs to help them become self-actualized.

Keen awareness of these differing work perspectives is critical. To illustrate we refer to an editor at a well-known newspaper. He had been in therapy himself and was a thoughtful, unthreatened manager, committed to supporting his employees' growth. When a bright and capable assistant was assigned to him, he conscientiously provided opportunities for more responsibility and autonomy and looked forward to being able to offer a promotion. The editor became sheepishly aware of his own projections when the assistant finally came forth and explained that he did not have ambitions of acquiring more responsibility, that the additional expectations and opportunities were a burden for him. This point was made also when, as a young graduate student and feminist, I interviewed assembly line workers, prepared to hear a litany of complaints about life on the line. My resistance to upsetting my own values and perspectives became clear only slowly.

Socialization and depressed expectations may certainly play a part in the fact that not everyone wants to become a plant manager or company president. However, accepting the aspirations and goals of others nonjudgmentally is an important facet of the occupational social worker's understanding of the work-worker-workplace complex and is vital to good practice.

We hope we have demonstrated the rightful place of person in the context of work, have made more understandable the concept of workplace milieu, and have provided a rationale for adding two analytical categories to the occupational social worker's body of knowledge. We next present a sampler of occupational social work roles.

CHAPTER FIVE
ESTABLISHED AND EMERGING ROLES IN OCCUPATIONAL SOCIAL WORK

OCCUPATIONAL SOCIAL WORK ROLE OPTIONS

The discussion of occupational social work must inevitably turn to the subject of roles: what they are, and how they develop and function within today's work organizations. This chapter will provide an understanding of the diverse roles of occupational social workers as the field has evolved and expanded.

The following profiles, selected from occupational social workers around the country in a variety of work settings, demonstrate the multiplicity of roles and functions within the field. To obtain these vignettes, interviews were conducted with eight occupational social workers. They were asked to describe their job responsibilities, their environment, and how their social work education and experience have affected their functioning within the organizations they serve. The profiles are intended to provide a sample of illustrative possibilities for the contemporary occupational social worker. Such vignettes cannot illustrate organizational dynamism because the interviewees were caught in time, so to speak, in their activities. Qualitative and longitudinal studies of occupational social workers are needed to understand fully the complexity of practice.

The profiles, presented in descending order of tradition and familiarity, are:

Employee assistance manager
Union social service director
Affirmative action specialist
Personnel manager
Director of employee development and training
Urban social affairs specialist
Human resource generalist
Marketing specialist

Employee Assistance Manager

The Employee Assistance Program (EAP) has opened more doors into the workplace for social workers than any other single development. The clinical aspects of the counseling role are generally known, while the program management activities represent a broad spectrum of skills and functions. Barry Donnely* is a corporate EAP manager for a high tech firm with over seventy thousand employees worldwide. The EAP that he manages is large and complex, with twenty-four separate sites throughout the United States and Canada. Over thirty-one thousand of the company's employees are currently served by EAPs. The work force is typical of high tech—highly educated and young, with an average age of thirty-three.

Reflective of the company's matrix form of management, the EAPs outside of corporate headquarters operate autonomously, reporting to a plant manager with consulting lines to the corporate EAP. Thus, Barry's responsibilities are twofold— serving the needs of employees at corporate headquarters and coordinating and consulting with the decentralized EAPs. His span of responsibilities includes supervision and development of standards for the delivery of mental health services to all company EAPs, work with EAP staff and consultants, collaboration with health service staff in development and training related to EAP services, and supervision of professional staff within the corporate program.

The program ethos relates to the corporate philosophy; that is, it encourages flexibility. Employees take responsibility for their own actions and roles in order to foster creativity. (This is valued in the EAP as an opportunity for fostering stress within the organization, just as it also stimulates creativity, growth, and self-actualization.) While the philosophy encourages employees to balance their personal and work lives, there is recognition that work and travel may require time away from family for many.

Barry's EAP philosophy reflects corporate goals. Therefore, he has constructed a program focusing on prevention. While services to individuals are provided, Barry's role as a corporate manager is primarily to facilitate access to outside human service providers. He spends a great deal of time

---

*The names in these vignettes have been changed to insure confidentiality.

developing referral sources and enlarging the resource network for his EAP staff.

Barry also consults frequently with company managers. Drawing on his knowledge of human behavior, he contributes an understanding of personality and character types and their influence on management style and employee reaction. Recently he initiated an extensive consultation on employee health and wellness. Another project involves mainstreaming EAP instruction into the company's management training and development programs. This will help integrate the knowledge base of his staff with that of the manager training group, thus enhancing programs on performance monitoring, effective communication, and problem-solving skills.

The scope of EAP responsibilities delineated by Barry includes prevention and education activities for employees; for example, regular lunch hour seminars to raise awareness of difficult life situations and basic information and resources to manage them. Collaborative efforts with the health services division are presented on such topics as stress, hypertension, and holistic health and wellness.

Barry is an innovator in the development of program evaluation methods and data. Over the past few years, he has constructed a data information system which enables the EAP to make recommendations on human resource planning; assist in the design of employee benefits for mental health services; identify special needs within the work force; and confirm trends seen by public relations and human resource staff.

For example, an analysis of case records revealed that 10 percent of the EAP caseload were single parents. Since the corporation had no data on this group, the EAP took the lead in examining policies and programs that affect this employee population. Job sharing, working at home, and day care have become topics of study and action.

Barry's future projects include identifying company divisions not covered by EAPs and initiating the development of such services with their management teams. His broad goals are to achieve total EAP coverage of the company work force in the United States and to develop an ongoing newsletter for all divisional EAPs to share trends, program innovations, and corporate goals. He envisions broadening the EAP through involvement in developing retirement policies and services for an aging work force, and in management of relocation, human resource planning, and health and wellness activities.

Barry represents an entrepreneurial approach to the delivery of EAP services. Without professional guidelines or program models, Barry and others like him are in uncharted territory, which provides considerable opportunity for innovation. His ability to assess organizational needs, to understand and integrate corporate culture, and to build effective program mechanisms has enabled him to create a respected and influential service in the corporation. As he and his staff team become more established and "earn their stripes," the EAP will play an increasingly significant role in meeting human needs within this corporate setting.

Union Social Service Director

Jane Jordan is associate director of the social service department of a large labor union at its national headquarters. She began her occupational social work career with the union during her graduate school field placement. She filled a number of roles as the union's social work mission evolved from provision of direct services to a broader emphasis on social issues and national concerns.

The mission of her social service unit is derived from the traditions of the union, which serves labor-intensive industries where member wages eventually plateau. Because of sizeable and well-managed health and welfare funds, day care programs, retiree programs, personal services, and prepaid legal services have been established. Provision of extensive health and pension benefits is seen as a crucial responsibility of the union. The union has a strong commitment to the quality of life of workers both on and off the job, with member participation as the centerpiece of its local social service outreach.

Through union conventions, the social service department exerts policy influence on both local and national issues. Resolutions concerning health and welfare benefits are reviewed and passed at these forums. Unions are as organizationally complex as corporations; what happens at the national level may be far removed from local issues and needs. For the social service department, this necessitates effective management and program implementation strategy within the complex structure of national, regional, joint, and local boards.

Some of Jane's achievements include

training local volunteer members as information and referral agents;
coordinating health, education, and hypertension screening programs;
developing low-cost medical and dental plans;
establishing a mandatory second-surgical-opinion program;
organizing and consulting with joint labor-management EAPs;
leading seminars on communication and problem-solving skills;
giving assistance to local social service committees;
publishing a newsletter for retirees.

The technical assistance program was developed at the national office to assist local unions in establishment and improvement of their social service and retiree programs. Jane's department monitors social service activities and the needs of union locals and affiliates to evaluate program effectiveness. Special projects developed at the national office include services to meet employees' physical, social, and mental health needs and to deal with job loss resulting from plant closings.

The extent of social service delivery to union members is no small matter. Social service programs exist in approximately eight hundred of the union's fifteen hundred locals. Social service activities in the national office provide support to locals through technical assistance, training, information, education, and referral. Unlike EAP social workers, who tend to focus on direct services, this union social worker is centrally involved in human resource policy. Where company EAPs do exist, Jane encourages local social service committees to collaborate with the EAP professionals to obtain the best community services for their members and to monitor the services and policy functions of the EAP.

Another activity of Jane's staff is teaching brokering skills to local committee members. The social service committees in local unions rely on a self-help philosophy in responding to individual and family needs, and brokering skills enable volunteers to be more effective in tapping community services for union members. This approach also helps establish strong community involvement in social service delivery through organizations such as the United Way. To support these activities, headquarters staff have developed standardized service forms to help local committees obtain information for appropriate referrals, develop case management expertise, standardize approaches for problem resolution, and collect data on service gaps in the community that might be filled by United Way agencies and other community service providers.

Jane feels that occupational social work in unions will in part be shaped by changes in the current economic and political arenas. In spite of difficult times for unions, the perceived needs of members are growing. For example, hospice and home care services are new areas of member interest and need. Social workers are well suited to evaluate benefits, policies, and service quality in these areas.

Health needs constitute a major priority for this union's national social service department, as issues of prevention, cost savings, and program initiatives increasingly fall within its purview. All of this continues to emerge as union membership and power decline.

Jane plays a very active role in meeting the needs of her union's members. As a result of the strong health and welfare mandates that union officials have adopted to serve their constituency, she provides direct services, contributes to policy development, and gives technical assistance.

Affirmative Action Specialist

Given the natural affinity between the philosophy and goals of social work and those of affirmative action and equal opportunity employers, it is surprising that occupational social workers are rarely found in corporate affirmative action programs. Jim Paris, a social worker, has served as a senior affirmative action administrator for several years since holding clinical positions in community agencies and serving a stint as an assistant commissioner of a state youth agency.

Affirmative action officers generally have several major functions within corporations:

to monitor affirmative action legislation and insure corporate compliance;

to work with protected classes of workers (women, minorities, the disabled, Vietnam veterans) to assure their assimilation into the work force and to guarantee equal opportunities;

to train and educate managers and supervisors on corporate affirmative action policies and procedures.

Social workers in affirmative action departments guard against discrimination and abuses to individual freedom and also attempt to create a positive environment for individual freedoms and justice in the work setting. Jim describes his work on affirmative action issues as difficult, falling between advocacy on one hand and impartial technical assistance on the other. He views his position as a broker or mediator. He suggests that there are three major approaches to corporate affirmative action: one in which technical assistance is provided to anyone in the company who needs it; an advocacy approach; and a span broker approach, which attempts to work with all parties—management, protected classes, and the majority employee groups—by building credibility on all sides. Social attitudes toward affirmative action and the heightened level of emotional and legal debate within a workplace call for a combination of the patience of Job and the force of Rambo.

At Jim's company the affirmative action department reports to the human resource vice-president. Jim's role and responsibilities include case management and intervention. In one case, an employee came to Jim to discuss a problem. Their conversation revealed that the employee had been reluctant to deal directly with his supervisor about the problem at hand. Jim assumed the role of what he calls a span broker—he met with the employee to discuss the problem, researched the situation, and then arranged a meeting with the supervisor and the employee to resolve the situation.

Other responsibilities include monitoring legislation and court cases related to affirmative action. Jim has chaired a task force with representatives from all major areas of the company to heighten awareness of issues for handicapped employees and to develop organizational mechanisms to deal with them. Training is another duty, which involves educating groups of managers and employees about equal-employment-opportunity legislation and corporate affirmative action policies.

Jim's work highlights a natural link between the human needs of a corporation and the knowledge and skills of the occupational social worker. The workplace is a microcosm of the larger society and consequently mirrors its problems and issues. Social workers in affirmative action identify and intervene in problems of injustice and discrimination. Although considerable activity is devoted to legal aspects of affirmative action, much time is also spent in troubleshooting, crisis intervention, and negotiating conflicts common to all work settings.

Personnel Manager

Peter Dean is a social worker whose pioneering efforts make him a doyen of occupational social work. Although he is currently a personnel manager for a company's worldwide marketing division, his twenty-five year career includes work as a counselor, a manager of human development programs, an employee relations consultant, and an ombudsman.

Peter joined the company in 1959 with a background in school social work. His initial charge was to develop a career planning and education department which reported directly to the company president. The president's goal was to nurture the program until it was integrated into the corporation. This was one of the first corporate uses of social work in post-World War II America. We note that the service began as a program for career planning and education; had an educator been hired, the outcome undoubtedly would have been quite different. Because of the undefined mandate for service, Peter and his fellow social workers took initiative to widen the program's scope. Within a few years, the program had developed into a broader counseling center in which career, family, group and individual counseling for employees with emotional problems at work or home were the primary foci.

Peter's present work as personnel manager is enriched by the many roles in the company which he has filled and by his extensive understanding of the organization's structure and unique culture.

A typical day for Peter would involve working with managers on compensation claims and budgets. Later, he might consult with senior managers to review personnel concerns such as employee relations, career planning, or termination programs. He characterizes much of his work as "fire fighting"—moving from one crisis to the next, working with managers daily to resolve a wide range of problems. The following case is a typical example:

> A middle manager was with the company for 14–15 years, skilled and talented but lacking in basic interpersonal skills. The employee was never confronted with this problem until her current manager indicated a desire to transfer her out of the department. The manager was told he couldn't transfer the problem out, but had to manage it. Peter met with the employee to discuss the situation, alleviating some of the pressure from her manager, thus functioning as a consultant and advisor to ensure that the situation was handled with respect and concern for all the parties involved.

Personnel departments have not traditionally involved themselves with interpersonal issues, but the movement toward *human resource management* is changing attitudes of felt responsibility. Peter sees this movement as beneficial to both social workers and employees; as the personnel department moves toward a more comprehensive delivery of services, its role in organizational change will increase, with partnerships with line organizations being formed in the process.

Peter outlines a number of skills that social work brings to human resource management:

> an understanding of individual and group behavior;
> communication and process skills;
> aptitude for managing organizational change;
> problem solving, mediating, and planning.

The various roles Peter has played in the corporation help him see social work and corporate goals in a balanced light. "Working for a profit making organization," he points out, "requires social workers to make decisions which are influenced by financial imperatives." For example, a social worker's knowledge of how both management and employees react to layoffs makes it possible for the company to be more responsive and to assist managers in handling such difficult decisions.

Peter oversees the personnel staff of a division comprised of twenty-five hundred marketing and sales employees. He reports to the vice-president of worldwide marketing and interfaces with the sales, advertising, market research, publicity, distribution, customer service, and export departments. His staff of seventeen includes a number of personnel generalists who perform the typical range of personnel functions. Their responsibilities include developing leadership and collaborative skills to enable others to become more synergistic (e.g., assisting engineering in working with marketing), dealing with personnel problems on the job, and identifying resources to assist employees with problems. He is aware of his role as a manager in developing people both as individuals and in their careers within the corporation.

The job of personnel manager is not one that a social worker would attain early in a career. It frequently encompasses broad human resource responsibilities, such as managing compensation, benefits, training, and employee development. Peter's long history with the company, his proven record as counselor, manager, ombudsman, and troubleshooter, and his understanding of the organization have equipped him for this role. His career path provides one example for social workers in the human resource field and suggests a direction that some skilled and seasoned occupational social workers may take.

Director of Employee Development and Training

Social workers frequently overlook in corporations people-related positions not specific to counseling programs. Those who begin in EAP or counseling roles may find themselves providing a range of human services which have little to do with their original contract or job description.

Jean Ball came to CSA, a company employing 750 people in manufacture of precision measurement equipment, without corporate experience. Her work experience was in community organizing, program development, and training. CSA, in an effort to expand and enhance its human resource programs, hired Jean to work on management development, to establish training programs, and to manage the employee tuition reimbursement program. It is typical that as a company grows in size and complexity, the need for training, human resource development, and staff enrichment becomes more apparent.

Because of the newness of her role at CSA, Jean found the boundaries of her position fuzzy at times, a fairly common situation for occupational social workers in newly created positions. She thus had to develop the parameters, roles, and functions of the position as much as possible to respond to her prescribed job description. This has led Jean down some creative paths. She has moved into organizational issues more quickly than this would happen in a company where the training function is already established. This move fit with Jean's own career goals and interests and has enabled her to expand the boundaries and scope of the job.

An advantage of working in small and medium-sized companies is the enhanced ability to influence the organization. Jean's mandate includes working to improve the poor relationship between the human resources and manufacturing divisions. Much of her effort has focused on breaking down barriers between line workers and management staff at CSA. As the human resource department has moved from a simple personnel function to a human resource management role, change has begun to take place.

Jean was surprised (as often are social workers in work organizations) at how little of human behavior some managers understand and how poorly trained they are in interpersonal skills. This is particularly common in companies where technology and managers with technical backgrounds, rather than those with people skills, predominate. Some newly created high tech companies with a technologically oriented perception of work can be traditional and conservative in their approach to human resources. Many of these companies are facing what Yankelovich characterizes as "new work values," in which there is a clash within the organizational culture. This results from a traditional management style in conjunction with employees whose motivation to work derives from their worklife satisfaction goals.

Part of Jean's job is to infuse this human dimension into a technological oriented company whose managers report spending less than 10 percent of their time in people management issues. The reality of this management style was probably best summed up by a manager who reported that he "wished his employees were machines because he could then turn them off when he was finished with them."

To generate greater interest in improved human resource management, Jean has initiated a discussion group on managerial issues. For each discussion she selects a relevant article that is distributed prior to the informal lunchtime meeting. The article serves as a vehicle to discuss management concerns at CSA and to broaden the thinking of these technologically oriented managers to the people issues and interpersonal skill aspects of management.

Organizational change occurs slowly, and much of Jean's work is aimed at creating an environment to meet the needs of a growing and changing company. Having to understand these changing needs led Jean to administer an employee opinion survey; approximately one-third of the employee recommendations were subsequently implemented.

While Jean sees that knowledge and skill in managing human behavior are necessities in industry, she is confronted with managers seeking formulas for working with people in much the same way as they have formulas for working with engineering problems. Many require considerable assistance in understanding the need to treat people and situations differentially.

Career opportunities are arising in small and medium-sized companies where human resource generalists are needed. Thus training, organizational development, and even career counseling roles offer social opportunities to meet diverse organizational and individual needs. For social workers entering this area, the challenge is to create healthy and productive work environments where individuals and the corporation can thrive mutually, rather than one functioning well at the expense of the other.

Urban Social Affairs Specialist

Social and environmental issues are very much on the minds of today's consumers, stockholders, and company officials. Most large corporations have a person or department to keep abreast of issues and maintain dialogue with key corporate and community leaders. Social workers, trained in assessment and intervention, are well suited to assist corporations in understanding and responding to social and environmental concerns. Lucy Hannon is a social worker who has pioneered in this area. Accountable to the corporate personnel department, she is a consultant on urban and social issues for a large high technology firm. The company is concerned with and involved in a wide range of social and environmental issues in the U.S. and abroad. The corporation's philosophy is to maintain a low profile while being responsive to community interests. This philosophy was manifested most recently, and notably, by building manufacturing plants, staffed and managed primarily by minorities in two urban centers.

Lucy was brought into the company six years ago by a group of senior managers concerned about community issues that arose as the company was constructing new manufacturing facilities. She advised them on cultural, educational, affirmative action, human resource policy, and local political issues of concern to the communities where these plants were built.

Changes within the organization have shaped Lucy's position and altered her reporting structure during her six years there. Her responsibilities have taken her into many areas of the company, and the tasks for which she is called upon indicate the diversity and unpredictability of corporate needs in a company which sees itself as a citizen of a community. Her work on corporate contributions and community and governmental relations requires cooperation with one vice-president, while her activity in public affairs involves working with another. Work on the issue of child care may best exemplify her position.

Simple demographics convinced Lucy that child care is a compelling social and corporate concern. The company's young work force is dominated by working parents. The corporation chose not to provide on-site child care due to cost and internal organizational and cultural issues. Undaunted, Lucy focused on community child care resources, assisting them in documenting need and in developing community inventories of services available to company employees. Simultaneously she advised the corporation to develop and support community-based resources. As new corporate operations open, Lucy assesses the corporation's impact on existing day care and other services.

Lucy has been instrumental in developing child care awareness for employees who are parents. To this end, she developed a survey to analyze employee needs. She now plans to develop an information and referral system, to include family day care networks. Corporate child care guidelines also are being developed for managers in one of the company's plants in another state.

Lucy spends a lot of time building awareness within the company on issues of local and national concern. Her goal is to provide a strong link to the community to enable achievement of shared goals. Using her knowledge of and familiarity with communities and institutions, she encourages local managers to be actively involved with issues that surface rather than taking the lead herself in setting position and response. She sees her role as a technical expert and facilitator and relies particularly on her group work skills. A project which managers became enthusiastic about was initiation of a science award program for minority youth. Lucy organized the award, given to outstanding black high school science students through the annual NAACP conference. The award program enabled the corporation to recognize and encourage aspiring minority scientists. By working with colleagues in the marketing division to help establish this program, Lucy gained credibility and formed relationships that would help her tackle more controversial projects down the road.

Two stories provide insight into the value of the social work skills Lucy brings to the corporation. A manufacturing plant was losing minority employees due to the lack of reliable transportation between the plant and several surrounding urban areas. Lucy developed a plan to expand public transportation to the industrial park by engaging active support from community leaders in the surrounding towns to convince the regional transit authority of the need. Company managers were inexperienced in dealing with local government and needed Lucy's experience to develop and carry out this strategy. This experience helped plant managers value positive community and government relations. By facilitating rather than directing the effort, Lucy left these managers with new skills. Through expansion of the transportation system, the company and employees benefited. Further, the enlarged transportation network has stimulated economic development in an area which suffers serious unemployment by linking manufacturers with a trained labor pool. The corporation feels some pride in having contributed to the expansion of economic development in the region.

Lucy used her group work skills when she staged a series of meetings to increase understanding of cultural issues by employees in another facility. A rural manufacturing plant negotiated a contract with a group of native Americans to supply the plant with materials. One goal was to promote minority entrepreneurialism. Lucy assisted the plant manager in the negotiation and helped bridge the cultural differences and expectations. Slow start-up on the contract resulted in higher-than-expected costs. While this can happen with any supplier, the fact that it was a minority group made the issue especially sensitive. Lucy helped the plant and financial managers address both the business aspects and the social impacts of the contract while addressing organizational concerns about cost.

Most companies now are involved with a long agenda of social and environmental issues. For social workers trained in organizational and community analysis and intervention, the role of urban social affairs consultant is a challenging frontier. As more corporations become sensitive to the dynamic interrelationship of corporations and communities and expand their traditional public relations perspective, the demand for trained social workers like Lucy will undoubtedly increase.

Human Resource Generalist

Donna Ryan began her career in occupational social work like many practitioners in the field. Her second-year field placement was in the affirmative action office of a large, high technology manufacturing company, and she was hired to work in that office after graduation. Through her work in this area, she learned a great deal about corporate human resource policies and was invited to transfer to a manufacturing site to become a personnel generalist. Donna developed innovative human resource programs for the division, approaching her work with a systems and ecological perspective. From her job in the manufacturing division, Donna was moved to her current position as a regional personnel manager in the international marketing division. The career route is not uncommon for social workers in the occupational setting. Moving from more traditional counseling roles to less traditional roles, such as personnel manager, is a typical direction taken by social workers, whose skills and talents have for the most part been unknown and untested in these work environments. It is also a natural process when the applicability of social work skills becomes evident.

Donna helped define the role of personnel services for a division previously unserved directly by the personnel department, relying instead on plant managers to interpret policies on a more idiosyncratic basis. She assisted in relocating employees and families to and from positions in various countries, managed compensation and benefits relevant to international marketing personnel, assessed the needs of the international organization, and worked on a performance management system that takes cultural and legal diversity into account.

Because the department is responsible for a worldwide work force, the job is complex, requiring the administration of personnel policy across many cultures, political climates, and governmental policies. There are twelve hundred employees in Donna's division, employed in twenty-two international subsidiaries. Donna's role at corporate headquarters is less administration than policy development and consultation with senior managers in the twenty-two subsidiaries.

International program development is more complex and challenging because of the cultural diversity of both the work force and the work environment. The twenty-two subsidiaries operate under different governments and widely divergent cultures. Donna credits her social work training and experience with helping her to recognize the significance of these differences and enabling her to deal with them more effectively.

A good example of her versatility in applying social work skills involved the closing of a major distribution center in Europe. This called for development of a support program for people leaving the company and for those transferring to other parts of the company. An out-placement process was established to assist and counsel employees applying for other jobs to link them with potential employment opportunities. The laws of the country required that the closing of any operation be worked out in conjunction with governmental and legal guidelines that protect workers. Donna met with personnel managers from other multinational and European companies to plan for the closing in such a way as to minimize the negative effect on employees and the company's reputation. Cultural factors were considered carefully because in the local work culture, employee loyalty is very high. This necessitated development of special supportive services during the termination period to enable workers to make positive transitions to new work environments.

A business decision to close down an operation, made for apparently sound financial reasons, presents multiple social ramifications for employees, communities, and governments. Donna's work in the process described illustrates the role of out-placement counseling by social workers, who may bring valuable understanding of personal issues affecting workers who face job loss.

Donna also was involved in a performance appraisal program aimed at improving performance feedback to employees. This complex and essentially face-to-face process is common to all organizations, but is often difficult to manage effectively. Donna approached the issue as an organizational problem, establishing a systematic approach to finding a solution rather than merely "fire fighting" as a function of the personnel department. Application of an ecological perspective in the workplace is a particular skill of social workers. A systems orientation, combined with an understanding of interpersonal and group dynamics, organizational skills, and sensitivity to multi-and crosscultural issues, helps illuminate the most intractable problems.

Relocation, experienced by hundreds of thousands of employees in this country every year, was assigned to Donna. She was asked to examine the corporate relocation policy. She began by conducting a survey of all employees relocated in the last three years, to reveal patterns and identify needs for new relocation policies, systems, and programming. She utilized a needs assessment tool to gather information and to develop an intervention plan. Prior to the survey, all relocations were managed on an individual basis. The survey permitted Donna to take the first comprehensive look at the total process of relocation. This approach, she believed, would impact multiple systems within the corporation. In fact, the survey not only provided data, but was also useful in educating managers about psychosocial issues affecting productivity that arise due to relocation. Although the survey was performed for the international division, Donna believes it will eventually impact the corporation's domestic organization as well. Thus the survey was both an information gathering device and an organizational intervention. While Donna was not given total authority over the company's relocation process, her intervention forced those involved to participate in a change process that significantly influenced relocation procedures.

Donna examined the relocation policies from both individual and systems perspectives, assessing the impact on individual employees, their family systems, and the work organization. She then created a process to manage the stress of relocation and minimize its negative impact on job performance. Social workers who can separate themselves from a pathological orientation to human behavior will be able to utilize their skills to address important and neglected human resource issues in work organizations. Line and staff personnel dealing with interpersonal problems on a daily basis can turn to such social workers to add a social dimension to management and a more systematic approach to problem solving.

Marketing Specialist

As the workplace has opened to social workers as an arena of practice, entrepreneurial organizations have sprung up within the treatment community to contract with business and industry to provide human services, offering corporations an alternative to in-house programs and services. This development has brought with it a relatively new phenomena—the social work entrepreneur, or vendor-marketer. What has resulted is a competitive market for contracted services among hospitals, mental health centers, family service agencies, and an array of private, for-profit agencies.

Victor Bates is the manager of Industrial Consultation Services (ICS), a department of a large psychiatric hospital. The program was established in 1976 as the result of inquiries from industries on how to manage their recovering alcoholic employees. Its first major contract was with the state government. A satellite office was opened near state offices. By 1978, ICS served a clientele of four thousand, including employees of state and federal government, several high tech firms, and a large retail organization. By 1983, it had expanded to serve twelve thousand employees and was experiencing an annual growth rate of 20–30%.

The hospital initially hired a social worker to develop the program, and this decision strongly influenced subsequent ICS staffing. Five other staff members are trained graduate social workers, who along with social work interns provide contracted counseling services. Victor's role was initially intended as a liason for the employed patients of the hospital's alcoholism treatment center and as a marketer of treatment center services. Today the program maintains no clinical relationship with the hospital, nor does it automatically refer clients to the hospital for in-patient treatment when needed.

The marketing of ICS is based on several factors: the product, a pricing strategy, knowing the competition, developing effective program presentation material, and identifying and contracting the market. For each new industrial client, a proposal is developed, tailored to its needs. Contacts made by staff determine most marketing targets. Victor notes that it generally takes eighteen to twenty-four months for program leads to develop into contracts. While he does rely on following leads and responding to requests from companies interested in services, a parallel thrust of his marketing strategy is to expand existing contract services. To maintain accounts, Victor stresses, ICS must constantly work with companies to carry out organizational, political, and public relations tasks while attending to service needs. Therefore, expansion of current contract services is a major marketing goal.

Marketing is not a function usually associated with social work training or activities. Yet the changing nature of funding, private-public sector relationships, and service delivery mechanisms have created a competitive marketplace. Victor enjoys the diversity of his position, which includes marketing and consultation roles that he sees as critical components of success of the program.

All staff, including clinicians, are required to have some understanding of the marketing function. Through in-service training, they learn marketing protocol, how to respond to a call, and what they should keep in mind when involved in program marketing. This last component includes

Learning to listen carefully to what people are requesting,

Getting a sense of where the person is in the marketing process,

Examining organizational needs, i.e., what types of cases are coming to the attention of company officials. Examination of sick leave policies, health insurance benefits, turnover rates, grievance patterns, etc., is used to determine numbers of employees falling outside the norm.

Determining what type of program the company wants, e.g., in-house, external.

The amount of counseling to be provided.

How ICS can work with the company to develop a program.

Unlike other employee assistance vendors, ICS helps corporations develop their own in-house programs by acting as a program consultant.

ICS is fortunate that Victor has both an MSW and an MBA. This dual education increases both his business and clinical credibility with companies and has provided him with a strong theoretical and practical marketing background. This combination of knowledge and skills also enhances his other function— consultation to programs already under contract. At one high tech company, this takes the form of monthly consultation with personnel officers to determine trends and identify problems. The personnel department, in turn, regularly provides ICS with information on organizational and staffing changes.

While ICS has been careful not to move into areas, such as organizational development, where it has no expertise, it does play a number of valuable roles in helping organizations address human concerns. A current example is consultation to a major retailing corporation, including developing a counseling resource director to be used by their EAP, educating their trainers to do EAP training, providing technical assistance to their EAP committee, assisting human resource managers in policy development procedures, creating a brochure, and providing backup clincial consultation service to EAP staff.

As marketing of human services to work organizations becomes more commonplace, it becomes increasingly important for social workers providing these services to be familiar and skilled in these marketing strategies and techniques.

SUMMARY

The roles portrayed above reflect growth and indicate directions in occupational social work practice. While the majority of social workers in work settings carry out counseling functions, a significant minority have begun to assume the varied roles described in this chapter. Many of these roles result from business and industry's expanded conception of human resource services. An equal number result from pioneering social work entrepreneurs who have identified a broad-based client and service system in which social needs and problems have not been addressed properly or have been handled inappropriately. The positions described are recent phenomena reflecting the quiet but progressive growth of the occupational social work field.

Some may criticize some of these roles as inappropriate or atypical for occupational social work; this strikes at the heart of the issue. What is the essence of occupational social work, and what are the boundaries of its practice? Since this brief period of growth should be viewed as part of a developmental process, it is not appropriate to dogmatically declare absolute answers to these questions. The variety of functions discussed in this chapter reflect the explorations of a developmental era that has attempted to identify the social needs of a newly discovered client system while simultaneously determining professional turf, new roles, and effective interventions. This era can be seen either as an exciting challenge opening up new fields of practice or as a threat to the perceived mission and role of social work. As these roles continue to evolve, expansion and experimentation will take place on many levels within many work organizations. New directions will continue to emerge as occupational social workers serve the employee assistance and human resource needs of educational, human service, health care, and mental health organizations. It is critical to understand where the boundary expansions are taking place; to learn from the entrepreneurial roles that are breaking loose in occupational settings; and above all to examine and learn as much as possible to insure that occupational social work is both effective and responsible to its client system, while remaining committed to the value base of the social work profession.

CHAPTER SIX
EMPLOYEE ASSISTANCE PROGRAMS

INTRODUCTION

Except for personnel systems, Employee Assistance Programs (EAP) constitute the largest program type among human service programs in the workplace.* EAPs have increased from an estimated 500 programs in 1973 to
more than 4000 by 1980 (NIAAA, 1981). Programs proliferate as corporations and unions perceive the benefits of EAPs to the organization and to
their employees or members.

EAPs have not evolved in an orderly, rational fashion; rather development is best described as idiosyncratic, producing numerous program types
and philosophies. Thus the occupational alcoholism/employee assistance
field lacks a universal model and is characterized by a variety of program
types (Shain and Groeneveld, 1980).

The study of EAPs is important for several reasons. First, they represent the most common machanism by which human services are provided

---

*A case could be made that personnel or human resource departments are in the
broadest sense a part of an occupational human service system. Indeed their origins and
functions do in part address the human needs of employees. While personnel departments
can and should be an integral component of any human services system, the current reality
separates the worlds of Occupational Social Work, Employee Assistance Programs, and
Personnel Departments.

within the workplace, and a majority of occupational social workers can be found in these programs. Second, the nature and function of EAPs constitute an increasingly complex field in itself. EAPs currently are the organizational context from which most occupational social workers and other human service professionals provide their services to work organizations.

This chapter will first attempt to define EAPs and then explore their assumptions, examining the rationale for this unique social intervention. The second part of the chapter will look at the ideological orientation and structural characteristics of EAPs. It is these variables that distinguish one EAP from another. Although there is little evidence demonstrating the effectiveness of one model or program over another, the presence of many variables warrant an attempt to place them in a typology so that a full range of alternatives can be considered when establishing or reconsidering EAP structure.

DEFINITION, MYTHS, ASSUMPTIONS, AND REASONS BEHIND THE GROWTH OF EAPs

A precise definition for EAPs has not yet been agreed on by either practitioners or theorists, due largely to the wide variance of program types. Nevertheless, EAPs generally refer to a set of policies and program procedures by which a work organization legitimately intervenes in identifying and treating problems of employees that impact and have the capacity to impact job performance. "As a generic entity, an EAP can be defined as a set of company policies and procedures for identifying, or responding to, personal or emotional problems of employees which interfere, directly or indirectly, with job performance" (Walsh, 1982, p. 495).

Others have suggested a core technology which uniquely defines EAPs (Roman and Blum, 1985), but there is little agreement at this point in time within the field on the components of this technology.

To better understand the nature and function of EAPs, a number of beliefs or assumptions should be examined. Discussions of four of these follow:

1. Prevention is more likely in occupational settings.
2. Work organizations share a responsibility for the health of their employees.
3. Substance abuse is affecting the workplace.
4. Problem invention is more effective when integrated into existing social institutions.

Prevention is more likely in occupational settings.   The EAP has been touted as an effective means of prevention, particularly for alcoholism. Whether this is so is subject to much debate. The prevention potential of EAPs can be attributed to the structure and nature of the work organization as well as the characteristics of the EAP itself. Work settings can use job performance criteria to identify problems, drawing on existing rules and roles in the workplace to justify constructively confronting problem drinking. The nature of work organizations and work roles, particularly the supervisory role, thus sets the stage for early intervention and prevention.

The public health model of prevention has provided the framework for prevention efforts in many health issues, including smoking, heart disease, and alcohol abuse, which has been attacked particularly through legislative initiatives concerning drunk driving. However, the EAP offers a new tool—the threat of job loss coupled with a structure that can legitimately intervene in the pattern of dysfunctional performance. The established relationships and roles of the workplace have a decided advantage over more diffuse family relationships and affective friendships in breaking through problems such as alcoholic denial. Prescribed rules and norms of behavior serve as standards against which manifestations of problem drinking appear in substandard job performance. Because alcoholism affects the physical, social, and psychological functioning of the individual, its disruption of acceptable and routine job behaviors and performance is often inevitable, though this fact is unconfirmed by good empirical data (Googins and Kurtz, 1981; Trice, 1962).

Deteriorating job performance as a means of early identification, prevention, and intervention has strengthened the need for EAP involvement. Despite the inadequacies of measuring performance (Trice & Beyer, 1981) and the ability of employees to perform successfully even in the face of grave personal difficulties the value of monitoring job performance to detect symptoms of problems is at the heart of EAPs and ultimately adds to the credibility of these programs.

Prevention has been primarily a public health concern, and its transference into the work setting has been slow. However, the relationship between the economics of the workplace and the value of rehabilitated and healthy employees is becoming clearer. This combined with the growing emphasis on health cost containment throughout our society may further fuel the increase in new EAPs.

Work organizations share a responsibility for the health of their employees. During the past decade, business has become more actively involved in the issues of employee health. This has come in part from legal mandates such as the Occupational Safety and Health Act (OSHA), informal coercion from citizen action lobbies such as Public Interest Research Groups, and the advocacy of employees themselves. These forces have exerted pressure to improve working conditions and safeguard the handling of toxic materials. This vigilance made health standards a higher priority with employers. Two factors, social responsibility and legal mandate, have particularly influenced corporations in this regard.

Social responsibility. The importance of a corporation's profile of social responsibility is contributing to increasing concern for employee health. That employers create healthy environments for their employees is increasingly becoming an expectation of communities and a felt responsibility of the corporation. Healthy employees are a necessary and positive sign of concerned and responsible corporate behavior; concern for employees' health is a pragmatic reality of enlightened self-interest. It has been alleged that the single largest factor behind the adoption and implementation of EAPs is a growing sense of social responsibility or humanitarianism. This view suggests that, all factors considered, EAPs are primarily established because they seem like a good, helpful, and humanitarian way to assist people who are hurting. There is in fact some evidence to buttress this position. Roman (1977), in analyzing corporate rationale for establishing EAPs, found that humanitarianism was the most frequent determinant of program initiation. Thirty-nine percent of those surveyed were started for this reason in contrast to 20 percent that were started because of a demonstrated or visible need and only 17 percent that cited cost benefits.

Numerous anecdotal reports exist of corporate executive officers who themselves were problem drinkers or had experienced other trauma such as divorce, death in the family, etc., or whose close family or work associates had problems that subsequently led to EAP development. Thus it is not uncommon to find EAPs whose existence is a result of an individual impulse or sense of noblesse oblige. Much of this humanitarian impulse can be traced to the precursors of EAPs—the occupational alcoholism programs. Alcoholism is on the cusp between medical and moral domains, carrying with it the strong cultural and value dimensions that historically culminated in prohibition and its repeal. Intellectually, at least, those in the work environment have adopted the illness or medical paradigm that has taken hold during the past three decades, and business and industry are institutions that reflect (and shape) larger social values. Thus the alcoholism movement grew dramatically in the 1970s primarily driven by a humanitarian response to an ill person. Later offshoots and developments such as the EAP share in this philosophical and moral heritage.

Social responsibility, while difficult to quantify and target as a rationale for the adoption of EAPs, nevertheless has been a force in the establishment of some EAPs. This is a positive development, but it is probably not enough to sustain EAPs. Changes in leadership, shifts in conceptions of social responsibility, and economic belt tightening may threaten programs when bottom line costs come in conflict with social concern. Nevertheless, social responsibility is increasingly an institutionalized concern particularly as it relates to a corporation's own employees. Thus social responsibility will continue to be an important force for program development.

Legal mandates.   Another force generating EAPs lies in the need for organizations to avoid legal action. Since the early 1960s legal decisions have been handed down which have redefined alcoholism as a handicap. Other decisions have cited employers as responsible for treating alcoholism as an illness. In the area of emotional well-being of employees, the courts have begun to define broad employer responsibility (Barrie et al. 1980). The 1973

Rehabilitation Act (Section 504, Public Law 93-1128), for example, defines a "handicapped individual" as one who has a physical or mental disability that constitutes or results in a substantial handicap to employment. The law continues, "no individual defined as handicapped shall, solely by reason of his handicap, be excluded from the participation in, be denied the benefits of, or be subjected to discrimination under any programs or activity receiving federal financial assistance."

Trice and Belasco (1966) were among the first to examine employer responsibility prior to the 1973 federal legislation. Their examination of court decisions up to that point led them to cite increased employer liability for employee disability. Traditionally, this liability has been applied under worker's compensation for injuries received while intoxicated on the job. Thus it is natural for alcoholism itself to be considered under compensation laws. Blue (1980) in his review of compensation for the mentally impaired worker found that the expansion of worker's compensation coverage is continuing and that this may result in the liberalization of benefits for all types of claims.

The Occupational Safety and Health Act is another factor in EAP development. In 1978, Senator William Hathaway of Maine introduced a bill which would have mandated occupational alcoholism programs in industries doing business with the federal government through OSHA legislation. Although this bill was never passed, it demonstrates an increased awareness of the linkage between alcoholism and health safety.

Maxwell's (1959) early study cited an accident rate for alcoholics three times higher than that of a control group. This has been confirmed by Asma et al. (1971, 1980) and Pell and D'Alonzo (1970). Manello, Paddock, and Seaman's (1979) study of the railroads graphically demonstrated the connection between alcohol and accidents and the potential liability of the railroad industry.

The increase of litigious activity has caused some companies to welcome the EAP as a means of avoiding further liability. The responsibility to offer treatment and avoid exclusive use of disciplinary action against the alcoholic or otherwise troubled employee makes it unacceptable to simply suspend or terminate such an employee. Trice and Belasco (1966) cite criteria used in arbitration such as "mitigating circumstances must have been taken into consideration such as prior good work record, or joining AA after discharge." (p. 485) It should not be overlooked that the costs, both direct and indirect, of processing the arbitration and pursuing avenues and appeals can be considerable for both management and unions.

The legal mandate, then, has become a powerful force behind the EAP. Some, such as Shain and Groeneveld (1980), argue that the process and structure of the EAP are so parallel with disciplinary procedure that the real reason behind the growth of the EAP is so employers can cover themselves in case of arbitration. "An employer who followed EAP practices to the letter would meet such arbitration criteria when firing eventually became inevitable. It is therefore a useful policy to have if employers wish to avoid fruitless and costly reinstatements of problem employees" (p. 17).

Substance abuse is affecting the workplace.   Prevailing myths to the contrary, there is ample evidence that alcoholism is commonplace in working America. The skid row stereotype, representing a very small proportion of the alcoholic population (3–5 percent), has gradually been replaced by a more scientific profile of prevalence. The early studies of Straus and Bacon (1951) as well as national survey findings (Cahalan, 1970) offer convincing data that demonstrate that the majority of alcohol problems exist within the intact (working) family.

Nevertheless, prevalence of alcoholism within the workplace is still a matter of much conjecture and little fact. Most reports of prevalance rates in particular occupations or industries are at best crude estimates (Hayward et al. 1975). One attempt at measurement reported rates of 9.2 percent presumptive problem drinkers in a public employee sample (Shain and Groenveld, 1980). In earlier studies Straus and Bacon (1951) analyzed the distribution of alcoholics who appeared in clinics by type of industry. No one industry was found to have a higher rate than another, and 10 percent has become the generally accepted figure indicating the prevalence of alcoholism in the workplace. The presence of substantial numbers of problems drinkers at the worksite is, however, solidly established, reflecting the trends within society at large—a Gallup poll in 1983 indicated one out of every three families reported a drinking problem within their family.

Problem intervention is more effective when integrated into the existing social institutions.   The establishment of EAPs in work settings marks a new strategy aimed at treating problems within the institutional environments in which they exist. This strategy acknowledges the inadequacy of separate boundaries between treatment and problem manifestation. EAPs provide a locus in the work environment for problem identification and prevention, necessary first steps for treatment.

The traditional detachment of treatment centers from other social institutions may well reflect a world characterized by specialization. Unfortunately, people do not leave personal problems behind as they step through the office door. Because employee personal problems negatively affect productivity, rates of absenteeism, and employee morale, introducing a means of problem identification and early intervention can be facilitated by the natural structure of the organization.

Benefits to Work Organizations

Behind program adoption lies the ultimate question: What benefits will accrue to the organization as the result of establishing an EAP? Or what negative costs will accrue to the organization by not adopting a program? In each instance the organization assesses the proposed intervention in relation with the total system. While each organization examines the decision in light of its unique needs, several broad benefits have been cited that buttress such forces as social responsibility and legal mandates.

Cost Effectiveness It is widely assumed that the major rationale for EAPs lies in its cost savings. If billions of dollars are lost to companies due to alcoholic employees' impaired job performances, EAPs may be viewed as a means of rehabilitating the alcoholic employee and reducing costs by decreasing absenteeism, tardiness, accidents, errors in judgement, and the like. By initiating the EAP, work organizations institute a cost-savings program that will, among other things, improve bottom line profits.

Cost savings have been examined from a variety of perspectives as a factor in EAP program adoption. Absenteeism, for example, as the most visible performance indicator is also the easiest measure by which to calculate a cost-benefit analysis. Observer and Maxwell (1959), for example, in comparing the absence records of problem drinkers with normal employees found that the alcoholic group was absent 2.5 times more often that their comparison group. Kennecott Cooper found that absenteeism decreased 52 percent following treatment (Skidmore et al. 1974). Others have attempted to quantify costs and savings. Mannello, Puddock, and Seaman (1979) in a comprehensive study of alcoholism in the railroad industry, reported the following costs of alcoholism among a workforce of 28,000: absenteeism $3.1 million; lost productivity $25 to $100 million; injuries $593,000; accidents and damages $650,000; grievance procedures $408,000. This cost amounted to almost $500 per employee. Asma et al. (1980) provide one of the more comprehensive cost-saving studies, done at Illinois Telephone Company. Of the 750 new clients admitted into their program over a nine-year period, the researcher estimated that 31,806 work days were saved due to the EAP intervention. Using an average of $40 per day, this one factor alone accounted for $1.2 million in savings. Foote et al. (1978), in testing their evaluation method of cost effectiveness found substantial dollar savings in four companies in the areas of absenteeism, accidents, visits to medical units, disciplinary actions, grievances, worker's compensation, and sickness and accident benefits.

Although these cost studies have methodological deficiencies, the estimated $40 billion annual cost of alcohol abuse to the country (President's Commission on Mental Health, 1978) and the $10 billion annual cost to industry (NIAAA, 1974) provide a convincing argument that the costs are indeed real. These costs, however, go beyond those mentioned above. Walsh (1982) argues for an even wider perspective on cost savings by examining health care costs themselves. Employers expend enormous amounts of money for health care for employees, their dependents, and retirees. Walsh argues that the EAP could help the company achieve substantial savings by assisting these groups with their individual family and social problems as well as crises of living. While this is currently being addressed in relatively few EAPs, it is a harbinger of future directions, making cost savings a more important EAP rationale.

Whereas the cost savings seem potentially great and in line with the values of the organization, this rationale does not seem to be the deciding factor, judging from the number of companies who have not instituted EAPs despite seemingly obvious cost benefits. Nevertheless, cost effectiveness will continue to play a part in interesting work organizations in EAPs and insuring the continuation and growth of those already in existence.

Aid to Management   A second benefit of EAPs rests in their potential for assisting management. It has been the experience of many companies that EAPs result in a reinforcement of basic management principles, particularly those relating to the supervisory role and its responsibilities. Because employers are concerned with the control of job performance standards (Shain and Groeneveld, 1980, p. 179), the EAP provides a supplemental mechanism that reinforces basic management practices. Although it would be unrealistic to expect employers to become particularly interested in types of problems, intervention techniques, or referral rates, they do have a particular interest in the ability of the organization and its subunits to achieve standards of performance, maintain a high level of productivity, and maintain an environment that is safe, humane, and condusive to the optimal functioning of employees. This interdependence between broad management goals and the EAP goals of identifying, confronting, and treating employees with personal, family, and social problems creates an ideal situation in which each can assist the other in attaining their goals.

Improve Labor–Management Relations   EAPs provide a forum for jointly addressing problems and issues, thereby temporarily suspending the conventional contentious relationship set up by union-management roles. Provided labor and management have agreed on policy and procedures, alcoholism and other personal problems can be defined and treated as such rather than as work issues and symptoms of poor labor-management relations. The enormous expense entailed by unions on behalf of just a few employees can result in as many problems for the union as they present to management.

Consequently, the organization benefits when the joint labor-management EAP has worked out procedures that unclog labor-management channels, minimizing appeals, grievances, and arbitration. Not only do management and labor signal to the organization that they can cooperate, but the employee escapes a gauntlet of labor-management charges and countercharges in which the employee becomes secondary to organizational struggles. However, where labor-management relations have deteriorated, unions may see the EAP as a device for weeding out undesirables, a tool that unions understandably would not want to grant to management. This natural suspicion of a program so intimately tied to job performance can only be overcome through joint union-management planning and cooperation from the inception of the program.

Enhance Corporate Image EAPs provide a variety of what can be called *image messages* both within the company and to the outside community. One of these messages relates to the nebulous qualities of caring, concern, and well-being. Properly established, EAPs can serve as a symbol by which the company communicates its active willingness to provide for and protect those employees who are experiencing personal problems. As an alternative to the more rigid disciplinary process, the EAP signals to employees a positive concern for the well-being of the work force and a recognition of the role of the company in attending to employees' needs where appropriate. This image may be equally effective in the outside community, where corporate image is essential to product viability. A company that is perceived as creating a healthy climate for its employees enhances its public image of attractiveness to the consumer.

Summary

Rationale for EAP adoption is complex. The factors presented above are neither all inclusive nor conclusive in their evidence of which factors account for EAP adoption. It is clear that all parties involved must benefit if the EAP is to become an integral and necessary component of the work organization. At this stage of development, humanitarian motives, legal mandates, and concerns over spiraling health costs have served as incentives for EAPs. While the benefits to the corporation and its employees are multi-faceted, the EAP and its rationale within the corporation are far from stabilized. As the EAP becomes more commonplace as a legitimate entity within corporations and unions, and as the benefits of EAPs become more clear, these programs will be more integrated into the organization, expanding and enhancing their roles and functions. Because EAPs have been established at a rapid rate, it is much too soon to define any framework for EAPs in terms of goals and design. The price for this developmental process is, as we shall see in the next section, the absence of a clearly defined program model.

PROGRAM TYPOLOGY

EAPs are commonly referred to in the singular case as if representing a single design. The development of EAPs has not, however, followed a single program model. Even those who have described models, such as Shain and Groenevald (1980), Wrich (1974), and Walsh (1982), have gone to great lengths to indicate the nonuniversality of any program type. Programs vary in ideological assumptions and program orientations, not to mention pragmatic considerations such as program sponsorship and type of staff. Walsh (p. 494) cites a number of these variations:

formality of policies and procedures
organizational locus of the program
process by which troubled employees find their way into the EAP
extent to which job performance is stressed as justification for referrals
types of problems the program tends to address
the use of outside treatment agencies
the nature of outside referral process and extent of follow-up
staffing of the program
financial arrangements

As programs mature and become widespread, a critical mass is beginning to develop in which these variants can be tested empirically and experientially.

For the outsider or one new to this field, the lack of a framework or a closely knit program model can be confusing and to a degree disturbing. It is difficult to press for adoption of an EAP when no consensus exists on such basic dimensions as program elements, characteristics, and orientation. Nevertheless, there does seem to be an accepted set of elements that every program should possess. These elements can be adopted and incorporated into the particular environmental conditions of the work organization and its culture. These are listed in Table 6–1 followed by a detailed discussion of each.

TABLE 6–1   EAP Program Typology

Program Context	Program Elements
A. Ideology 　　Alcoholism 　　Employee Assistance 　　Employee Wellness	A. Organizational Components 　　Policy and Procedures 　　Outreach 　　Marketing 　　Supervisor Training 　　Employee Education
B. Orientation 　　Individual 　　Environmental	B. Program Mechanism 　　Identification 　　Record Keeping 　　Assessment & Monitoring 　　Referral 　　Advocacy 　　Evaluation
C. Structural Characteristics 　　Program Sponsorships 　　Organizational Placement 　　Program Designs 　　Indigenous 　　　Contracted 　　　Consortium 　　　Association	

Ideology

Perhaps the most fundamental EAP variable is ideology. The term is used to indicate a set of values and ideas that are reflected in discrete program philosophy, design, and treatment. Ideology is often set by programs and staff. There are three distinct ideologies: alcoholism, employee assistance, and mental wellness. Each of these represents a specific program approach.

The Alcoholism Program   The alcoholism ideology has its roots in the early development of occupational alcoholism programs (OAPs). Concerned about the effects of alcoholism in industry, the early pioneers of this field established a straightforward method of identifying and assisting employees with alcoholism. The Yale Plan for Business and Industry (Henderson and Bacon, 1953) established the first program model. Major elements of the plan included an educational component for management and labor on the causes, effects, and prevention of alcoholism. The program limited participation to employees whose job performance was impaired by alcoholism. It was this model that characterized programs established from the 1940s into the early 1970s.

The alcoholism ideology approaches alcoholism head on, citing the cost incurred by companies as the motivation for detecting the problems within the work environment. Its characteristics are derived from trends in alcoholism policy of the 1940s and 1950s which attempted to destereotype the prevailing skid row image of alcoholics and to diffuse the moral attributes associated with the alcoholic. Thus its function was to bring the treatment of alcoholism into the open at the workplace, thereby giving legitimacy to alcohol programs within the occupational context.

The majority of these programs included alcohol in their program title. Although they conceptually included other personal and behavioral problems, there is little evidence to substantiate programmatic efforts at problems other than alcoholism. However, the alcoholism orientation historically and programmatically did introduce several elements that are at the core of all three orientations. The first was the use of job performance as a criterion by which alcoholism could be identified and confronted. This bold device made use of an already existing mechanism to intervene in the development and continuance of problem drinking. By using supervisors as gatekeepers, a new mechanism could be used to identify the alcoholic at an early stage. In addition, the use of constructive confrontation or coercion (Roman & Trice, 1972) introduced a novel approach to breaking down denial and the alibi system of the alcoholic.

A second element of this model is alcohol specific policies and procedures. This sanctions the alcoholism program within the work organization, thereby supporting the view of alcoholism as illness. It also provides program guidelines by which alcoholic employees can be handled by the supervisor.

These innovations gave rise to a program which developed steadily over thirty years. When the National Institute on Alcohol Abuse and Alcoholism (NIAAA) was established in 1971, it identified employed alcoholics as a priority target population. However, the federal initiative embraced a new model, the Employee Assistance Program, which would trigger intense ideological and programmatic debates within the occupational alcoholism field.

The Employee Assistance Program   The Employee Assistance Program traces its origins to NIAAA. Under a variety of names—behavioral problems control (Presnall 1972), troubled employee (Tucker 1974), employee assistance (Wrich 1974), and broad brush—the programs responded to a range of personal and work-related problems that might impact an employee. Like its predecessor, the OAP, it uses deteriorating job performance as the primary method by which problems are identified.

The EAP tends to focus on a broader spectrum of problems than the OAP but retains more of the job performance focus than the wellness model. The core functioning and activities of the EAPs, although subject to numerous descriptions, are best captured in Figure 6–1, the Erfurt-Foote Schema (1977).

The service delivery functions will be discussed later in this chapter. Suffice it to say that EAPs provide a linkage between individual employees, their problems, the policies and constraints of the organization within which they work, and the array of community treatment resources that are in a position to assist with the resolution of the problems.

While this is the essence of the EAP system, it does not capture the ideological strains that exist on the macro—micro continuum. Those arguing for a clinical focus would center the EAP on a problem approach that details with alcoholism, emotional, family, legal, and the usual range of problems that enter any social service system. Others argue for a more macro focus that provides clinical services, but uses a client system rather than a problem focus. Thus the corporation is the community or client system, and all employees, not just those affected by a problem, are part of the EAP focus.

Does alcoholism tend to be "lost" in the employee assistance approach? This has been an ongoing concern by those espousing the alcoholism approach. By expanding programmatic efforts to include all problems (marital, legal, emotional, financial, etc.), it was feared that EAPs might deemphasize alcoholism amidst the multitude of other problems, thereby diminishing the focal point of the program and abandoning the strategy necessary for combatting alcoholism's social stigma and breaking down the denial. The transformation from alcoholism programs to EAPs was seen as broadening both the goals of occupational programs as well as their constituencies, consequently deprioritizing alcoholism as the primary concern

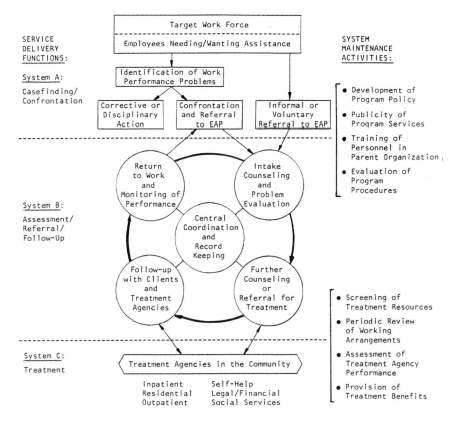

FIGURE 6–1 Erfurt-Foote Chart of EAP Activities.

(Roman, 1981). The counter argument rested on the function of the EAP in accelerating early identification and increasing alcoholism case finding by casting a wider net.

The major ideological differences that characterize these programs (EAPs and OAPs) have substantially different impacts. Schlenger's (1976) evaluation of fifteen occupational programs found that self-referrals were nearly twice as common for employee assistance programs than for alcoholism-only programs. The same study found major differences with regard to the skill level of clients. Alcoholism programs tended to reach the unskilled or semiskilled, while the EAPs were successful primarily in reaching the skilled and clerical employees.

In summary, the EAP seems to represent a second stage of development. Drawing on some elements of the occupational alcoholism program, EAP built its foundation on job performance and used behavioral outcome measures as the means for identifying, confronting, and treating the troubled employee. The move from alcoholic to troubled employee broadened the operational base but created ideological and programmatic conflict with the adherents of the occupational alcoholism model.

The Employee Mental Wellness Program   A third ideology is represented by a group of programs that are focused on the mental wellness of employees. This is a more recent development, but nevertheless does have an identifiable constituency.

Employee wellness programs are primarily centered in the mental health field and are oriented toward emotional and mental health problems. While resembling the EAP, the wellness program is much more apt to be staffed by professionals (physicians, psychiatrists, psychologists, and social workers) and based on a view of the workplace as a potential resource for the prevention of mental health problems.

In 1980 a conference on Mental Wellness Programs for Employees (Egdahl and Walsh, 1980) was held in Washington, D.C. sponsored by the Washington Business Group on Health and the Boston University Center for Industry and Health Care. It was a substantial exposition of employee wellness programs. Definitions and concepts focused on emotional illness and support, stress, and personal well-being. Four questions were raised that mark the parameters of this orientation (p. 9):

What is mental wellness, and how is the relationship between mental wellness and job performance accurately measured?

Is there sufficient evidence that companies can provide programs for mental wellness that reduce the costs of alcoholism, drug abuse, and mental illness?

Can supervisors and managers be taught to recognize mental wellness needs within the work environment, and is this an appropriate role to assign?

What legal and financial responsibilities do employers have for the emotional well-being of their employees, and what risks are incurred in the acceptance of such responsibilities?

In some respects, Employee Wellness takes the EAP a step further and advocates the broadest health and prevention stance of all three ideologies.

Indeed the next stage is the development of occupational health activities including EAPs, health prevention, and health fitness, among others. The rising costs of health care, the fragmentation of occupational programs, and the changing definition of health into broader context all argue for bringing EAPs under the health prevention and promotion umbrella (Case 1985; Shain & Boyle 1985).

These three ideologies constitute one variable in the typology. For the most part, they are the "soul" of these work-based programs, giving impetus and direction to each program. Clearly, elements of each can be found in most programs. Nevertheless, distinct characteristics can be identified and adherents found for each ideology. What is most important in considering the three is their contribution in the development and evolution of human service programs in the workplace. Each has specific dimensions that orient the program and influence staffing, program goals, and treatment options. Their separateness and their interrelatedness must be understood to fully comprehend the Employee Assistance Program history and development.

General Orientation

In addition to ideological variations, two orientations have emerged, marking distinct approaches to servicing work populations. These two orientations—individual and environmental—cut across all three ideologies. The individual orientation defines problems within the person, and consequently all programmatic effort are aimed at assisting the employee to overcome depression, for example, and participate in one's work group.

The environmental orientation sees problems within the social context, i.e., the work environment. Consequently, definition and problem resolution require environmental intervention and change. Thus stress is not simply a stressed employee in need of counseling, but a problem in which environmental stressors can be identified and appropriate remedial steps initiated.

The distinction between individual and environmental philosophical assumptions is important. The choice and the degree of intensity to which either the individual or environmental orientation is adopted and incorporated into program goals, objectives, roles, activities, and strategies influence the interventions that effect the workplace and the nature of the delivery of human services within the workplace.

Shain and Groeneveld (1980, p. 11), using alcohol as an example, cite an Addiction Research Foundation Survey in Ontario, which made the following distinctions:

INDIVIDUAL ORIENTATION

1. The excessive use of alcohol is considered wholly dysfunctional to the individual.

2. The causes of alcoholism may be largely sought within the individual's own psychological makeup.

3. The prescribed treatment for the condition of alcoholism is some form of rehabilitation focusing on the individual's psychological makeup. Many variations on this theme are possible, including psychoanalysis, behavior therapy, casework, crisis intervention, reality therapy, and transactional analysis. The concern of some interventions is improved psychosocial functioning, that of others, simply improving job performance.

ENVIRONMENTAL ORIENTATION

1. The excessive use of alcohol is considered under certain conditions to be functional for the individual: relief from monotony, stress, or feelings of

powerlessness. Also, the "drunk" role may be a part of a broader social role which is important in the industrial peer group situation (Dentler and Erickson, 1959).

2.   The causes of alcoholism may be sought not only or even mainly in the individual, but also in the social context (economic and political disadvantage) and in the specific organizational context (the nature of some kinds of work or the structure of some types of organization.)

3.   The prescribed treatment may not be for the individual, but for society and for the specific organization within which alcoholism is found. A reorientation of the worker to the means of production (control over) may be more relevant than psychotherapy.

Although these orientations exist occasionally in extreme forms, strains of both can be found in most programs. When analyzing a program, it is important to assess the degree to which the individual or environmental orientation is manifest organizationally and programmatically. Still, it is essential to recognize that both exist within occupational programs regardless of primary orientation.

These two orientations have become more pronounced over the past several years as the field of occupational social work has grown in prominence. The ecological perspective brought by the social work profession tends to align itself with the environmental orientation. Within the workplace this orientation tests the boundaries of existing EAPs, suggesting new roles and responsibilities for program staff (Googins, 1984). This is often a source of friction between the proponents and staff of EAPs and those of wellness programs. Obviously these are two extremes on a continuum, and most programs tend towards either the individual model or the center. It is interesting to note that the orientation of European industrial social work tends toward the environmental orientation. As EAPs in general mature, this issue will intensify since it touches upon the very nature and function of EAPs.

Structural Characteristics

Structural configurations constitute another set of variables that differentiate EAPs. Because EAPs evolved idiosyncratically, individual companies constructed the EAP functions within their organizational structures, resulting in this variety of structural arrangements. Location of the program is one example. Some EAPs have been an appendix to medical departments, while others are free-standing units responsible to a vice president for personnel.

Programs also differ by sponsorship. Although most come under the auspices of corporations, others are sponsored by unions, labor organizations, and professional associations. Some are cosponsored by both labor and management. Still others delegate partial sponsorship to a consortium. Finally, a growing number of programs have entered into contractual arrangements with external agents, usually treatment centers.

This amalgam of sponsors, program locations, and organizational design often presents a confusing picture. Decisions governing design, location, and sponsorship are influenced as much by idiosyncratic organizational culture and politics as by an informed body of knowledge. As EAPs have developed, little consideration has been given to the consequences of these decisions except from the perspective of organizational constraints and realities. Conscious attention to these variables provides an opportunity to compare the effectiveness of one arrangement to another. Following is a discussion of the dominant configurations that have evolved to date.

Program Sponsorship The original EAPs were initiated by the management of large corporations like Dupont, Eastman Kodak, and Consolidated Edison in New York, all of which were initiated in the 1940s. During the 1970s, as occupational alcoholism programs gained momentum, three primary sponsors emerged: management, unions, and joint labor-management sponsorship. Management-sponsored programs represent the majority of EAPs. The corporation is the sanctioning agent due to the availability of resources and the ability to promulgate corporate policy in the early stages. However, countervailing forces within the labor movement and the alcoholism field have argued for and secured new sources of sponsorship. One alternative is the union-sponsored program of which the Longshoreman's Union and the Communications Union EAPs are examples. These programs are modeled on other health and welfare programs created as union benefits. Although some of these programs were initiated with federal funding, all are now self-sustaining from union funds.

The third model is joint labor-management sponsorship. Labor leaders such as "Lefty" Henderson (Trice and Schonbrunn, 1981) and Leo Perlis (1977), argued that unless a program had both management and labor support, labor would be suspicious and management tempted to misuse the powers inherent in EAPs. Consequently, joint cooperation and sponsorship was pushed during the 1970s to mitigate the traditional contention between labor and management.

Nevertheless, because labor-management cooperation is still an elusive ideal, sponsorship has primarily been assumed by management. In the 1977 Washington Business Group on Health's report on Employee Wellness Programs, union involvement was minimal despite the fact that more than 70 percent of the responding companies were unionized. Only 11 percent reported joint labor-management efforts (Kiefhaber and Goldbeck, 1980).

Organizational Placement EAPs are often located in the personnel or human resources departments. The natural assignment of "people" issues to these departments dictate the logic of this. However, EAPs often chafe at the negative connotation associated with personnel departments. Many of the traditional functions of personnel—i.e., terminations, disciplinary enforcement, grievance hearings, benefits, and the management position in labor-management relations and negotiations—are sometimes feared as threats to the integrity of the EAP.

Each company, therefore, struggles with the positioning of its program. Because location is both politically and symbolically powerful, the decision often affects the perceptions of the program. For example, if the program is located within the medical department, the EAP will be colored by the status and range of the department. If the medical department is seen as a disciplinary arm of management to insure that employees are not abusing medical leave, the EAP will share that image. Conversely, where the medical department is perceived as a benign autonomous unit whose primary function is to improve environmental health and flag potential hazards, the EAP will share that image.

Options for placement of the EAP are relatively limited. In most organizations that group programs on the basis of compatible or complimentary functions in the interest of collaboration, communication, and organizational functioning, EAPs are most often directly or indirectly under the umbrella of personnel.

Since this is not always known or understood by employees, the situational placement of the EAP will influence its credibility and accessibility. EAPs have been assigned to medical departments, personnel units, training units, labor-management units, and so-called autonomous units. There is no ideal. What determines placement must be established within the particular organizational context. An informed decision is made based on the subjective judgement of all available information, taking into account such factors as organizational climate and culture, reputation of potential sponsoring agents, labor-management relations, resources, and support.

Program Designs   There are a number of program types or designs that exhibit different structural characteristics. Each type carries a set of advantages and disadvantages that will affect the fit with the particular nature and needs of the company itself.

Relationship to the host company and treatment configurations are the distinguishing characteristics of four program types: indigenous, contractual, consortium, and association.

Indigenous (Figure 6–2)   The indigenous or internal design places the program in the mainstream of the work institution, solidifying identity with the organization. Typically, staff are employed as members of the company, and the program bears the company name. Such indigenous programs represent the early occupational alcoholism programs, and EAPs are found today in most large corporations. The program functions as a unit or organizational entity within the hierarchical structure conducting specified activities sanctioned by the organization—in this case, the assessment and

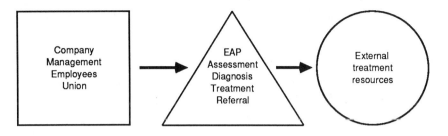

FIGURE 6–2 Indigenous EAP.

treatment of employees with personal and work-related problems. The indigenous model usually includes assessment, diagnosis, and referral capabilities and linkages to outside treatment programs. The focus of this design is on assisting in problem identification and aiding both the employee and the family member in receiving the appropriate treatment.

Certain advantages as well as disadvantages accrue to the indigenous EAP.

ADVANTAGES

Organizational belongingness. The nature of the institution is such that any unit integral to the organization has a relationship that differs from any outside unit. When EAP program staff are bona fide members of a work organization, they automatically align themselves symbolically and functionally as insiders and can more easily build relationships based on common organizational traditions, norms, and respect. Because of their membership these EAPs are in a better position to influence structural as well as individual change.

Organizational positioning. As an integral part of the organization, the EAP is better positioned to link problems and resolutions. For example, recent research on supervisors, (Googins and Kurtz, 1981) indicates that knowledge of the program is a high predictor of whether supervisors will use an EAP when faced with a problem employee. A program indigenous to an organization is more visible and accessible to both supervisors and employees.

Organizational positioning also affects internal communications. What one communicates and how it is communicated is influenced by one's position. Being *of* the organization is advantageous to the EAP staff in being able to communicate in a way outsiders cannot. For example, if the EAP works with employees facing layoffs or retirement, chances are its sensitivity and understanding of the organizational dynamics and culture will make it more effective than the external provider.

Ability to respond.   The remoteness of contracted programs minimizes accessibility and opportunities to intervene when help is most needed. Programs indigenous to the organization can respond to crises immediately, with none the delays caused by scheduled hours or site distance.

DISADVANTAGES

- is the most expensive for company
- forces work organizations into the treatment business
- tends to replicate a community service agency, thereby limiting other roles and activities, i.e., consultation, training, etc.
- relies too much on particular skills of staff
- may cause conflict between treatment and management issues

Contracted   The contracted or external design places the major functions of the EAP outside the organization but responsible to it. The outside agent, usually a treatment or service agency, contracts with the organization to provide specified services. These can vary from a narrow contract, in which problems that emerge are referred to the contractor, to more encompassing contracts, in which policy and procedure development, onsite counseling, and supervisory training are all part of the contractor's responsibility. The staff are not members of the company but are somewhat more autonomous and separate from the company or union. When discussing contracted services (Figure 6–3) it is important to distinguish these two types. In one type of treatment agency, such as a hospital, contracts with a company to provide an EAP include a treatment component that is funded through third-party reimbursement. The second type is a free-standing contractor who does not provide treatment services funded through reimbursement, but refers employees to appropriate community-based treatment facilities.

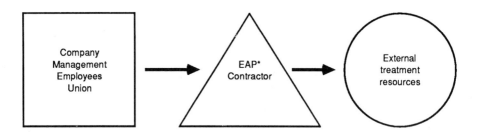

* These contractors are either located in their offices outside the company or have use of company space for a contracted amount of time to carry out the assessment diagnosis treatment and referral function.

FIGURE 6–3   Contracted EAP.

ADVANTAGES

Confidentiality.   The contractor's apparent independence suggests that employee rights are safe and information will not be compromised in organizational decisions. Whereas this may or may not be true in a contractual relationship, the organization can appear to draw clearer lines between the employee's problems and right to treatment and the organization's need to maintain order and discipline while insuring adequate levels of productivity.

Suitability to smaller organizations.   Although some have cited 3,000–4,000 as the break-even number of employees needed to support an indigenous program, no such norm has been clearly established for a contracted program. What is apparent is the inability of the smaller work organization (which accounts for the majority of businesses and industries) to provide EAP services of indigenous design. The contracted design allows the smaller company to take advantage of an array of services without having to pay for full-time staff.

Richness and diversity of resources.   Economy of scale works inversely in regard to treatment resources. Whereas the indigenous program may rely on one or two individuals, the contracted program can provide a greater array of skills and treatment resources. Consequently, the services of the larger treatment staff can be channeled to meet the particular needs of the troubled employee or even organization needs.

DISADVANTAGES

- treatment possibly too narrow, reflecting the particular skills and treatment preference of contractor
- low degree of understanding and incorporation of work-environment issues
- less accessible for supervisors
- least able to respond to crisis

Consortium   An attempt to find a solution for small work organizations whose employee population and resource base were inadequate to mount a full-fledged EAP resulted in the consortium design (Figure 6–4). Fossen (1975) described several consortia models.

1.   A group of employees or employer-union combinations in a given geographic area share resources and services.

2.   Each employer engages the services of an alcoholism consulting firm or aligns with a local council on alcoholism.

3.   Employers involved pool their service money but do not share operational or functional responsibility.

4.   Funding comes from public sources and third party payments, while employers determine program policies and proceedings.

5.   Employees share fiscal and governing responsibilities.

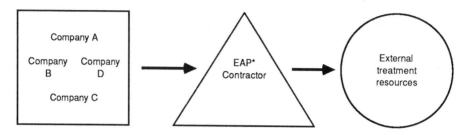

* Similar to the contracted design, the EAP functions of assessment, diagnosis, treatment and referral can be carried out either within the companies on a contracted basis, and/or at a central external site.

FIGURE 6–4   Consortium EAP.

Although consortia sponsorship appeals to companies that otherwise would not be able to participate in EAPs, they have not proliferated or endured primarily because of the inherent complexity of multiple sponsorship. Fossen (1975), in analyzing consortia, cited three major determinants of program failure:

1.   They are not allowed realistic time and financial support to establish credibility among employees.
2.   They are not staffed according to a well-identified set of delivery capabilities and according to a systematic plan to deliver services in an effective and timely manner.
3.   They do not maintain their quality service delivery.

Association   A fourth design is the association (Figure 6–5). This is a type of consortium in which occupational groups establish a program for their members. Examples of this are the Association of Air Line Pilots, lawyers in a state bar association, and professional athletes such as found in the National Basketball Association. The benefit of such an arrangement is its sensitivity to unique professional and occupational issues. These associations provide services to members who either work in a very autonomous manner or whose work affiliation is more to a profession than an organization. The association simply serves as the vehicle by which the EAP can most effectively reach these "employees."

It should be noted that the association design has allowed individual companies to avoid the potentially negative publicity of programs for substance-abusing employees. Thus the Atlas Tire Company, by joining the National Tire Manufacturer's EAP, avoids being singled out as the "tire company with all those problem employees."

Advantages and disadvantages are similar for both the consortium and associational EAPs.

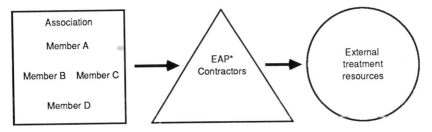

* Same as the consortium design.

FIGURE 6–5   Association EAP (same as the Consortium Design).

ADVANTAGES

Flexible.   The structural arrangements of consortium and association EAPs lend themselves to small corporations of dispensed groups such as are often found in associations. By pooling resources a full-fledged EAP is possible, which could not be achieved independently.

Avoids stigmatization.   Establishing an EAP has often precipitated negative corporate images. In the competitive market, an airline, for example, wouldn't want to risk being the only one with an EAP because that might be used by competitors or perceived by consumers as: "Northern Airlines—the airlines with drunken pilots." By bringing a number of competitors into an EAP under the association umbrella, stigmatization can be avoided.

Accommodates dispersed populations.   Consortia or associations can better handle employee populations who are widely dispersed across the state or country as well as employees who are mobile rather than anchored within a particular work site.

DISADVANTAGES

- individual organizational needs are subject to the needs of consortium or association
- high degree of interorganization communication and cooperation is required
- policy making becomes more complex
- individual member organization's input is considerably diminished.

Summary   These are the four major types present at this time. Although there are gradations and alterations in individual programs, essentially all EAPs could fit under one of the four. These designs are key variants influencing programs and outcomes.

The indigenous design was the most common in the early stages of EAP establishment and still is predominant in most large companies. However, during the past several years the contracted design has gained much favor due in large part to the meteoric rise of treatment facilities and their successful marketing strategies.

Orientation, ideology, and design are the primary concepts in an EAP typology. Because so little standardization exists at this time, typology must be viewed as dynamic. This dynamism, though frustrating at times, indicates a level of energy, creativity, and thoughfulness that bodes well for workers and their workplaces. As the field matures throughout the next decade, a more definitive typology will emerge in which consensus around these factors will be more apparent.

No research has yet linked a particular orientation placement or design with its outcome. Without such information, typology can only be tied to personal preference or other idiosyncratic variables. This lack of outcome data represents a problem in that EAPs cannot assure sponsors or constituents of effectiveness. Likewise, those who contemplate developing such programs lack adequate guidance as they attempt to match a program type with the needs of their organization.

PROGRAM ELEMENTS

Universal components of EAPs have evolved in spite of the varying ideologies and implementations of those components. These are represented schematically in Table 6–2.

Three broad categories—organizational components, program mechanisms, and treatment services—constitute the essentials of EAPs necessary to establish a minimal level of functioning and effectiveness.

Organizational Components

An EAP is not simply a human service agency set in a work environment. It is a program designed to work in and with a specific *kind* of environment and population. In order for an EAP to be effective, the organization

TABLE 6–2   Program Components of EAPs

Organizational Components	Program Mechanisms	Treatment Services
Policy & Procedures	Identification	Alcoholism
Outreach	Record Keeping	Other Drug Abuse
		Health Problems
Marketing	Assessment & Monitoring	Mental Health
Supervisory Training	Referral	Family
Employee Education	Reintegration	Legal & Financial
	Advocacy	
	Evaluation	

has to prepare itself for this new program and insure that its members understand and utilize it. Specific organizational components aid this task.

Policy and Procedures   Personnel policies are sanctioned and approved statements that guide the relationship between a company and its employees. These policies reflect a set of values and establish mutual expectations. Trice and Roman (1972, p. 180) cite three major purposes for a written policy related to alcohol and drugs:

1.   informs employees of the consequence of using alcohol and drugs in conjunction with job performance
2.   spells out the distribution of authority and responsibility involved in policy implementation
3.   eliminates the possibility of ambiguity or favoritism

A policy supporting an EAP program is important, but it is not sufficient for success. Policy must be operationalized to be effective. In addition, policy should be viewed within a political context and from the dynamic perspective of organizational receptiveness and commitment as well as from the more static dimensions of presence. Just as the constitution is the life blood of American democracy so is corporate policy the essential force of a work community.

In addition to philosophical congruence, program policy writers need to remember that compatability with performance appraisal systems, grievance processes, disciplinary procedures, insurance policies, and above all, the protection of employee privacy through strict confidentiality are important to the viability of the EAP. To achieve policy integration requires constant interaction with all stakeholders in the work community to safeguard the integrity of policy and procedures.

Intraorganizational Outreach   Where EAPs are a staff function within an organization, they must establish relationships with other staff and line groups in a multitude of semiautonomous units. The EAP must interface with union, personnel departments, equal employment opportunity offices, medical departments, groups of retirees, and training groups to establish working relations. Without such outreach the EAP may be an isolated appendage, contributing little to the dynamics of the work community. Linkage to relevant organizational units assures two-way communication as well as functional integration into the culture and operations of the company.

This interface requires outreach and policy diffusion. These activities can be formal or informal. The normal contact of the EAP with troubled employees can often lead beyond the individual problem to a larger systemic problem in a department or division or of corporate policy. Thus, as the EAP counselor works with a supervisor on a specific employee-focused problem, he or she may establish more permanent relationships. Individual cases then become a vehicle for the EAP staff and work groups to better understand one another.

Marketing: Developing a Constituency   After adopting policy and procedures, some EAPs still find themselves underutilized. The EAP needs to establish methods of calling attention to its services in such a way that appropriate use is made of those services. Often called a marketing plan, it is simply an assessment of and response to the needs of the work system. Demographics and psychographics can be used as a way of aiding this process. Any new or unorthodox program must learn to convey its presence, its purposes, and its usefulness. The EAP must be understandable to its constituents and demonstrate an intimate understanding of the organization. No organization is a monolith, and the need for the EAP, its receptiveness, and points of access to it, differ among and between organizational units. For example, professionals in a purchasing division may practice excessive lunchtime drinking in the course of doing business, resulting in tardiness and lost afternoons, while a productions unit's greatest problem might be high levels of stress due to forced overtime. The EAP must be able to understand and respond to the special needs and circumstances of each.

Supervisor Training   Training is essential to a successful EAP. In a 1976 survey compiled for the Association of Labor and Management Administrators and Consultants on Alcoholism (ALMACA), training constituted the third largest proportion of staff time spent after clinical activities and program administration. Training helps bring about changes in knowledge and attitudes that enable the EAP to realize its objectives within the organization.

Training is a powerful tool for communication and change. Frequently, its content includes information regarding company policy and procedures; an explanation of the EAP itself; and training supervisory personnel in procedures for identifying, confronting, and referring an employee with job performance problems.

While training curriculum and purpose varies (Etchen and Roman, 1977; Googins and Kurtz, 1981) the necessity of training is undisputed. Without such a component, the EAP will be less effective with supervisors, personnel administrators, and others who might not otherwise understand how best to work with and utilize the EAP.

Employee Education   Employee education, although not as well established as staff training, is of growing importance. The objectives of employee education are prevention and intervention. Through brochures, presentations, and articles in the company newsletter, the EAP informs employees of what the EAP is and how to use it. As any introductory marketing student knows, no program can survive without visibility, recognition, and exposure.

Another goal of employee education is to reduce stigmatization (as in the case of alcoholism), provide updated information on a wide range of health problems, and develop a culture of prevention. Problems that affect society as a whole also affect the workplace, which is an appropriate environment to increase awareness and improve knowledge about smoking, stress, alcohol, drugs, and other social problems such as battered children and spouse abuse.

Program Mechanisms

Program mechanisms are vehicles for smooth and routine identification, documentation, confrontation, and referral. Those listed below represent the collective wisdom of the field and do not purport to describe a totally circumscribed set of mechanisms.

Identification The identification of employees with problems in work organizations has been the basis for EAPs. Mechanisms exist for identification and for assessing and monitoring job performance. It is assumed that an employee's personal problems will manifest themselves in negative behaviors within the workplace and that deteriorating job performance will indicate signs or symptoms of underlying behavioral problems.

Thus each EAP must have some way of utilizing existing workplace mechanisms for monitoring job performance as an aid in identifying the employee with problems. Because these signs are manifested in absenteeism, tardiness, sickness, accidents, and overall employee deterioration, identification mechanisms are linked to these areas. Hence, monthly absenteeism forms, employee appraisal sheets, accident reports, and other such procedures are potential first-line identification mechanisms through which alcoholic employees become known and linked to the EAP. While there are a number of these formal identification mechanisms, occupational social workers also bring a number of skills that further enhance them. Listening, environmental sensing, and relationship building are essential in identifying problems on both the individual level and the organizational level. Although these identification mechanisms are traditionally used on individual problems, EAPs also need to draw on mechanisms for identifying systemic and environmental problems that impede the health of the organization as well as the individual employee.

Record Keeping Record keeping is intimately linked to identification mechanisms. Records are an essential element of any personnel-oriented program. This is particularly true since performance information is often critical in clinically confronting an alcoholic and breaking through the denial and alibi system.

The EAP record-keeping system consists of scrupulously guarded confidential material gathered through approved organizational channels and from outside treatment agencies as well as from the client. These records are tools for assessing the problems, confronting denial, and evaluating outcome. While the record keeping mechanism can be useful in other functions, such as promoting the EAP within the organization, its primary function is as a tool for confronting problems and monitoring and evaluating treatment outcome.

Assessment and Monitoring   Most presenting problems are complex, multi-dimensional ones that require attention over time. Each EAP must be able to provide an initial assessment, monitor problems, and help resolve them over time. The most effective means of accomplishing this is through staff who are trained in interviewing and assessment skills and in the use of an intake procedure designed to aid the initial assessment.

Assessment is particularly important in EAPs where referrals for extended treatment are frequently made. Because the solution of a problem flows from its definition, an erroneous or poorly defined assessment may lead to misguided treatment. The sharper the assessment and monitoring, the more likely are positive outcomes.

Monitoring is perhaps the most neglected function within EAP. Because treatment is often outside the EAP, monitoring the progress of both treatment and performance within the work site is important. Without a well-defined mechanism for case monitoring, EAP staff will tend to place emphasis on the initial stages of treatment and not allocate sufficient time to monitor progress or identify relapse and recidivism within the workplace. Follow-up groups and routine checks with treatment centers and work supervisors (where appropriate) are effective monitoring devices.

Referral Mechanism   EAPs are rarely complete treatment centers, and referral mechanisms are necessary to link the program with external treatment systems. The art and science of referrals through interagency coordination is made complex by an array of service providers, each with their strengths and weaknesses, their eligibility criteria, waiting lists, and fee structures. Couple this with the formal and informal elements of each system and the constantly changing characteristics of the system, and the complexity of good referral becomes apparent. Failure to establish a referral mechanism securely within the EAP severely limits the ability of the program to provide employees with appropriate and effective services.

EAP staff must be familiar with community-resources. Their relationship with outside agencies goes beyond sufficient understanding of the agencies to facilitate effective information and referral services to employees. They also need to educate agencies and individuals to the realities of the workplace. Because their practice has been isolated from work organizations, these agencies have to be informed and trained as to the nature of work-based programs, the treatment-management issues involved, and the treatment needs of the EAP staff and the work organization.

Reintegration   For employees who have completed treatment programs, reentering the workplace or work group may be difficult. If the employee has had a history of absenteeism, missed assignments, or other performance problems that caused resentment among co-workers and embarrassment on the part of the employee, the process may be more complicated. A full treatment plan will include a mechanism to follow employees after treatment and rehabilitation, identifying and assisting with reentry problems. This may be accomplished by working with the employee's work group supervisors and union stewards to create a welcoming climate in which problems of reentry and reintegration are mitigated.

Advocacy Advocacy is a basic tenet of social work practice. A carefully thought out advocacy mechanism is appropriate and necessary. Advocacy affirms the rights and responsibilities of all employees regardless of level or role. Advocacy may mean opening avenues of communication that are blocked or closed off.

As the EAP grows within the organization, securing credence and sanction, it is able to advocate for institutional changes within the broader environment. This type of advocacy transcends a particular case and may argue for environmental change that will benefit the organization and the health and welfare of all the individuals within that environment. Because this emerges at a later stage of development, few EAPs have yet adopted such a mechanism.

Evaluation Evaluation mechanisms vary from simple enumerations of cases to highly sophisticated research to determine program effectiveness. While many organizations require some evaluation, only recently have programs attended to the need and usefulness of evaluation both within the company and in the external environment. The need for evaluation has encouraged better record-keeping systems and the recruitment of researchers and program evaluators to assist the EAP. In summary, the presence of a program evaluation mechanism adds to program credibility and provides information that can be used to improve service.

Treatment Services

The third set of variables which constitute the essential program components of the EAP are treatment services.

The most common services involve treatment for:

Alcoholism
Controlled substance abuse
Mental illness
Family problems
Legal and financial problems
Stress
Interpersonal problems
Work-related problems
Intrapsychic problems

Each EAP must be prepared to identify and treat these problems (among others) either within the confines of the EAP or through the auspices of specialized human service agencies, practitioners, and self-help groups. By coordinating internal and external resources, the EAP creates professional treatment services in which the company, the union, and the individual employee recognize and trust the treatment as an aid to them in solving their individual and collective problems.

Providing treatment services within a work setting involves both an understanding of treatment within this context and a thorough knowledge of outside treatment resources. Business is not used to, nor is it in the business of, providing treatment. Consequently, treatment by the human service and mental health community has to account for the parallel tracks of managing and treating employee problems (Googins, 1975). Identification, documentation, and confrontation are all part of this enlarged treatment process. A typical treatment path would look something like Figure 6–6 (Walsh, 1982).

Throughout this process, treatment staff (EAP as well as community agency staff) work separately and together at different stages of the process. Although managing and treating a problem require different skills they are inexorably intertwined. As supervisors continue to insist on an employee getting to work on time, the EAP counselor focuses on the abandonment of the denial and alibi systems of the problem drinker. Just because an employee accepts EAP treatment does not exempt him or her from rules, norms, and expectations of the workplace. The two operate in tandem, and if job performance is impaired, treatment should lead to improvement and not serve as an escape from the real demands of the workplace. On the contrary, part of treatment is the accountability of ordinary life tasks, such as are required at work, and to suspend these hinders treatment.

At each decision point in the flow chart, problem treatment and problem management work together. If treatment is refused or not followed, disciplinary action is needed (if job performance does not improve), not solely as a requirement of the workplace, but as an additional treatment tool.

In summary, treatment services have to be understood and incorporated into a workplace framework. The parallel paths of treatment and management, although complex and touching on legal, labor-management, and confidentiality issues, represent the realities of treatment in work organizations in an opportunity to utilize work-based mechanisms in the treatment process.

SUMMARY

The description of core mechanisms, components, and services in this chapter is one attempt to provide an overview of the nature and function of

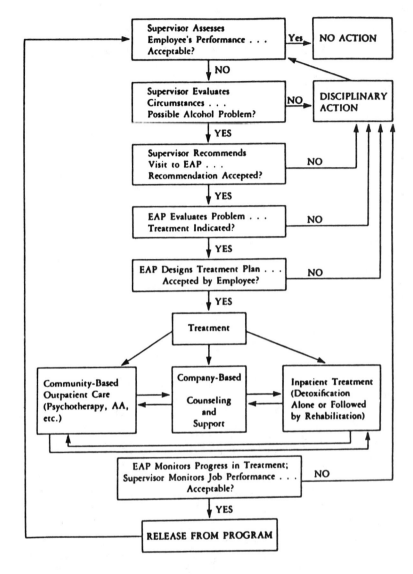

FIGURE 6–6 A Typical Occupational Alcoholism Treatment Path.

EAPs. It suffers from several deficiencies not the least of which is the evolutionary stage within which the EAP is developing. The next decade will see a continuing evolution of ideology, program structure design, and the boundaries of EAPs. As this occurs a more standard program format will emerge with less variation and idiosyncratic practice. The accumulated wisdom of time and growth coupled with a widening research base will yield a more consistent and conceptually clearer Employee Assistance Program.

CHAPTER SEVEN
ALCOHOLISM IN THE WORKPLACE

INTRODUCTION

The problem of alcoholism[*] constitutes a primary focus of human service programs and activities in business and industry. A spurt of occupational social work in the mid 1970s was caused largely by the introduction of occupational alcoholism programs from which employee assistance programs and other occupational social work initiatives were spawned. Without the catalyst of occupational alcoholism, it is doubtful that the dramatic rise of occupational social work would have occurred. During the past decade businesses and industries have established programs and policies on alcoholism or contracted with community agencies for the treatment of alcoholism primarily because alcoholism has become a major problem both in financial and human loss. Trice and Roman (1972, p. 2) cite three specific work-based costs of problem drinking: (1) those stemming directly from the employee's work behavior; (2) those caused by the impact of the deviant drinker on other employees; and (3) the costs of "doing something" about

---

[*]The term alcoholism will be used in this chapter although substance abuse or chemical dependency might be more fitting since the use of alcohol is usually accompanied by other drug use, including prescription drugs. Nevertheless, since alcohol is the most widespread drug problem in the workplace we primarily use the term alcoholism.

the deviant drinker once the limits of tolerance are reached. Others have referred to the alcohol problem in work organizations as industry's "billion-dollar hangover." Regardless of the true measure of cost, the plain facts are that alcoholism is a concern and a cost to the workplace that far outweighs and often causes other concerns such as stress, child care needs, marital problems, and emotional illness.

Social workers entering the workplace face two handicaps: a lack of knowledge about work and work environments as well as the traditional ignorance and avoidance of the disease of alcoholism in particular and of substance abuse in general. However, since the client-system's needs have demanded an alcoholism focus, it has served to stimulate alcoholism training and education as an essential qualification for practice. Unfortunately, social workers and human service and health professionals are still woefully undertrained in alcoholism diagnosis and treatment (Googins, 1984). This chapter will examine alcoholism in the workplace in the context of occupational social work rather than as a primer or basic text on the subject.

ALCOHOLISM IN THE WORKPLACE: AN HISTORICAL PERSPECTIVE

Occupational Alcoholism Programs (OAPs) are a relatively new phenomenon, the first program having been established in the 1940s. Although organized programs at the work site are recent, the problems of alcoholism in work organizations are not new, and attempts to intervene and to solve those problems go back to the early years of the industrial era in this country. As corporations strengthened themselves institutionally, new mechanisms for dealing with the alcoholic employee were developed, and a unique set of interventions tailored to the needs and dynamics of the work place emerged.

Underlying these attempts to intervene in problem drinking at the workplace are empirical data and assumptions that differ from the beliefs of the early industrialists. (1) Alcoholism cuts across the population at large and is relatively evenly distributed. This has been corroborated through research studies (Cahalan, 1970; Straus and Bacon, 1951) that have demonstrated that the majority of alcohol problems exist within the spectrum of intact working families. (2) Furthermore, the workplace as a central institution in society is directly affected by problem drinking in terms of costs, inefficiency, and impaired work environments. This suggests that, (3) the work place is both an appropriate locus for intervention and uniquely suited for disrupting patterns of dysfunctional drinking behavior and further that (4) the treatment of alcohol problems must be integrated into the basic institutions of society rather than isolated among social welfare agencies and their staffs (Trice, 1974). (5) Alcoholism is a treatable illness as is evident in the widespread growth of Alcoholics Anonymous (AA) and the large cohort of recovering alcoholics and drug addicts.

These last points are particularly important. Although occupational alcoholism programs are still in their infancy, both in the alcoholism field and in the workplace itself, their uniqueness forms the rationale and essence of such interventions. From the perspective of alcoholism professionals, EAPs represent a form of intervention that stresses the use of coercive force to break down the alcoholic's denial. These forces are most readily available at the workplace through such mechanisms as company policy, performance reviews, and supervisory mandates. Though concentration may be on the individual, the workplace also benefits from EAPs. This is particularly true when therapeutic imperatives coincide with the managerial exigencies of the workplace (Walsh, 1982). Since performance criteria are already established in work settings, the workplace is an ideal location to confront the alcoholic's dysfunctional behaviors. Threat of job loss due to deteriorating and alcohol-affected job performance is often sufficient to penetrate denial.

Nevertheless, "selling" the suitability of EAPs for the workplace has not been easy. Considering that the first programs began less than 40 years ago and that the majority of companies have yet to adopt such programs, it is clear that universal acceptance is still some time away. On the other hand, the establishment of programs is spiraling upwards geometrically. Recent statistics on EAPs indicate that the number of programs has increased from 6 in 1945 to 50 in 1950, 500 in 1973, 2,400 in 1977, and more than 4,000 in 1978–1979 (NIAAA, 1980).

The roots of today's programs for alcoholism intervention in the workplace rest on a series of responses that emerged in the early 1940s. Those responses formed the nucleus of modern OAPs. In the 1940s the nation was just beginning to overcome that volatile and confusing period during which prohibition was adopted and then rescinded. That social experiment left a philosophical and policy lacuna. The dissatisfaction with a moralistic and legislative paradigm gradually gave way to an attempt to develop a more scientific understanding of alcoholism. Under the leadership of the Yale School of Alcohol Studies, a group of prominent health professionals and social scientists began the first systematic study of alcoholism. One of their significant contributions was the development of the first comprehensive model of OAPs (Henderson and Bacon, 1953). The Yale plan for business and industry sketched out, for the first time, guidelines for companies on how to deal with alcoholism among its employees. At about the same time, the National Council on Alcoholism (NCA) began a campaign aimed at big companies in the heavily industrialized Northeast (Presnall, 1967). Largely through the efforts of the NCA and the Yale Plan, a number of pioneering companies — Kodak, DuPont, Consolidated Edison, and Allis Chalmers — began to identify and treat alcoholic employees. The impetus for these programs was the realization that alcohol problems were of sufficient magnitude within the company to warrant an institutional response. The initial results of these programs were considered successful. The medical director of Eastman Kodak, in a presentation to the First Industrial Conference on Alcoholism in the mid 1940s, reported that 2,000 of the 2,800 employees treated during a five-year period were successfully rehabilitated (Norris, 1950).

From all historical anecdotal accounts, the OAPs established from the 1940s until the late 1970s resulted from the inspirations and dogged work of AA members who argued, proselytized, negotiated, packaged, and marketed programs within their own companies and in the larger industrial and union worlds. It is not accidental that the rise of occupational programs parallels the AA movement itself. From 1938 to 1944, membership in AA grew from 100 to 10,000 and from two groups to 3,000. Within the next six years it had expanded to 90,000 and more than 3,000 groups (Trice, 1957). It was during this period of AA's early growth that modern day OAP's came into existence, the majority of which were staffed by "recovering" AA alcoholics. The occupational alcoholism field, despite its rapid professionalization, continues to reflect a strong orientation due to the activism of its members.

The early OAPs were primarily management oriented; unions played only ancillary roles. The Yale Plan suggested no role for unions, nor was there any mention of them. However, during the late 1940s and 1950s union interest and involvement with these programs grew (Trice and Schonbrunn, 1981). Through the leadership of Leo Perlis and the community service arm of the Congress of Industrial Organizations (CIO), unions participated in seminars and conferences on alcohol and the workplace. Perlis himself characterized union involvement during this period:

> Our records show that we first initiated a nationwide program on alcoholism in 1950. This was under the National CIO Community Services Committee. While there was even less enthusiasm among corporate executives this was so even though we proposed joint union–management sponsorship and a policy to keep alcoholism outside the controversial area of collective bargaining (Trice and Schonbrunn, 1981, p. 43).

The 1940–1960 period represented the nascent stirrings of present-day OAPs. While developments were slow and somewhat unsophisticated by today's standards, they did represent a significant departure from the moralism of the prohibition era and the paternalism of the earlier industrialists' attempts to intervene in the problems of alcohol in the workplace. These developments paralleled events throughout society as the problem of alcohol was recognized as a problem that cut across socioeconomic boundaries. Straus and Bacon's (1951) classic study on social stability presented data that demonstrated the presence of alcoholism among the so-called healthy, intact, and working population, while simultaneously demythologizing the skid row image as the preeminent alcoholic. This set the stage for the development of alcoholism programs in the workplace. Because of the gradual acceptance of the sociological data and the slow process of attitudinal change, the actual number of OAPs remained small, and companies and unions were slow to initiate alcoholism programs.

If the 1940–1970 period represented the evolution of OAPS, 1970–1980 signaled the revolution. In 1970 the Hughes Act (Public Law 91-616) established the National Institute of Alcohol Abuse and Alcoholism (NIAAA). The mission of NIAAA was to initiate and fund national efforts for combatting alcohol problems. One group, the Occupational Programs Branch, had as its primary target the employed population. NIAAA established a three-year demonstration program to grant $50,000 per year to each state to develop OAP consultation. Following a national training program for the consultants hired under the demonstration program, other consultants began to approach employers in the private and public sector to offer assistance in developing and marketing OAPs throughout each state. Although results were mixed (Adams, Roman, and Greene, 1977), this pioneering effort opened the American workplace to the potential of work-based alcoholism programs.

The NIAAA initiative, through its Occupational Programs Branch, accelerated the process of developing EAPs in the private sector, systematically reaching vast numbers of work organizations. The NIAAA programs reinforced the emphasis of the OAP on the importance of using deteriorating or impaired job performance as criteria for identifying problems. Subsequently, identification of impaired job performance, the first step in the OAP model, became the responsibility of the supervisor, whose role it is to monitor and evaluate job performance (Googins and Kurtz, 1981). This strategy strengthened the OAP model by reinforcing existing supervisory roles while releasing supervisors from a diagnostic role with which they were ill-equipped to deal. The rationale for this was that intervention in alcohol problems lay outside of the role mandates of supervisors (Kurtz and Googins, and Williams 1980) and when attempted, simply made the employee defensive, encouraging denial and a search for alternative ways to account for behavior (Roman, 1981).

While the OAP was essentially the same program under the NIAAA as before, the emergence of Employee Assistance Programs (EAPs) introduced both a new strategy and an expanded version of OAPs and created a spirited debate throughout the 1970s. The EAP introduced the so-called broad brush or expanded scope program that transformed the OAP into a program in which job performance expectations legitimized the addition of emotional, personal, and behavioral medical problems as part of program staff responsibility. As discussed in the previous chapter, EAP moved toward a program model in which alcohol was seen in a broader context. This program model mitigated two perceived negative qualities of the OAP—alcohol stigma and unrealistic demands on supervisors. Although arguments comparing these two models still exist (Roman, 1981), the majority of programs have been influenced by the NIAAA strategy and have adopted the EAP model.

Federal initiatives and efforts of the occupational program specialists within the privately funded NCA proved to be the catalysts for rapid adoption of programs in the early 1970s and show indications of continuing to be catalytic forces well into the future. A professional organization, the Association of Labor and Management Administrators and Consultants on Alcoholism (ALMACA) was begun with NIAAA assistance. Today it reflects the field's growth, serves EAP's and has created a network of 4,000 members.

THE CHARACTERISTICS OF OCCUPATIONAL ALCOHOLISM PROGRAMS

The requirements of work organizations facilitate an early identification of problem drinkers and legitimize sanctions necessary for constructive confrontation and intervention. The preventive potential of the work setting represents an opportunity rarely found within alcoholism treatment systems. Historically, the alcoholism treatment community has been hindered by the absence of settings where legitimate and effective interventions can be used to "breakup" a pattern of excessive drinking and halt the progression toward alcohol addiction (Trice and Belasco, 1966). Roman and Trice (1976) list four assumptions underlying the preventive potential of the workplace:

1. Drinking patterns that are prodromal to chronic problems of drinking and alcohol addictions become manifest in impaired job performance early in the sequence of problem development.*

2. The relationship between employer and employee provides for legitimate intervention by the employer upon documentation of impaired job performance.

3. Problem drinkers and potential problem drinkers tend to be concentrated among employees with relatively heavy investments in their jobs in terms of seniority, fringe benefits, and the centrality of work in their lives.

4. Confrontation regarding impaired performance directed to relatively long-term employees tends to precipitate a crisis that, in turn, motivates the individual to "do something" about his or her drinking, thereby increasing responsiveness to treatment efforts.

These early assumptions are currently being examined in light of new developments. For example, most EAPs are reporting large numbers of self-referrals. This might be the result of the broad brush strategy, which may be reaching earlier-stage alcoholics who self-refer for other problems, or it may

---

*Many practitioners believe that the employee is already in the later stages of alcoholism by the time impaired performance surfaces within the work setting.

be a new developmental stage in the evolution and maturation of these programs.

These assumptions support the role and legitimacy of work organizations for identification and treatment of the alcoholic employee. As work organizations began to offer services and develop programs, specific properties emerged that characterize the occupational alcoholic program.

Performance Orientation

The workplace is an institution with prescribed rules, behaviors, and roles, all of which are intended to serve the overriding goal of performance — i.e., getting the job done. Because alcoholism generally interferes with the individual's ability to function over time, its impact on the employee's work is manifested in job performance deterioration. A well-documented phenomena of alcoholic employees is the gradual (or sometimes dramatic) deterioration in their job performance, evidenced by increased absenteeism, tardiness, missed assignments, accidents, sloppy work, and repeated customer complaints, or through difficulties in getting along with co-workers. Thus alcoholism often causes a direct violation of basic work rules, norms, or standards. This provides both a rationale and a basis on which the organization is able to legitimately intervene with the employee.

Early Identification

In most alcoholism treatment programs, the alcoholic has usually arrived for treatment after many years of heavy drinking. This late-stage intervention is a result of the stigma of the problem and the denial of alcoholism by the alcoholic, his fellow workers, his family, and the environment in general. Treatment becomes more difficult and prognosis for total rehabilitation and sobriety less certain. Early identification is often even more difficult, however, because many alcoholics in early and middle stages are exceptionally good employees whose performance is often superior when they are sober.

The work organization is an environment in which early- and middle-stage alcoholics are more likely to surface and begin treatment. The early prevention and identification of the alcoholic can be tied to the nature of the workplace. For most jobs the visibility of the employee's behaviors, and the routine expected functions of employees are highly visible to fellow employees, supervisors, and union officials. Although the alcoholic employee may go to great lengths to cover up alcoholic drinking and any accompanying job performance slippage, over time problem patterns will become visible. This stage of the problem is much more conducive to treatment and greatly enhances the desired outcome — sobriety and rehabilitation.

Early recognition is more likely in blue and pink collar jobs than in white collar. As one moves vertically upward in the organization there is a greater ability to hide the drinking primarily because of the loosening of controls over employees in management or professional roles. Even within this environment, however, telltale signs will usually emerge that point to employee alcoholic behavior.

Role of the Supervisor

The supervisor's role provides the work environment with another advantage. Conceptually a gatekeeper between the individual and the organization, the supervisor is in a pivotal position to identify performance problems, confront the employee, and get him or her into treatment. Supervisors by reason of their organizational role and functions are not only in an ideal position to identify, confront, and refer employees for help, but are expected and sanctioned to identify and resolve deteriorating job performance (Googins and Kurtz, 1981).

Because of the routinized interaction that occurs between supervisors and employees, the supervisor is the individual with both the responsibility and the opportunity to observe dysfunctional performance. Early OAPs defined deviant behaviors as those commonly associated with alcoholism. Supervisors were trained specifically to look for job-related and personal behavior that indicated excessive drinking either on the job or outside the workplace (Roman and Trice, 1976). While this made sense from a definitional stance, operationalizing the role within the workplace was problematic. The supervisor was, in effect, entrusted with witch-hunting, trying to spot those employees whose obvious symptoms—alcohol on the breath, blurry eyes, stumbling, slurred speech, etc.—fit the diagnostic category of alcoholism. Because supervisors are not trained as diagnosticians, this role added a burden to an already difficult job. Thus, this model did not meet with much success (Googins, 1978, pp. 16–17).

A more recent approach shifted from identifying alcoholism to observing and monitoring job performance. This enables the supervisor to avoid defining or identifying alcoholism by sticking more closely to the identification of deteriorating job performance. Thus, deviant drinking behavior is not defined in terms of medical signs or symptoms but in terms of behaviors endemic to the occupational role. Looking for alcoholics is replaced by monitoring and evaluating deteriorating job performance, a responsibility already entrusted to the supervisor. (A secondary effect of this has been a broader understanding of poor job performance—how such changed behavior may be viewed as symptomatic of other problems rather than evidence of character defect.)

Constructive Confrontation

Another property of the OAP is its use of constructive confrontation. Alcoholism is difficult to define or describe. In addition, denial and the rationalization process constitute a tremendous obstacle. Getting the alcoholic to "own" the alcoholism and accept treatment is a formidable task.

In the workplace the presence of identifiable job performance criteria provide a means of operationalizing the definition of alcoholism. Further, the treat of job loss through constructive confrontation of the alcoholic employee is an ideal mechanism for breaking down resistance and rationalizations and provides motivation for the problem drinker to seek treatment.

The major assumption underlying the confrontation method is that the drinking employee has a heavy investment in maintaining employment. Because of individual and social values surrounding an employee's work or job, the threat of unemployment poses grave consequences affecting self-identification and self-worth. Work and the workplace play an important role for individuals within our work-centered society. The confrontation strategy capitalizes on work values held by the individual, and the authority inherent in the work organization compels the problem drinker to accept treatment.

The coercive element borrows a tenet from AA, modifying it to fit the occupational setting. In AA parlance the psychological experience of "hitting bottom" is a necessary prerequisite for the individual to accept a drinking problem and to develop the motivation to do something about it. In effect, confrontation provides the alcoholism treatment community with an instrument that is unique to the organizational setting. By employing authorized group sanctions, the problem drinker is faced with the threatened sanction unless he changes his drinking behavior (Trice, 1980). Implicit in this measure is the assumption that changing the deviant behavior on the job (absenteeism, tardiness, and the like) will require the alcoholic employee first to remedy his drinking problem.

The supervisor, having observed impaired job performance, gives the employee the alternatives of disciplinary action and potential termination or the option of seeking assistance through the company's alcoholism program. The confrontation can precipitate a crisis, forcing the employee to do something about his or her problem.

All of these factors operate to create a program by which alcoholism is identified, confronted, and treated. The fact that these characteristics are endemic to the work organization provides both a prevention mechanism and a legitimate and effective tool for intervention.

THE WORKPLACE AND DRINKING: A CULTURAL PERSPECTIVE

Debate continues over the causes and conditions of alcoholism. In most discussions sociocultural variables represent one theoretical approach that attempts to explain the complexities of alcoholism. Work and work organizations are extremely influential in shaping and socializing individuals, thus it is not surprising that these same environments produce distinct cultures in respect to drinking, drunkenness, and alcoholism. What is surprising is how little attention has been paid to this perspective.

Most if not all work organizations have explicit norms and policies on drinking. For example, drinking on the job is either implicitly or explicitly forbidden. Organizational culture, however, ultimately determines members' behaviors. Trice (1983), in discussing rites and ceremonials in organizational culture, describes two ways of analyzing ceremonial behavior: (1) a network of meaning producing ideologies and (2) forms and mechanisms whereby these messages are delivered to members; for example, myths, symbols, rituals, and legend-stories; these forms combine "to form ceremonial behavior" (p. 4).

Messages about drinking and alcoholism are understood in part by analyzing the cultural attitudes as well as the symbols, rituals, legends, and stories that are passed throughout an organization. This culture differs from organization to organization and within the subcultures of the organization itself. Some examples are offered here to clarify these differences and to indicate how culture transmits messages about normative behavior and attitudes.

Three executives regularly have working lunches at which drinking is an integral part. Although the company has a strict policy against drinking on the job, this is generally interpreted as applicable to the blue collar hourly employees within the manufacturing division.

Members of a telephone repair crew in one section of the city drink their lunch. Although everyone knows this goes on, no one intervenes despite obvious safety problems because of groups norms around "ratting."

A boss notices his secretary's performance problems and, based on the office grapevine, is sure it is a drinking problem. Although he has confronted employees in the past with this problem, he hesitates to do so in this case because the fact that she is a woman makes it too touchy an issue.

Harold returns to work after spending thirty days in an alcohol rehabilitation center. He is met with warm but distant greetings by his co-workers, who find his new-found sobriety a threat to their drinking habits, which are not all that different from Harold's past drinking patterns.

Organized culture cannot be separated from the societal culture because the interplay is strong. But the intensity of the workplace environment is likely to effect a stronger influence. Fine, Akabas and Bellinger (1982) cite several types of information that are transmitted to employees through existing cultural norms: (1) the social benefits of alcohol use, (2) the tradition of alcohol use among coworkers at the worksite, (3) the expectation of alcohol use among coworkers at the work site and (4) the toleration, camouflage, or other support of alcohol use by coworkers at the worksite.

Work organizations (and subgroups within these organizations) are important in defining what is and is not alcoholic drinking, who is and who is not abusing alcohol, and the acceptable circumstances for drinking.

Drinking is sanctioned within organizations for ceremonial purposes, fraternizing, or "doing business." Because work is comprised of groups, group norms concerning drinking set the standards, and membership in the group may be effectuated by the acceptance of these norms.

There have been some studies of drinking in specific occupations. For example, police, doctors, construction workers, and entertainers have the reputation of being heavy drinkers with an above average number of problem drinkers. This may be explained to a certain extent by the drinking norms in these groups. To develop an effective strategy for identifying and treating alcoholism, cultural and subcultural contexts must be carefully assessed.

The issue of the cultural aspects of occupational alcoholism must also take into consideration the organization's impact on or contribution to employee alcoholism. There is a widespread belief or concern that the etiology of alcoholism may well lie within the work environment itself. This linkage of alcoholism to the workplace often examines such factors as work stressors, repetitive and nondemanding jobs, and informal requirements of alcohol use on the job (business lunches). Although there is little research to substantiate this proposition, numerous proponents contend that the workplace contributes to the emergence of problem drinking (Fine, Akabas and Bellinger, 1982). Because of a parallel with family environments, we can postulate that workplaces do play a role that needs further study and research.

While it is helpful to examine the cultural influences within the workplace, this in no way displaces the more complex issue of the etiology of alcoholism. The scientific quest for understanding the root causes of this problem is a well-researched arena in which physiological, psychological, and sociocultural theories compete with each other to explain the mystery of alcoholism. Although many competing claims exist, at present no definitive findings have emerged. There are some exciting projects in the biochemical field that are focused on endorphins, compounds such as tetrahydroisoquinolines (TIQ), and chemicals within the central nervous system. While still within the research stage, their promise is of pharmacological intervention in the addictive process. Because it is likely that psychological, sociocultural, and biochemical factors all play a role in the etiology, it is clear that research in all three areas is increasing our understanding of addiction.

MANAGING AND TREATING THE ALCOHOLIC EMPLOYEE

During the past decade treatment procedures have emerged which have been found to be effective with the alcoholic employee. The process entails a series of steps beginning with identification of the problem and culminating in reintegration of the recovering employee to the workplace. Figure 7-1 (Kurtz and Googins, 1979, p. 19) illustrates this process.

These stages constitute the steps by which the employee, the organization (supervisors, personnel staff, union staff), and the treatment resource (EAP staff counselor, outside or contracted services) interact in relation to the alcoholism problem.

Identification and Documentation

The identification of problem drinkers in work organizations is triggered by mechanisms within the work environment that identify problem drinkers in the incipient and middle stages of alcoholism as well as in the late stages when intervention has been delayed. Identification measures are directly related to deteriorating and impaired job performance as perceived and monitored by supervisors and managers within the organization. (Googins, 1975)

The logic behind the identification and documentation of alcoholic employees is appealingly simple. Because of the universal supervisory monitoring responsibility, the ability of employees to hide or cover up alcoholic behavior is, theoretically, minimized. For the incipient or developing alcoholic, the "spillover" effects of drinking into the workplace usually

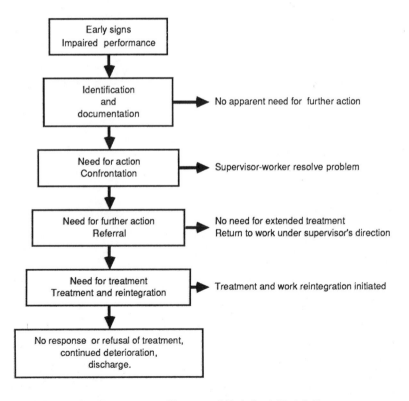

FIGURE 7–1 The Management and Treatment of Alcoholics in Work Settings.

increase over time. Consequently alcoholism will manifest itself in deteriorating job performance: absenteeism, tardiness, accidents, and other signs of impairment. While earlier occupational alcoholism programs focused on physical symptoms (blearing eyes, tremors), recent programs place emphasis on declining job performance as the identifying symptom.

Linking job deterioration and measures of work performance is also a means of protecting employees from excessive intrusiveness into their lives. Drinking habits are none of a corporation's business unless they interfere with the contract between employer and employee. Any such interference is manifested most clearly in job performance.

Maxwell (1960) used a list of forty-four signs which were administered to 400 alcoholic males recovered or in treatment. Of the forty-four on-the-job signs, the following occurred most frequently (in percentages):

Hangovers	(84)
Increased nervousness	(83)
Greater irratibility	(75)
Putting things off (procrastination)	(72)
Red or bleary eyes	(70)
More spasmodic work pace	(69)
Sensitivity to opinions about own drinking	(68)
Hard tremors	(68)
Avoiding boss or associates	(67)
Neglecting details	(66)

Trice (1962) in his study of the work behavior of 602 AA members cited several other signs that occur frequently: decrease in work efficiency, cover up, and job turnover.

No one sign can be associated with the identification of a potential drinking problem, although absenteeism is often cited as the most reliable. Alcoholism is accompanied by numerous problems and seldom occurs in isolation. As the disease progresses, the number, frequency, and complexity of attendant problems multiply, thereby heightening the vulnerability of work habits.

The documentation process is the written record of identified job deterioration, routinely kept by most organizations. There can be no formal identification without documentation of the problem. Documentation has three functions (Kurtz, 1981). First, it is required by the employer as assurance that action in regard to an alcoholic is not discriminatory. It also serves as the basis for cooperation between management and labor for helping the alcoholic employee. Finally, documentation is the primary tool of the supervisor in initiating action with a problem employee.

As noted above, identification and documentation are ideally suited both to workplace organization and the needs of an OAP. However, there is a considerable gap between the ideal model and actual behaviors within the workplace. Job performance criteria are universally suspect due to the vagaries and ambiguities of application and interpretation. The subjective aspect of determining, measuring, and evaluating job performance clouds the superficial logic of scientific management. The rich reporting of anecdotal episodes from both the occupational alcoholism field and the management field reveal the deficiencies of relying too rigorously on job performance as a surefire mechanism for identifying the alcoholic and getting him or her into treatment. Uneven and unreliable record keeping and human tendencies to overlook problems or attempt to solve them have long frustrated the rational process of identification and documentation. Despite their shortcomings, many of these procedures are widely used and have become the first step in solving the complex problem of alcoholism within the workplace, providing the supervisor and treatment personnel with a tool for initiating aid for the alcoholic.

Confrontation

Confrontation is the second mechanism available within the field of occupational alcoholism treatment. Although the symptoms described in the identification process are endemic to the individual and the organizational environment, they are insufficient to actively engage the problem drinker in treatment. To initiate treatment a linkage must be made between identification and referral for treatment. The confrontation stage is this bridge.

The concept of confrontation emerges from the dynamics of the work organization. Alcoholism is difficult to define and operationalize. Because denial and the rationalization are formidable obstacles, convincing the alcoholic to accept treatment or even to be referred to a treatment program may be the primary goal of the alcoholism program. In the presence of clearly impaired job performance behaviors, the threat of disciplinary action or job loss at the time of confrontation may penetrate resistance, rationalization, or denial. Subsequently, the problem drinker may seek treatment. Without documentation of impaired job performance there can be no productive confrontation.

As discussed earlier, constructive confrontation provides a means for coercing the employee to face his or her pattern of performance problems and the role of alcohol in that pattern. As in the identification stage, the supervisor's position is pivotal. Using documented performance decline, a supervisor exercises his or her prerogatives guided by basic policy, such as (Trice and Roman, 1972):

> 1) drug dependency behaviors produce unacceptable job performance, and these behaviors are likely to become health problems; 2) since these are potential health problems with physiological and psychiatric consequences, the organization will provide typical health coverage similar to that for other disorders; 3) unless job performance returns to an acceptable level, however, a crisis precipitation strategy will be implemented (p. 171).

Because denial is an integral part of the alcoholism illness, the need to exercise confrontation is absolute. Conversely, not to have confrontation as a tool deprives the supervisor (or spouse, friends, etc.) of a strategy by which the alcoholism can be treated. The supervisor weakens the alcoholic's defenses and breaks through alibis and rationalization by confronting the employee on documented job deterioration. Confrontation also serves to precipitate a crisis by which the continued pattern of drinking and subsequent problems associated with it cannot continue without a counterbalanced set of consequences, i.e., termination of employment. This crisis precipitation is often seen as "raising the bottom." Rather than waiting for the alcoholism to run its course (move into the late stage of utter defeat, alienation, and despair with life threatening complications), confrontation makes "hitting the bottom" more imminent by threatening the ultimate loss of the job.

Confrontation can occur formally or informally. Formally, confrontation follows the policies and procedures set forth by the company. The strength of denial will indicate the degree of force required in the confrontation: without such a correlation the confrontation may fail. Consequently policy, in conjunction with the appropriate personnel and disciplinary guidelines (especially in union organizations), will be employed to bring the confrontation to a successful conclusion.

Informally, confrontation may occur in numerous situations, without initiating the formal process. Many program staff report this phenomenon occurs more frequently and effectively than the formal process. "Off the record" confrontation may take place over a cup of coffee, in passing comments in the hallway or via a heart to heart talk between colleagues. Because of the supervisor's natural avoidance of the hardhearted role and reluctance to fire an employee, the informal approach may function as an early warning with the same coercive message and effect without formally entering the confrontation into the record. This maintains the supervisor's "goodhearted" sense of self and eliminates both paper work and bureaucratic involvement. The employee "gets the message" but still feels there is a chance to act before the company becomes formally involved.

Every alcoholic may not need confrontation. And though powerful as a tool, it is not infallible; some alcoholics will find their drinking and its rewards stronger than the confrontation and the perceived and anticipated negative consequences.

Confrontation is fraught with ambivalence, primarily because the act of confronting is difficult and goes against the grain of most human beings. On the other hand, it has proven effective for those who use it (Heyman, 1976). As supervisors become more attuned to assistance programs and see confrontation as a device for helping a troubled employee, rather than punishing, the use of confrontation increases. It can also be expected that a more informal use of the strategy will be utilized thereby relieving the perceived onus of invoking formal company sanctions.

Referral

The referral stage represents the natural culmination of identifying and confronting the problem. Interestingly, not much attention has been paid to this step. Basically, the referral of an alcoholic employee to a treatment resource within the company (an EAP) or to an outside resource (a community clinic or hospital) marks the beginning of the rehabilitation process by which the alcoholism is dealt within a therapeutic framework. The referral may be coercive or self-initiated.

Coercive referrals are those in which the employee comes into treatment as the result of a confrontation. In the EAP, confrontation is initiated by the work supervisor as discussed above. However, the coercion to treatment may come from other members of the work environment, such as union officials or fellow employees, or from outside sources such as family members, church or civic organizations, and friends and relatives.

Self-referrals are those in which the employee brings himself or herself into treatment. In the occupational field, most EAPs refer to self-referrals as those employees who come into the program without supervisory or union coercion. This causes some conceptual vagueness since the notion of self-referring alcoholics seems at odds with the denial aspects of alcoholism. Because an essential part of the disease is denial of the problem and since an alibi structure serves as a defense mechanism to allow the drinking to continue, referring oneself to treatment seems contradictory if not unlikely. Nevertheless, over the past several years EAPs have reported a significant increase in self-referrals.

One explanation is that self-referrals, while not reflecting supervisory or work confrontation, may have felt pressure from other sources not reported or obvious. A spouse who has handed the alcoholic an ultimatum to get help may be the factor that propels the employee into treatment. The referral may show up as a self-referral, however, because the reporting interest of the EAP is dichotomous—supervisory or self-referral.

In the occupational setting, supervisory referral is a unique tool because of the supervisor's opportunity to spot emerging problems through deteriorating job performance and refer the employee to treatment through confrontation and threat of disciplinary action or job loss. Nevertheless, though the potential of this model is great, it is not always realized. For a variety of reasons supervisors may not carry out their roles, and consequently referrals are not made. Trice and Roman (1972, pp. 159–160) identified several factors that encouraged and discouraged supervisors regarding the act of referral.

DISCOURAGING FACTORS	ENCOURAGING FACTORS
It was my duty to handle the	I had to watch him/her more closely.
He/she was often an able worker.	She/he was out a great deal.
Referral would mean separation from the company.	He/she was lacking in self-respect.
I felt "in between" employees and management.	My boss would back me up.
	I never knew what to expect.
Referral would hurt her/his family.	She/he was a safety risk.
He/she might be "bugged".	I needed to do something as soon as possible.
Referral would mean inconvenience for me.	I would help his/her family if I took action.
Referral would get me mixed up with the union.	She/he had a bad effect on fellow workers.
She/he "snapped out of it" frequently.	He/she wasn't getting work out.
I had come up through the ranks.	He/she put me in a bad light. I wanted a replacement.

In a more recent study Googins (1978) identified a different set of barriers. These were supervisors' lack of knowledge about the EAP; the tendency for supervisors to handle the problem themselves; the perception that referring might reflect badly on their ability to supervise. Kurtz, Googins, and Williams (1980) also identified as barriers fear of harming the employees' family, fear of involvement, burden of responsibility, and fear of the disciplinary process.

The referral stage is a complex one that may put an onus on the supervisor while establishing a bridge between recognition of the problem and initiation of rehabilitation. Because it is an unfamiliar and therefore uncomfortable role, it remains a stage that will be tentatively approached by supervisors as programs mature.

Treatment and Reintegration

Early OAPs relied heavily on AA both in principle and in treatment. Alcoholics Anonymous meetings and counseling by recovering AA members were the primary treatment modality. Although some hospitalization for detoxification was used, it was not until the late 1970s that the hospital became an important treatment vehicle. Despite the absence of substantive evidence on the effectiveness of hospitalization, in-house treatment has proliferated. Major national corporations have been formed to capitalize on this growth. In-house programs usually last between three and four weeks and include detoxification, alcohol education, individual and group counseling, and a range of other activities from recreational therapy to Outward Bound expeditions.

A more recent innovation is the day treatment model in which the employee remains in the work environment, lives at home, and returns to the job after two weeks of intensive treatment similar to the hospital treatment program. Few such programs have yet been established (Frankel, 1982), but it does suggest an alternative to the more expensive and time-consuming hospitalization.

As treatment alternatives have evolved so have reservations about theory and even necessity of treatment. Roman points to "rush to treatment" in which treatment programs self-perpetuate, undermining the use of confrontation (Roman, 1976, p. 499). Confrontation by supervisors may be sufficient by itself or used in conjunction with AA meetings to reverse the alcoholism and constitute the treatment. However, the alcoholism treatment business has overshadowed this simple and at times effective tool by its marketing of long-term hospitalization (Googins and Collier, 1985).

Treatment within the occupational alcoholism and employee assistance programs has continued to develop, primarily in external treatment centers. While the process of treatment begins with identification and includes the critical stages described above, Roman's fear of a rush to treatment—that is, a precipitous movement into treatment programs without exploring less drastic steps such as simple confrontation—has in large part been realized. Treatment today often means deferring to the vendors whose hospitals have been relegated the "treatment" function.

As yet there is little discussion or research concerning the reintegration of the recovering alcoholic into the workplace. It can only be assumed that long periods of problem drinking have caused considerable disruption, frayed relationships, and altered attitudes in the alcoholic employee's environment. Although this has been recognized and discussed as it pertains to the family environment (McCrady et al., 1979), there has been scant mention of it in connection with the workplace. Reintegrating the alcoholic employee requires an aftercare plan to insure continued sobriety and develop successful alternatives to drinking as well as an examination of the work environment to assess prior damage and facilitate reintegration. Such a plan might include meeting with the alcoholic employee's work group to help educate and sensitize them and building social supports for the returning employee by encouraging contact with other employees who are AA members, for example.

BARRIERS TO TREATMENT

The importance of alcoholism prevention and treatment has been clearly documented. The advantages of early identification and confrontation mechanisms make the workplace a legitimate and effective locus for intervention in which the problem of alcoholism can be treated with a higher degree of success than other treatment contexts. Nevertheless, social work and the other helping professions have not demonstrated a strong record of effectiveness in treating alcoholics. The early success of OAPs was due primarily to their administration by recovering alcoholics, the majority of whom were uncredentialed and nondegreed. As human services have developed in the workplace, professionalization of the field has accelerated. However, as social workers and other professionals become involved in programs, their lack of alcoholism training will be a problem for workers and the workplace. Several barriers exist in the social work profession that serve to hinder the effective delivery of services to alcoholics. Although it is difficult to distinguish between social influences, professional biases, and organizational constraints, these barriers exist in almost all human service resources including occupational programs such as EAPs.[*]

Myths Surrounding Alcoholism

Ignorance about alcoholism is still relatively widespread among social workers; basic alcohol information is by and large absent. Consequently, practice is informed primarily by a "layman's" understanding that is often inadequate and misinformed.

Myths about alcoholism that have evolved are both informational and attitudinal. Because alcohol use and abuse is so prevalent in American society, understanding is tempered by the social context in which information is diffused. The history of society's attempt to define, control, and legislate substance and use provides a graphic picture of the ambivalence and currents of controversy that remain with us.

The informational myths that have evolved cover a broad spectrum. For example, many people do not understand that alcohol is a drug with all the properties and characteristics of any other drug. Others perceive beer drinking to be much less likely to lead to alcoholism than whiskey and other so-called hard liquors—a myth built on an insufficient understanding of alcohol and its effect on the central nervous system. Others believe the myth that coffee and cold showers will help sober up the party-goer who had had "one too many" (whatever that means). These are examples of the misinformations that permeate the drinking and drunkenness mores of our society.

Attitudinal myths, however, constitute an even more prominent barrier. Because of the devastating consequences of alcoholism and the historical involvement of churches in efforts to curtail and control this problem, the prevailing attitude toward alcoholism and especially toward the alcoholic has been moralistic. We have laughed at and jailed the alcoholic. The shame and guilt surrounding alcoholism in the family results in an intense cover-up by the family to the external world. Thus, attitudinal myths that cast alcoholism in a moralistic and negative framework constrain the definition of alcoholism and inhibit the development of a new paradigm that has

---

[*]An expanded version of this point can be found in Googins (March-April 1984). Avoidance of the Alcoholic Client. *Social Work*, 29(2): pp. 161–166.

social and medical dimensions. Despite the official acceptance of alcoholism as an illness by the American Medical Association in 1956 and by other professional organizations since then, there is still ample evidence that the alcoholic is seen as a morally inferior person (Googins, 1978).

This attitudinal barrier is particularly problematic for clinicians. Attitudes, whether moral or treatment biased, become subtle screening mechanisms by which alcoholics are seen as undesirable, unemployable, or unmotivated. Coupled with such barriers are the ambivalences reflected in social and agency policies and practices. Until these attitudes are brought to the foreground, discussed, and clarified, there is little hope that alcoholics will be brought into the mainstream of agency practice, or that individual practitioners will be able to assist them.

Therapeutic Nihilism

A second means by which myths are operationalized at the agency level is a pervasive sense of therapeutic nihilism. Briefly, this refers to the therapeutic stance of the social worker, whether conscious or unconscious, that there is little hope in treating the alcoholic. Although there is not an abundance of hard data to support this contention, an overwhelming collection of anecdotal evidence exists. Under this banner, the alcoholic is viewed as a resistant, hard to work with, unmotivated client for whom the prognosis is guarded at best. Most will continue drinking and, despite occasional periods of sobriety, relapses will be frequent. Thus, alcoholic clients in most human service agencies stand little chance of being identified, diagnosed, and treated for their alcoholism because of the negative images, feelings, and attributes held by the social worker and the subsequent labels attached to the alcoholic client. As a result, alcoholics who have little self-esteem gladly conspire with the social worker to avoid discussing the drinking problem and agree to concentrate on family problems, depression, or any other problem that offers some hope for solution.

Symptom Versus Cause

A major conflict between the health and human service professions and self-help movements such as AA lies in the conceptualization of alcoholism. Although alcoholism has been defined as an illness by the health and social work professions, it is most often treated as a symptom. Based in part on the influential psychoanalytic tradition, many social workers perceive alcoholism as a manifestation of an underlying problem. Deal with the depression and the dysfunctional problem drinking will disappear; any actions that improve the mental health or family functioning will at the same time serve to reduce rates of alcohol problems. Beauchamp (1976) observes that one of the standard myths about alcoholism is that alcohol does not cause the behavior of the alcoholic; the blame for behavioral factors is located inside the victim.

While this view, like the disease model, excuses the culpability of the drinker, it nevertheless focuses treatment on an underlying pathology whose successful resolution will rid the client of the symptomatic drinking. This, of course, runs directly counter to the AA conception of alcoholism as a unique physiological entity that has to be treated prior to other related problems. Gitlow (1980, p. 7) forcefully confronts the symptom approach: "A return to the psychoanalytic approach to alcoholism as a symptom dependent on some deeper psychiatric defect is a therapeutically bankrupt concept abandoned by all but the most naive or inexperienced." This very issue of symptom versus cause accounts for chronic friction between the alcoholism field and the helping professions. Addressing alcohol-related problems without directly dealing with the separate illness of alcoholism denies the reality of the drugged state of the alcoholic.

Fear of Confrontation

Successful treatment of alcoholism often requires a confrontation component to break down the denial and alibi network that operates in the disease process. Unfortunately, many social workers have not incorporated this strategy into their treatment repertoire, and therefore are subjected to the protracted and convoluted series of excuses, denials, and confabulations the alcoholic weaves to protect his or her denial. In part, this fear of confrontation conflicts with some of the basic professional images of the helpful, nurturant practitioner. When a social worker allows such fear and uncomfortableness to prevent confrontation, the alcoholic remains unchallenged and free to continue deviant drinking, and the social worker is left without appropriate tools to achieve the treatment goal.

Agency Denial

Denial is at work not only within the individual alcoholic and the clinician, but also within human service agencies. A subtle set of dynamics is present in many agencies that denies the alcoholism problem throughout the organization and "conspires" to avoid a reasonable response. In examining the discrepancy between the widespread evidence of alcoholism and its infrequent occurrence in the caseloads of human service agencies, one can only speculate to what extent the agency allows this to continue. Obviously there is no insidious conspiracy; rather a combination of factors operate to maintain denial. First, the agency attempts to adhere to its goals. For example, a family and children service agency tends to define itself, hire staff, attract board members, and raise funds to serve the needs of children and families. Because its major identity is syntonic with its mission or goals, the skills, sensitivity, knowledge, and policies concerning alcoholism are at best subjugated to the agency's overriding goals. At worst (and this is much more common) the agency, in attempting to stay current and competitive within its own sphere, stresses in its activities, hirings, and in-service training programs those things that are necessary in its own field, such as new modalities, techniques, and information pertaining to families and children.

A second source of denial results from the combination of misinformation, negative attitudes, lack of skills, and therapeutic nihilism discussed above. These factors converge to deny the existence of the problem in much the same way denial works in the alcoholic family. At the root of this is a sense of hopelessness: "What can we do with a problem that has almost no chance for success, about which we know little, and which we feel unskilled to remedy?" Under these circumstances agency denial becomes functional to the organization and the individuals working within it.

Agency denial is particularly pertinent to the occupational social worker when linking work organizations to external treatment services. Unless organizational awareness of the nature of alcoholism has been realized by the agency, referred employees will run the risk of being treated for those problems in which the agency specializes. Alcoholism and substance abuse will be glossed over to the detriment of the employee and, by association, of the EAP.

Use of the Specialized Alcoholism Agency

For most human service agencies caught in the binds described above, referrals to specialized alcoholism agencies and clinics offer a way out. Agencies, reflecting the specialization that has taken place throughout society and confronted with numerous other problems (marital, learning disabilities, sexual, etc.), turn to problem-specific agencies established primarily for alcoholism. Both specialized agencies and the self-help movement of AA and Al Anon have formed the core of the alcoholism treatment network. The expertise in alcoholism developed in specialized programs allows the human service agency to utilize them through the referral process. From an organizational perspective this suggests a coordinated network of services, drawing on the strengths of each unit and negating the concept that any one unit can be all things to all people. Even though this information and referral system may work well with most problems, with alcoholism it does not. Denial functions in such a way that alcoholics and alcoholic families rarely identify alcoholism as the presenting problem. In order to make a referral to an alcoholism clinic, the social worker must break through the denial and assist the person in identifying alcoholism as the problem, a set of therapeutic activities already discussed as difficult, requiring specialized skills, and occurring rarely within human service organizations.

What does occur is the use of specialized alcoholism agencies to serve as a referral agent in the event alcoholism emerges or when the problem is too overt to ignore. Agencies then are lulled into a false security, knowing that AA and the alcoholism clinic at the hospital are there when the alcoholic appears. What happens in practice, however, is that the alcoholic comes into the agency not as an alcoholic, but as a person with a family problem or a depressed individual, and the alcoholism remains hidden. Thus the specialized alcoholism agency becomes dysfunctional—even a barrier—in that the agency states it can deal with alcoholism (through referral), but in reality deals only with the minority of those who identify themselves or those for whom alibis have run out.

These barriers indicate the extent of the avoidance of alcoholism among social workers and other professionals working within the human service system. These barriers—some attitudinal, some inherent in social work education—are carried into the workplace with predictable results. Alcoholism problems are avoided, deferred, or set aside in favor of more treatable or comfortable emotional, family dysfunction, or parent–child issues.

Behind these feelings is a fear that social work will undermine the efforts of AA-oriented workers by broadening the intervention to such a degree that the original alcoholism emphasis will be lost.

> Psychiatric social work training emphasizes skills in counseling and treatment reflected in work-based programs that move troubled employees away from their supervisors and into counseling or treatment without delay. Because social workers have been successful in generating standards for licensing and certification, their increased involvement in occupational programs may lead to stratification in such programs, restricting employment to certified professionals, and as a side effect, deemphasizing alcohol problems within broad treatment-oriented employee assistance programs (Roman, 1981, p. 259).

In addition to institutional and professional hindrances, the treatment of the alcoholic is not easy. In one to one settings, most alcohol and drug abusers can convince the most highly trained social worker, psychiatrist, or physician that their substance abuse is social and not compulsive. The classic clinical training conceptualizes the client as the informant; client-centered casework with all of its techniques (such as its care of transferrence) does not prepare the clinicians to question the client's accuracy and perceive the denial, projection, and rationalization as part of the illness. Disbelief disrupts the essence of the relationship. These barriers, though pervasive and real, are by no means insurmountable. First, they are not unique to social work but to professions and professional training. Second, social work is ideally suited to treating alcoholism because of its ecosystem approach. If attitudes can be addressed and basic information and training added to educational programs, social workers will make a genuine contribution to assisting alcoholics regain sober and productive life styles, and create an environment within work organizations where alcoholics can be treated and alcoholism prevention integrated into the culture of the organization.

CHAPTER EIGHT
DEVELOPING
PROGRAMS

INTRODUCTION

Occupational social work (OSW) is a relatively new field and consequently lacks history, models, and well-developed guidelines for practice. Not only does it entail entering an environment of work organizations virtually unknown to social workers, but the goals, activities, and functions under which occupational social workers operate are constantly evolving and developing. The rapidity of the field's development has brought excitement and opportunity of dramatic proportions. The "downside" of these emerging trends, however, lies in the uncertainty surrounding practice roles and procedures. How does one begin to effectively practice occupational social work? What are the steps of program development? What skills and roles are utilized?

Most trailblazing efforts are fraught with uncertainty. In the beginning anecdotal reports constitute the primary resource for program development, model building, and learning. Only after a considerable period of practice do well-developed guidelines and models emerge. Guidelines, according to a dictionary definition, are indicators of policy or conduct. Thus, articulating a set of guidelines for developing OSW programs provides standards that fix a point of departure and enable development of some purposive plan toward achieving program goals. This does not mean delineating a rigid set of roles, but rather defining principles gained primarily from practice wisdom that foster credibility and act as a means of allaying the anxiety of those receiving the OSW services. This chapter, therefore, offers guidelines for practice, using the EAP as a case example. The EAP is chosen both because of the predominance of EAPs within OSW and the generalizability of EAP practice to other OSW roles. These guidelines draw on an accumulated experience within the occupational field as well as traditional social work practice, particularly in the community organization. Although social workers confront a new environment and subculture when entering work organizations, they bring to it a rich social work tradition and knowledge base that is eminently transferable and extremely useful.

Program development is a difficult and often illusive process in which the political, interpersonal, and operational roles often resemble a sensing procedure. Braybrooke and Lindblom (1963), in a more conceptual framework, refer to the process of incrementalism in which the practitioner bumbles along in an orderly and purposeful fashion (referred to by Lindblom as "muddling through") rather than operating from some well-conceived, rational, and comprehensive plan. The challenge of this chapter is to offer a framework and propose initial guidelines for the social worker entering the occupational arena (EAP or other) with this common set of questions: Where do I begin? What anchors or handles can I hang onto? How do I develop a plan and a constituency? How do I provide quality services to the client system?

GUIDELINES FOR GAINING ENTRY

Entering the corporation as an occupational social worker is much like a social worker reporting to a mental health center or a settlement house. In each case the practitioner is faced with a complex system within which a role must be assumed and services delivered. The occupational social worker is at an initial disadvantage because the program concept is often vague, poorly defined. Role expectations of corporate management reflect either a very rigid, narrow directive ("let's get these alcoholics out of the marketing division") or a mandate so broad and amorphous as to preclude definitive program directions so that no one knows what to expect. Because OSW is new to work organizations, managers' understanding of its role and functions and even of the company program is usually fragmented, poorly assimilated, and based on hearsay. Most EAPs have few models and little history to draw on, and consequently, social workers are left to assume proactive roles, develop programs, and gain sanction and acceptance in order to succeed.

The concept of client system is a useful one in determining initial steps and outlining preliminary activities. The client is best described as the primary beneficiary of the practitioner's activity (Cox 1979). Within work environments, as within all social organizations, this determination is not as simple as it may appear. It would be easy enough to identify employees and employer as the primary client system, but this ignores the complexity of the organization, the role of stakeholders discussed in chapter four, and the delicacy of developing social programs within work organizations. Although it is obvious that some aspects of labor and management will ordinarily constitute the client system, equal attention must be paid to the context and internal structure of this system. Sensitivity to the company's links and attitudes toward a union or employee group will thus influence the strategy and design of the EAP.

In a similar vein, other human service subsystems, broadly defined, may feel threatened by the development of a program such as the EAP or the inclusion of a new role such as OSW. Medical and personnel departments; organizational, development, and training units and corporate educational programs could feel threatened by a new program or person that, in their perception, infringes on activities, roles, or functions that had been in their domains. This reality must be taken into account and somehow recognized lest unreasonable energies be expended fighting "rear-guard actions." Organizational support and allies are absolutely crucial; any unnecessary alienation from those who would logically, philisophically, and functionally constitute this support network should be avoided through proactive strategies.

Building organizational support becomes one of the initial steps. The social worker will want to carefully analyze the client system for natural allies as well as potential opposition or resistance. Simply responding to those who knock on the door for service may create some initial feelings of goodness and fulfillment, but ultimately this overlooks the social and structural realities of the client system. Establishing a foothold for the program (and the practitioner) is basically a political process. For the EAP this has two immediate implications.

1. As a new type of program, the EAP introduces a very different element into the work organization. EAPs are essentially social interventions, a relatively recent phenomenon in modern-day corporations. In recent years major shifts in this ideology have taken place in such areas as child care and flexible time to reflect a changing environment and employee population. Nevertheless, in dealing with and treating social, family, and individual problems, the EAP contradicts the prevailing norms of corporate life in America, whose personnel policies have followed its economics in creating a laissez faire doctrine of minimal intervention. To overcome this situation, EAP social workers have to go beyond responding to those individuals who for whatever reason are able to seek assistance. They must also develop a purposive strategy and program to educate and persuade the various elements of the client system of the value and appropriateness of the EAP.

2. The general implications of the political nature of the EAP is that the EAP becomes a parallel component within the environment alongside purchasing

departments, marketing operations, data analysis sections, and the like, working together toward the goals of the organization. Like all subsystems, the EAP will be competing for resources, influence, power, recognition, and position. Not to recognize this reality of organizational behavior, or to opt not to engage in such behavior, is to segregate the EAP from the mainstream of the organization and to endanger its political viability and ultimately its survival.

Thus, analyzing the client system and incorporating the results of the analysis into the overall strategy and operation of the EAP is essential if occupational social workers are to develop an integrated, useful, and politically viable program.

A second initial step relies on the principle of "beginning where the client is." This time-tested tenet of social work practice deserves particular attention within the context of OSW. The client, as discussed above, is often of a quite different attitude than the occupational social worker. Not accustomed to dealing with the social needs of employees, the corporation has for most of the century successfully kept the world of work and production quite distinct from the world of family, personal problems, and external environments. Over the past decade Kanter (1977), O'Toole (1974), Yankelovitch (1978), and others have documented the counterproductiveness of maintaining these separate worlds. More recently corporations have begun to operate out of a new paradigm that requires them to assume new roles and responsibilities regarding the social and human needs of employees and their environments.

Consequently, for social workers to begin working with corporations and unions will require a patient understanding of the client's former and present attitudinal stance in order to develop an effective strategy for realizing program goals. All change occurs slowly, and corporations, like most large social systems, are inherently conservative and resistant to core change. Social work itself has an additional problem in that its image as perceived by the client system is often contrary to that which it wants and needs to project in order to achieve its goals. The widespread image of social workers as softhearted do-gooders and welfare workers checking under the beds for errant husbands is a perception that occupational social workers need to recognize as they begin to relate to the client system.

Even whether to identify oneself as a social worker becomes an issue. Should the occupational social worker expend energies to change negative stereotypes in forming and developing the professional role of OSW? There is obvious debate on this between those espousing the need to anchor practice within a professional base and others who point to the cultural norms of organizations that rely more on performance than credentials. Lawyers operating across the spectrum of the organization rarely utilize their credentials in performing nonlegal roles any more than those managers with master's degrees in business administration use initials after their names. How to resolve this issue will be guided primarily by an assessment of the organization, historical antecedents, and ultimately a decision about which image the occupational social workers determines will best promote the program and his or her goals.

Just as employers and employees have stereotypic images of social workers, social workers also have preconceived notions about the workplace. As the OSW field and individual social workers within it become more acquainted with work forces and workplaces, understanding will help break down myths and generalizations and naiveté will be replaced by a more balanced view of the dynamics, the politics, and the organizational behaviors and constraints of the work environment.

Operationally, starting where the client is will involve a great deal of face-to-face contact. Much of this interaction will involve assessing the expectations and needs of the client system concerning the EAP. Many EAPs were established to deal with alcoholic employees, undoubtedly a real need within the organization. As OSW and EAPs evolve, however, a broader perspective of individual and organizational needs emerges. Some of these needs relate to employees who may be feeling stressed, overworked, and undertrained and to supervisors anxious over an uncertain economic outlook or disturbed by the climate of labor–management relations. To build linkages to the EAP, some strategic activities should be undertaken to recognize and respond to the existential realities of the client system. Beginning "where employees are" enhances the image and legitimacy of the EAP while responding to legitimate needs. Of course a developed strategy will take into account many factors, political and programmatic, that will weigh proposed boundaries, level of resources, and appropriate expertise. Thus labor–management discord may well be too politically volatile and removed from the expertise of the EAP. However, creating a corporate-wide vehicle for addressing the stress resulting from the discord and offering stress management services may well be the best strategy.

GUIDELINES FOR RELATIONSHIP BUILDING

Building relationships and developing a contract move program development beyond initial considerations. If an EAP is about to begin or is just getting off the ground, the nature of the contract, formal and informal, will be an important factor in guiding its development. Although few programs have formal contracts, most have some form of business plan containing policies, job descriptions, and budget documents that were used in gaining corporate approval. These documents spell out in some detail the initial program expectations and goals.

It is worth mentioning at this point that companies contemplating the creation of an occupational program should attempt to develop these documents as a strategy for insuring corporate-wide acceptance and support. Too often programs such as EAPs evolve from "side deals" in which a corporate decision maker approves a program based on a personal relationship or dramatic event that had precipitated a crisis. Although these origins are as legitimate as those of a rationally planned program, such a program runs the risk of laying its foundation on sand. Written materials have longevity and provide a formalized mechanism by which the organization can approve and integrate the program into its mainstream. Programs built on informal relationships most often lie on the periphery of the organization. Thus when organizational politics intervene or the godfather relationship ceases through transfers or retirement, the viability, credibility, and survival of the program is placed in jeopardy.

The development of a contract or charter acknowledges the realities of organizational structure and politics. Clearly defined goals and objectives assist in relating the program to the organization's goals and objectives. Job descriptions and business plans help establish the need for and legitimacy of the program within the company while defining boundaries and avoiding unnecessary intramural friction and "turf invasion." Initiating these contractual documents will help the EAP or the OSW program gain universal acceptance and at the same time set realistic goals by which the program can be evaluated.

Understanding the culture and history of the company is essential to any program. No program exists separate from the company, and an integral part of that company is its cultural uniqueness and historical development. Consider for a moment how the following questions can be answered quite differently from company to company, and how the answers can markedly influence the development and effectiveness of the EAP.

1. What is the overriding management philosophy and style?
2. Has there been dramatic growth or gradual evolution?
3. Is the workforce primarily blue collar/white collar or pink collar?
4. Is this a male- or female-dominated culture?
5. What is the history of labor relations?
6. Is the personnel department highly valued?
7. Have there been any major crises in the company over the past 10 years?
8. Have there been programs similar to the EAP attempted in the past?
9. How are employee problems currently dealt with?
10. How and where are the decisions made?

The list could go on at considerable length. The complexity of cultural norms and values within a work organization are difficult for an outsider or newcomer to understand. Time and immersion are the primary teachers, and history is an essential key to understanding the present. EAPs need to utilize and build on historical antecedents and cultural norms as well as on formal and informal policies and mechanisms. Programs, to be effective, have to develop within the context of the organization linked as carefully and strategically as possible to the organization's norms and values. Thus from the outset the practitioner must be attentive to and appreciative of these factors in order to insure the integration of the program into the mainstream of the company.

A parallel analysis examines how the functions of OSW are carried out in the organization and by whom. Many people within an organization take on caregiving roles and constitute an informal caregiving system. In one organization the EAP administrator, aided by a social work intern, conducted an elaborate organizational study of counseling services provided by employees who were not formally designated and found there were a significant number of informal counselors. Consequently, there is a need to identify these individuals during the early stages of exploration and anticipate any resistance from these informal counselors, who may feel resentment towards the new formal venture.

A final consideration at this stage lies in understanding the history of the instigation of the program. Nothing comes from nothing; all phenomena were instigated for specific reasons and by a discernible process. Occupational practitioners would be wise to be aware of the history and context of the program's instigation for its value in assessing real and potential allies within the corporation as well as perceiving what events or activities get corporate attention.

Instigators—i.e., reasons for instigation—can be positive or negative. A highly valued employee who got into trouble with drugs or a report from a benefits section detailing potential cost savings through alcohol rehabilitation can both account for program initiation. Instigators or triggering incidents will provide excellent data for understanding corporate culture and consequently will result in a more accurate picture of the underlying rationale for program adoption, implementation, and expectations. Understanding program roots puts future development of the EAP on firmer ground.

In summary, beginnings are extremely important in program development. Occupational social workers and programs such as EAPs represent a new and bold step for unions and companies. Thus the attempts to introduce and develop programmatic activity take place in a cultural context in which survival and effectiveness are influenced by cultural norms, corporate values, and organizational politics.

DEVELOPING THE PLAN

Organizing and developing a new service or program such as an EAP requires a great deal of careful planning to insure that the program becomes institutionalized within the company or union as integral and indispensable to the organization's interests (Perow, 1972, pp. 92–132). Adopting and adding to Hasenfield's (1979) principles of program development, the following stages of a plan can be extracted:

1. identifying and establishing relationship with the client
2. identifying the need for the EAP
3. mobilizing support for the EAP
4. assigning responsibility to an advisory board
5. defining the mission of the EAP
6. specifying the objectives
7. developing a monitoring and evaluation process

Identifying and Establishing Relationship with the Client

From the outset building a program involves two major vectors: task and process. The task is concerned with achieving the primary goals of the program. Much of this programmatic outcome can be measured against the program's objectives of developing a design, designating a site, hiring staff, reaching a particular percentage of the population, conducting training sessions, etc. Thus the task can be most directly related to the more traditional phases of rational planning: assessing needs, setting goals, deciding objectives, mapping strategies, and evaluating the program.

The second vector, process, forms a different set of program goals that relate to the maintenance and political context of building the program. These process goals affect the maintenance and enhancement of the EAP, aiding employees and employers in achieving self-defined goals (Cox, 1979, p. 187). Process recognizes that in addition to achieving set goals, individuals involved in task activities (and their organization or environment) have needs extraneous to the goal but important to the individual or the environment. For example, managers, who have to be trained by the EAP to identify and document deteriorating job performance (task goal), may have factional rivalry with personnel or medical departments that needs to be addressed before it sabotages the task goal. Consequently, social workers have to be attentive to the process of achieving program goals and develop strategies for addressing these process needs.

Identifying the Need for the EAP

Under normal circumstances the social worker arrives to begin the EAP with a cloudy mandate and only a fractionalized and biased estimate of the program's need. Ironically, most OSW programs, particularly EAPs, give little attention to need and need assessment activities. This is due in part to the assumed or, more accurately, presumed estimation of need in narrowly focused programs. Thus, to cite the most common example, alcoholism is the focus of programmatic activity and, since the literature speaks of a 6–10 percent population at risk, there appears to be little need for assessment. There are two flaws in this approach. First is the assumption that alcoholism is *the* pressing need, and that an alcohol-focused program is the best strategy for reaching the alcoholic employee. The evolution of EAPs from occupational alcoholism programs took place in part because the strategy of focusing on alcoholism was defeating the very goals of the program due to realities such as stigmatization and the imposition of clinical roles on supervisors. By focusing on a single problem the program has publicly proclaimed its mission and thus its certitude of need. By taking this approach it runs the risk of not being able to start where the client is and build linkages to the problem focus nor be open and sensitive to other client needs within the work organization.

The second flaw is the assumption that there exists an adequate assessment of the problem. To return to the case of alcoholism, the widely used rates of prevalence and incidence are in fact based on crudely designed guesses that have become accepted over time. Variables such as age, sex, education, organizational size, and occupational type most likely have tremendous impact on the nature and size of the problem. Any EAP which ignored this would be operating on very soft data.

There are a number of ways for identifying and analyzing needs within work environments. Weinburg (1983) urges compilation of demographic data on employees as essential to any design process. Information should include:

wage and sex distribution of the work force
employee residence
employee marital status
employee length of service
the number of salaried/hourly workers represented by the program
broad categories and descriptions of work performance

The intelligence-gathering function consists of pulling together existing data through personnel, employee relations, and annual reports. Informally, occupational social workers should draw on the more time-tested methods of listening to the community. This can be achieved by walking through assembly lines, having lunch in the company cafeteria, and "hanging out" in an appropriate fashion to learn the procedures and problems of supplying the product or service provided by the company. These activities have a secondary gain in that the social workers will also acquire a better understanding of employee agendas.

Another secondary gain of a need assessment process is its usefulness in educating the company by raising the level of its awareness of the needs identified through the study. In fact, if there is sufficient participation by key personnel in the company in planning the study and disseminating its findings, the process may yield more results than the more rational purposes of supplying the program staff with accurate data. Identifying needs within work organizations can meet both analytical and political goals if carefully thought through and implemented.

Mobilizing Support for the EAP

As discussed earlier, EAPs and other social work programs are often "strangers in a strange land." Both functionally and ideologically they may represent marked departure from previous company approaches to human needs and consequently face cultural dissonance. Luckily, changes in many corporations throughout the past decade have resulted in a more culturally compatible environment for EAP operation. Nevertheless, most programs are isolated from the mainstream of the organization (particularly in the beginning as the "new kid on the block") and will ultimately need to move toward gathering and mobilizing support to insure their viability, relevance, and survival within the organization.

Accomplishing this mobilization of support is no easy task. The program and its services have to become known, needed, trusted, and accepted throughout the corporation or union. This entails spending a good deal of time meeting with people throughout the company trying to find out what this program may mean to them or could mean to them. This can obviously be a time-consuming process, but is well worth the effort if seen as a long-lasting investment in solidifying the program. This stage is more of a process than a task, since it will occur over time and will build upon preceding stages throughout the life of the program. It requires gathering resources and support from influential people for the program to enable it to root and flourish. Much of this mobilization serves as a defensive deterrent. If threats to its mission (pressures to weaken confidentiality) or survival (cuts in program budget) arise, the mobilized resources and people can act as advocates and buffers. Often this mobilization can become formalized through an advisory board or committee.

Assigning Responsibility to an Advisory Board

As in all social work activities, a solid relationship with the client has to be achieved if any change is going to occur. In the case of the EAP, the occupational social worker has to develop a relationship with a variety of stakeholders or persons within the client system: labor, management, personnel, labor relations, medical personnel and others within the system who are in a position to assist the realization of the EAP goals if positively disposed, or obstruct or resist program goals if negatively disposed.

Thus the first activity is to build support and legitimacy for the program. The primary strategy utilized is the involvement of key people from throughout the company. Obviously this determination of key people differs from company to company, but usually involves some combination of labor or union leaders, medical staff, and personnel or human resource managers. These individuals are invited to participate in shaping the program and developing its policies and to have a stake in the decision-making process. By involving these key individuals through some advisory board, the EAP is drawing on the organizational, cultural, and political expertise of the client system. Those with a stake in having the program succeed will help guide the program through the potential mine fields of ignorance, "turf fights," and the lack of legitimacy. This group also becomes drawn into the EAP itself, assuming a degree of ownership that can only assist the program in its quest for legitimacy by becoming staunch defenders and boosters.

Defining the Mission of the EAP

Establishing a new program such as an EAP within work organizations requires a clear, well-defined mission both to focus the resources and energies of the program and provide information to the client system about the nature and purpose of the EAP. Because of the importance of a clearly focused, easily understood mission, the EAP staff should expend some energy to carefully define that mission and choose a strategy by which the mission can be widely known and understood.

Mission involves policy and programmatic decisions concerning which *services* it will provide to what *population* to meet which *needs*. This may seem to be obvious in the case of an EAP, but experience in the field indicates just the opposite. Some programs let the mission be dictated by the flow of events, while others have a specific mission from the onset. Many programs begin with a preconceived mission, only to find the needs of the organization changing causing the stated mission of the EAP to become obsolete in relation to actual program needs. Still other programs have such a diffusion of services that any attempt at defining a mission results in one that is very broad and almost too general to have any significance. There is currently much debate over this very sensitive issue concerning the boundaries and missions of EAPs. Despite widespread dissensions within the social work or EAP field on the definition of mission, it is essentially an intracompany issue: the program is conceived and transmitted to company employees so as to meet *their* needs. Thus, mission is ultimately shaped (or should be) by the needs and politics of the company system to serve the major function of conveying to potential users its purpose and goals.

Specifying the Objectives

As any good program planner or manager knows, missions or goals are simply wish statements outlining the overall intent of the program in broad general (and sometimes idealistic) terms. While these are helpful in providing general direction, they need to be operationalized if they are to be useful in everyday living. Objectives are defined in concrete specific, and measurable statements that allow lofty goals to become operational in the world of everyday programs. Unfortunately many programs tend to wallow in the generalized world of goals: "To help employees in trouble"; "to treat alcoholics." All this does is allow the program to meander along without a plan whereby staff can carefully weigh all of the client needs and zero in on a few areas to receive concerted efforts. Making a choice between client needs to define areas of concentration—objectives—is consequently difficult since it sets specific targets, thereby eliminating major expansion. If training forty supervisors over the next twelve months to become proficient in monitoring and evaluating job performance becomes an objective, a company program might not have the resources to begin a group for recently divorced managers. Thus it becomes necessary to establish realistic and qualifiable measures that reflect goal attainment.

Objectives also serve the purpose of evaluating outcome or results. Without carefully constructed objectives to specify program goals there is little to evaluate. Because goals lack data to quantify specific program expectations they are open ended and meaningless from an evaluation perspective. Program objectives, on the other hand, map the route the program will travel over a specified period of time and provide concrete measures by which program success or failure can be measured.

Developing a Monitoring and Evaluation Process

Once the program is fully operational, the challenge of the staff is to insure that program goals and objectives are being met and that the quality of the program is adequate. Meeting this challenge requires assessing the program through a variety of tools ranging from "gut feeling" and immediate feedback to highly sophisticated evaluative research conducted by outside researchers. What level of assessment is possible and necessary for a particular program will be determined by a number of variables such as expectations and pressure from the corporation, ability of staff to conduct monitoring and evaluation, and available resources. The function of monitoring and evaluation is universal, however. Usually this function depends on the program's record keeping and management information system (MIS). By monitoring basic record data, program staff can assess client load, characteristics, and alignment with program objectives.

To move beyond a monitoring function, EAP staff may choose to evaluate the program to provide an estimate of achievement or to guide future program development. Using some type of process impact or outcome evaluation method the EAP can feedback to itself or others within the corporation a measure of the program's influence or impact on clients and the organization's environment. Although the use of such monitoring is all too scarce in occupational social work programs such as EAPs, its value as an integral part of program development is increasing. Ongoing monitoring and evaluation fosters program improvement and provides vehicles for adjusting to the changing needs of employees and work organizations.

SUMMARY

This chapter has provided some general, albeit brief, guidelines that inform program development within work organizations. For most social workers, assuming the role of occupational social worker is a formidable task since few role models and even fewer program models exist. Faced with the unfamiliar and sometimes even hostile environment of the workplace the social worker is charged with the mandate of becoming an explorer and entrepreneur. The guidelines above are considerations and practice wisdoms that help eliminate some of the unknown and provide structure to alleviate anxiety. As the years pass and occupational social work becomes more integrated into the fabric of corporations, these guidelines will be supplanted by program models and research findings to replace the current trial and error approach with a well-developed field of practice.

CHAPTER NINE
INDUSTRIAL SOCIAL WORK IN EUROPE

INTRODUCTION

Industrial social work (ISW) throughout Europe has been largely ignored in the midst of burgeoning growth in the United States and Canada. Despite several decades of existence, European ISW is virtually unknown to practitioners in North America, and consequently its practice wisdom has not been made available. As occupational-based social work has emerged in the United States, it refers to contemporary cultural and social phenomenon as the basis and stimulus for program form and direction.

The purpose of this chapter is to examine European ISW as a developed body of practice whose models and experience may well be useful to American occupational social workers[*], who are struggling with the issues that confront an emerging field.

A few words about the background of this study are in order. The authors[†] became aware of the apparently widespread occurrence of indus-

[*]While the term *Occupational Social Work* has been adopted in the United States to convey the realities of a postindustrial society, European practice continues to use the more established Industrial Social Work.

[†]This chapter was written by Bradley Googins, Ellin Reisner M.S.W. and Jonathan Milton and first appeared in *EAP Quarterly*.

trial social work in Europe through the visits of several European social work educators and practitioners to this country as well as through publications that surfaced from time to time. In order to explore the nature and extent of this specialization, the authors organized a structured examination of the subject through a series of interviews with professionals in the ISW communities in France, Holland, Germany, and Switzerland. The primary purpose of the study was to gather information about the history, stages of development, roles, and unique characteristics of this work in each country as an informative and potentially heuristic device for occupational social work (OSW) in America. Visits and interviews were held in each country with leading practitioners and educators. Their openness, cooperation, and degree of sharing was extraordinary enabling us to gather a great deal of information in a very short period of time. We would caution the reader that this exploration by no means serves as a comprehensive compendium or analysis of European ISW, but is, rather, a series of "snapshots"—initial impressions that may offer a basic understanding.

INDUSTRIAL SOCIAL WORK IN EUROPE: AN OVERVIEW

Industrial social work in Europe is not a standardized field but comprises, in fact, a variety of different models and methods. Each country has incorporated its unique cultural and social values into the field's practice. However, several commonalities were observed. Social work involvement at the workplace generally was a post war development as the devastation of those wars dictated a need for reconstruction. Consequently, the needs of employees concerning housing and living situations prompted many companies to engage social workers to assist them in meeting these worker needs. A second common base is the virtual absence of social workers within unions; there was no evidence of any social workers directly employed by or working within a union organization. A high degree of interaction occurs between social workers and unions through various work councils, but no autonomous practice was observed. Finally, although practice varied from country to country, examination of the four countries revealed the existence of definite stages of development through which ISW practice has evolved. In all the countries, the focus of social work, which had begun with a focus on individual employee needs, has evolved into a systems oriented field. In several countries, the stages correlate with the program's degree of integration within the corporation, moving from a mostly peripheral and extraneous function to an internal, highly integrated function. For other countries, however, development involved an increasingly broadened scope of practice—from housing to psychiatric and substance abuse problems. These stages of development seem to confirm Ozawa's (1980) projected stages of development for American OSW. While the particulars may differ, the importance of placing ISW within a developmental framework is reinforced.

Thus what is ultimately the most useful result of examining European ISW is not simply comparing one particular aspect or model with another, but perceiving the almost predictable stages of development. Before American OSW becomes frozen into a particular mode or is circumscribed by definite boundaries, it will be instructive to recognize the developmental stages of European ISW and to examine the future and potential of the American field within this perspective.

To better appreciate both its common denominators and the unique differences, brief descriptions of the practice of European ISW in each country is presented beginning with the least developed, Switzerland, and progressing through the increasingly developed practices of Germany, France, and Holland.

INDUSTRIAL SOCIAL WORK IN SWITZERLAND

Industrial Social Work in Switzerland is neither widespread nor well-developed compared to its counterparts in Germany, France, and Holland. Although there are social workers in scattered industries, neither the profession nor the business community has developed an identified practice arena. Dr. Hans Kneubuehler, a leading Swiss social work educator, carried out an extensive survey of ISW in the country's twenty largest corporations in conjunction with the authors for the purpose of this study. Major findings included: (1) very few had industrial social workers, (2) much of what is considered ISW is carried out by personnel departments, (3) the emphasis of ISW services is recreational and resembles traditional social welfare capitalism, (4) for many the problems don't exist (i.e., we don't have problems with alcoholism because it is forbidden). Unions also did not have an ISW orientation, but do carry out a great number of social work functions under the banner of education.

Switzerland's relatively undeveloped state of ISW resembles the early stages of development in France and Holland. Practice focuses primarily on a case approach that deals with personal problems of children, family dysfunction, or alcoholism. These are problems that have progressed so far that they can usually no longer be avoided. Prevention of any type has not generally been incorporated into practice.

A unique feature of Swiss industrial social workers is their involvement with foreign or guest workers who have come from less-developed countries to fill low-level blue collar and service positions. Although ISW in Germany, France, and Holland also addressed the problems of guest workers, none did so to the extent of the Swiss, perhaps because their rigid social structure has created serious integration and assimilation problems for this population. Recent studies within Switzerland indicate that guest workers have ten times more psychosomatic problems than native Swiss workers due primarily to cultural conflicts and to working in low-level, hierarchically structured roles in which psychosomatic illness becomes a normal way of coping. In Lucerne a consortium arrangement has been developed by companies to provide social service to foreign workers by a central agency to which the companies involved pay ten Swiss francs per employee. The industries contract with the agency to take referrals, and the agency employs social workers who are fluent in Italian, Turkish, Spanish, and Serbian and thus can more efficiently and effectively treat this foreign working population than could social workers within individual companies.

Social work is not particularly integrated into companies in Switzerland. Where social work exists, it lies at the periphery of the company, dealing with personal or family problems that have impinged on the workplace. Much of this lack of integration can be traced to a negative image of social work in Switzerland. In this very conforming culture, social workers often are perceived as aberrants, particularly because of their informality in dress and hair style, casual living, and political views. Combat fatigues, sandals, etc., are often worn by social workers in the community who work with youth. This is apt to be a company's image of social workers, and consequently they are not brought into the corporation in any significant role.

The size of companies is also an issue related to the degree of integration. There are less than a handful of large companies in Switzerland; in fact, most companies are quite small (70 percent have under 100 employees). Most companies would suggest that they are economically unable to hire a social worker. Because of these limitations, several deans of social work schools in Switzerland are currently in the planning stages of developing a strategy to overcome the lack of ISW and the negative social work images. Personnel and company executives are being brought into schools of social work as adjunct lecturers as a strategy for initiating contact between the business community and the social work field. The expected interaction between social work students and faculty with corporate personnel will provide a vehicle for defusing the negative images and conveying the positive aspects and importance of social work in dealing with problems found within corporations.

For social workers who do operate within companies, it is significant that the vast majority have been trained while employed at the companies and then moved into personnel and management roles, dropping the social worker role. An interesting phenomenon occurs within some schools that serve as an entree into personnel work. Because Switzerland is a highly stratified society with firmly defined roles and social class distinctions, gaining entrance into management has to occur through academic training.

Fifteen years ago there was no path into personnel work except through a university degree. However, a person who lacked this training and was working as a clerk, for example, had the option of going part-time to a school of social work, gaining the professional status without the full-time academic training, and thus becoming eligible to assume a personnel manager position. Interestingly, many companies value the social work training as preparation for the personnel field, and thus encourage their employees to follow this path.

The matter of social work identity in occupational practice is a grave concern. While social work in industrial settings in the United States is primarily clinical and perhaps too new to have confronted this identity issue, it will become increasingly important as practice roles broaden, particularly in the human resource or personnel field.

INDUSTRIAL SOCIAL WORK IN GERMANY

Industrial Social Work in Germany has roots in the early part of this century. For example, the program at Siemens, which today has over eighty social workers, began in 1911 as a program for women, children, and orphans. Yet, even with such a long history, the presence of ISW throughout Germany is uneven. A number of large industrial concerns have extensive programs, and clusters of programs exist in particular industries, but there is no universal mandate or widespread practice. The presence or absence of ISW seems to be dictated largely by the personal and idiosyncratic nature of each industry. Those companies founded by individuals, whose culture is imprinted by individual or family characteristics, tend to have social work programs, whereas companies with more bureaucratic organizational roots tend not to have developed social work programs. Thus Siemens and Beyer, large electronics firms with strong family ties, have extensive social work programs. In other electronic firms, however, and in most of the automobile companies that have no personal or family identity, few social work programs have been developed. Bilick (1984), in her analysis of the industrial alcoholism program movement in Germany, found industrial social workers mired in a practice of primarily resolving personal work-related problems and dealing almost exclusively with blue collar employees. She cites a 1981 journal article published in a well known German social work journal,

> Social Work (is) still of very little importance in the area of production. The hardly 500 industrial social workers in Germany are in an isolated position. Their work is insecure from all legal, sociopolitical and organizational points of view. They depend on the good will of management and the authority structure, hardly allowing them to develop a strategy of action.

Despite these problems, it is through social workers that some of the most recent industrial alcoholism programs have developed throughout Germany. The development of programs in companies is quickly increasing primarily because of the growing awareness of alcoholism. The automobile industry, Lufthansa Airlines, and some of the public utilities have recently begun addressing alcohol problems that effect their work forces and have hired social workers and psychologists to set up programs. It was the assessment of several industrial social workers in German industry that a movement regarding alcohol problems similar to the EAPs in the United States was beginning to emerge, and there has been a dramatic growth in interest and in program development within the past year.

A broad characterization of ISW in Germany would portray a primarily person-centered practice with fewer instances of systems orientation and methods. Some have characterized the practice as paternalistic, similar to the welfare capitalism found in the early industrial era in the United States. Given the family origins discussed earlier, it is not surprising that traces of this benevolence can be identified in those companies that have long-standing social work programs. Nevertheless, a curious mixture of clinical focus and environmental intervention exists in much of industrial social work in Germany. A large part of the social worker's role involves assisting individuals with problems of housing, disability, and linkages with appropriate community agencies. The range of clinical concerns includes depression, schizophrenia, and other mental illness problems. An equal amount of time is spent with employees who have recently had heart attacks or cancer, however. The industrial social workers are also operating in roles of environmental manipulation and adjustment, educating supervisors and the employee's colleagues on the nature of disabilities, and making plans for reintegrating the disabled back into the workplace. This paves the way for reentry which, though done on an individual case level, requires considerable understanding of the formal and informal work environments. These social workers must also possess the political skills to create a hospitable, informed, and accommodating work environment.

Extensive system change as it is carried out in Holland, which will be described later in this chapter, is generally not found in the mainstream of German ISW. There is no mandate for such action, but even this is changing in today's environment. The chief of social work of Siemens, for example, played a significant advocacy and leadership role in getting her company to deal with the problem of alcoholism. For more than a year and a half, she worked closely with the workers' committee, the medical services, and the social insurance bureau to get corporate support and sanction for a company-wide effort. This resulted in a policy requiring every plant to have an alcoholism committee and a plan for dealing with alcoholic employees. Thus, though the ISW role is not conceived of or mandated as an agent of change, some examples of system change are beginning to emerge as corporations address company-wide issues. The degree of integration differs between those companies in which paternalistic practice predominates and others, such as Siemens and Beyer, in which there is exceptionally strong sanction and support.

Considerable evidence exists, however, of a relatively high degree of social work integration within companies. This is accounted for not only by the relatively long history of ISW, but also by the structural characteristics and placement of social work programs within the companies. Social work services are, in most instances, on the same organizational level as medical, social welfare, and labor security (occupational health and safety) services. By reporting to personnel offices, social work does not have the kind of hierarchical problems often associated with reporting to medical departments, as can often be observed in the United States. However, it has the disadvantages of not having mandated services, for which medical services and worker committees have a legal base.

Social workers in many companies work closely with the legally mandated work council, whose role is to assess individual and system problems within the company and provide feedback. Because this is an essential part of the German work organization, it is important for social workers to work closely with the council. Often the issues of personal, family, or financial problems are referred to the social worker through the work council. However, the larger systems issues, such as corporate response to alcoholism or guest worker problems, are dealt with by the social work department and the work council.

The practice of ISW in Germany is changing rapidly. Many companies which had no ISW component are becoming interested in the problem of alcoholism, and older companies with ISW programs are broadening their scope beyond the individual problems of employees. Some companies, such as Beyer for example, are examining social work services with regard to handicapped employees, child care, and the special needs of young employees and older workers. As these developments accelerate, the movement toward system change will undoubtedly follow, as may a broader legal mandate for Industrial Social Work.

INDUSTRIAL SOCIAL WORK IN FRANCE

Industrial social work in France can be traced at least to the years immediately following World War I. In 1919, French companies were assisting the families of their workers in a fashion borrowed from the English welfare model. At Citroen, a combined medical/social service existed, providing direct service for worker injury, minor ailments, and welfare-oriented giving to individuals and families in need. This combined service split in 1935, with each profession requiring separate training and separate practices in the workplace. In 1936, the first legal text was written in France for the practice of what had informally become known as "social advising." By definition, industrial social workers were allowed to become more involved with the "life" of their organizations, rather than simply acting as welfare "givers" in particular times or instances of hardship. It was in the Vichy Government during World War II that the groundwork was laid for what exists today as the "service social." The practices codified during that period (1943) are operative today, although the focus of ISW has even further evolved, shifting from primarily providing material assistance to aid workers and their families to a larger and more professionalized focus on organizational/societal concerns and the "fit" between the worker and the enterprise. In fact, this past year saw the 36th Congress of The Study of Work, which has been sponsored by the National Association of Social Service Assistants.

The four companies in France that the authors studied provided for interesting comparison and indicated a wide spectrum of ISW involvement. These companies were the Citroen automobile company; Credit Lyonnaise, the second largest bank in the country; Phillips, a large, multinational corporation with operations in France; and Total, a multinational petroleum company headquartered in France. Within these four companies a consistent attention was given to the concrete needs of the workers, mostly in the form of assistance with housing, financial aid, vacation and holiday provision, and special attention to guest workers. A wide range existed in the degree to which industrial social workers were included or included themselves in "advising" functions to the corporation. As in Holland and Germany, in most instances ISW in France has evolved into a more integral organizational function, and social workers are viewed as intraorganizational team members. This membership increases in importance as technology expansion impacts the lives of all "team" workers. Social workers function at the interface between the person, the performance of the task, and the company's goals, expectations, and human resource policies.

The ISW service at the Total petroleum company provides a wide variety of services to management and line employees, and maintains a relationship with the union or "syndicat." The ISW service reports to the director of social relations, as do the departments of personnel, law, information, and work relations. The ISW service includes eight regional workers throughout France, managed by the director in Paris. All of the social workers throughout the company must respond to a variety of ongoing concerns and social issues—reclassifications of person-to-job in the case of accidents, work conditions, health promotion (including alcohol awareness campaigns), financial and budgeting problems among employees, housing problems, family vacations, relocation (especially domestic assistance with housing, school, job, and information), career and job counseling, employee relations (especially employee–supervisor problems), psychiatric opinions in the case of medical disability, psychiatric referrals, retirement counseling, and orientation of all new employees. The above represents a tremendous direct service responsibility and may account for the service's expression of frustration at the lack of time to attend to administrative and planning concerns, a lament well know to American occupational social workers. The point must also be made that the direct service responsibilities mentioned here also exist for industrial social workers in many other companies in France.

The ISW service at Total is responsible for an ongoing relationship with trade union representatives and with the "comité," a body elected by workers from various unions/syndicats. The ISW director meets twice yearly with the comité to discuss organizational and social problems but has no voting position. The industrial social worker also meets once yearly with the comité to discuss accidents and security issues and to review problems and procedures. The industrial social worker seemed careful to maintain good relations with the comité and with all union representatives, as their needs and goals are often similar. For the "service social," it appears that while the unions would rarely initiate contact, they would not refuse assistance if appropriate to their particular need and overall agenda. Union activists in France, as in the United States, remain suspicious of assistance that is basically management driven, but accept the relationship if it serves their goals. No social worker hired solely under union auspices could be identified in France.

At the Citroen automobile company, the ISW department provided many of the same services that were available at Total. There seemed to be, however, a closer relationship between the ISW and the medical department, as was the case before the 1936 law was enacted to separate the two services. This was especially true in areas concerning work conditions and the fit between person–job–machine–company. A team consisting of the industrial social worker, an engineer, the physician, and a personnel representative (in the United States this person might be known as a human factors engineer) work together to discuss all aspects of the relationship between the person and the technology. It was explained that this is especially important in those cases where a disabled person's condition necessitates alterations in specific work (such as the operation of the machine), the design of the machine, or perhaps in other aspects. The social workers at Citroen were emphatic in their opinion that their success depended on their ability to know the life of the organization by going into the factories, meeting with all employees, and knowing the business plans and the day-to-day realities of the products. They saw as their main task the treatment and management of individual problems existing between workers and management. While such discretionary problems might lead to policy discussions with management, this possibility seemed less likely at Citroen than at other companies that were observed. It did not appear that the social worker had a regularly mandated task of advising with regard to broad policy formulation. In fact, the ISW function at Citroen seemed quite close in some ways to an employee relations position in the United States.

At Credit Lyonnaise, the industrial social worker made it a point to describe how the annual social service report, a report that is mandated by the state to be submitted by all corporate social service organizations, could be utilized organizationally. This report documents social service activity in all of the areas that have been noted above, attempts to quantify the organization's utilization of the social worker, and offers some hypotheses about worker demographics and trends. The chief of social service at Credit Lyonnaise brings together management, union officials, and various personnel representatives to discuss areas in which their responsibilities may need clarification; to explore whether their roles may need to be more separate or distinct; and to identify needs in the bank that are not being responded to effectively. The social worker described this report as an effective means of developing and clarifying organizational communication and cooperation. This forum appeared to be most crucial with regard to the impact of emerging technology on work conditions and employee well-being. At the bank, operations previously done by hand are now being handled by computer, and the industrial social worker as well as other personnel are involved in the management of the shift to new technology in the workplace. This brings to industrial practice concerns such as retraining, work for older employees, retirement planning, and early retirement plans for those who choose to retire early.

The ISW at the Phillips Company is much more fundamentally a person-centered service. The social worker's primary purpose is to manage the company's vacation, housing, and financial assistance services; perform casework; and look into other employee problems that might require assistance. It did not appear that this function had developed into a strategic part of the life of the enterprise. Placed in the medical department suite, services are viewed more as an employee benefit than as an integrated organizational function.

Many of the issues facing French ISW, indeed many of the issues facing social workers in many of the companies and countries encountered, dealt with the issue of integration of ISW practice. The term "integration" in this case implies the desegregation of the ISW function from other necessary organizational functions. The "integrated" social worker would exist and perform as a valued participating member of an organization joined by common goals and purposes. The industrial social worker's purpose would be both clear and emerging, and his or her influence would be determined by the nature of and dynamic relations with other intra- and extraorganizational players. With this operational definition in mind, it must be remembered that responsibilities historically linked to the "friendly helper" still exist in most if not all French companies that utilize ISWs. In fact, in some enterprises this "Stage I" (see Ozawa, 1980) function represents the totality of ISW practice. This is not surprising, as these tasks are so traditionally linked to the profession. Other tasks that have accrued to the French industrial social worker are more given to influencing policy, creating services, supporting change, and evaluating programs in a variety of dimensions of organizational life. A current emphasis on the issue of social service accountability and profitability suggests the degree to which our French colleagues are being asked to join with other parts of the company organization in taking responsibility for the current state of French industrial affairs. As in the United States, French ISW practitioners are being asked to justify their interventions and to account in economic terms for their usefulness to management, employees, and unions. This demand for economic accounting offers social work the challenge to justify in economic terms that which is often evaluated in non-quantifiable, human terms. Cost-savings is more difficult to prove that product profit, yet French ISW is being asked, as we are in the United States, to present a formula which will rationalize this phenomena.

Although the task may seem unenviable, the suggestion may in itself be further evidence of the fact that French ISW has achieved greater integration, position, and influence in the enterprise. A function without influence, without a stand, is generally not asked to share in the process of accounting for the welfare of the entire organization. In France, industrial social workers are facing the problem of how to support the enterprises' long-term objectives—reinforcing the business image—while at the same time not totally accept the logic of management's profit-making decisions. This seems to be a consistent social work dilemma—how to coexist with the different agendas of the various constituencies while gaining trust and effectively serving the organization. In France today, within a sluggish economy, industrial social workers are attempting to establish themselves as integral and influential organizational operatives, serving all, accountable to all, and with a purpose and practice unique in the workplace.

INDUSTRIAL SOCIAL WORK IN THE NETHERLANDS

Industrial social work in the Netherlands represents some very unique practice models that operate on a more integrated, macro and intraorganizational level than the other three countries we have described thus far.

Since World War II, the field of industrial social work in the Netherlands has undergone extensive development. The initial interest in industrial social work emerged later than in France and Germany. In 1939, the director of the Post and Telecommunications (PTT) approached the director of the Amsterdam Social Academy concerning the development of a role for social work in that organization. Due to the events of World War II, no action was taken until the war ended.

At the PTT, a centrally administered department of social welfare was established in 1946. By 1950, there were twenty-one social workers. Today, the PTT has 103 social workers serving a workforce of 105,000. Similar to industrial social work in other European countries, the initial focus of the department was providing material assistance for workers who had lost their homes and possessions during World War II. As the need for material assistance decreased, attention at the PTT was shifted to addressing personal and family problems in a fashion similar to French industrial social work. This approach was taken because it was believed that assisting workers with these problems would contribute to improved work performance and "favorably influence" workers' attitudes.

Over time the focus of social work intervention at the PTT and other Dutch companies shifted to yet a third stage that placed a greater emphasis on work-related problems. In the Netherlands, industrial social work during the 1950s came to be viewed as having both internal and external responsibilities, with the internal function taking greater precedence. External work is characterized by its emphasis on housing, family, and financial problems. Internal activities include assisting individuals or groups of employees with psychosocial problems, working with vulnerable populations in the workplace, consulting with management, influencing personnel policies, and counseling employees affected by reorganizations. Management had supported the shift to an internal focus because this emphasis is viewed as having greater value to the organization and is seen as less paternalistic. These internal activities, which characterize much of the Dutch ISW model, have placed Dutch social workers in new practice roles and arenas.

Like their social work colleagues in France, Dutch workers are involved in addressing the major social impacts arising from technological innovation, increased competition, privatization of industry, and provisions for aging workers. Social workers also deal with issues such as the adaptation of guest workers and immigrants to Dutch culture and work organizations. Alcoholism, women's issues, and work and family life conflicts are matters of increasing concern, but not to the same level as in the United States. In addition, current economic problems in the Netherlands are increasing the need for financial and career-counseling assistance from industrial social workers.

The external functions remain important areas of concern due to severe housing shortages in some cities, inflation, and economic problems within the country. Some districts in the PTT and other work organizations have social service staff whose sole function is to address these external problems.

The development and integration of industrial social work in the Netherlands has occurred in an advanced capitalist welfare state. There is far greater government involvement in legislating business practice, as well as considerable government ownership of service and manufacturing enterprises. This has led the government ministries, and a few companies like the PTT, into a leadership position regarding the development of industrial social work in the Netherlands. Both of the enterprises examined in this study, the PTT, which is wholly operated by the Department of Interior, and Hogovens Steel Manufacturing, a partially government-owned corporation, are dealing with major thrusts toward privatization and increased marketplace competition, conditions well known to American counterparts. These economic and strategic changes affect industrial social work practice in the Netherlands, as they do in the United States, thereby forcing a reexamination and response to the social, organizational, and technological impacts that result.

For American social workers the most interesting aspects of ISW practice in the Netherlands are, perhaps, its evolutionary development, it high degree of integration into the work organization, and its legitimate position of influence in addressing macro-level organizational issues. Its involvement with the workers' council provides a concrete example.

Government legislation in the mid 1920s establishing workers' councils in all work organizations employing more than ten people has facilitated the development of an atmosphere in the workplace that enables industrial social workers to both support workers' rights and advocate for workers with far greater ease. Recent legislation has increased the supervisory role of workers' councils, and at the PTT, for example, the workers' councils are now required to review the annual objectives of the Industrial Social Work Branch. Although not a participant in the workers council, the social worker's ability to act as an intraorganizational team member is enhanced through this review process, through participation on social teams, and by the consultative function.

The integration of ISW in the Netherlands and particularly at the PTT, which serves as a national model, is evident in both the formal and informal dimensions of the organizational culture. Within the formal context, five elements identified are decentralized hiring and deployment of industrial social workers in all districts and departments; a social-marketing focus fostered by the central branch; district level development of social teams with the initiative to reorganize these teams to address individual and policy issues more effectively; and management support for the shifting of ISW practice from individual problem solving to organizational consulting.

Other elements contributing to integration have been noted in the informal culture. They include role flexibility that permits the social workers to function within the hierarchical structure with considerable independence (40 percent to 60 percent of social workers' time is spent in informal contacts with workers and managers); attention to cultural aspects in which all organizational subcultures are viewed as very important to effective organizational management; and collaboration with other social experts in the enterprise, which is encouraged at the central and departmental levels.

The progressive movement of ISW to this advanced stage of functioning has also been enhanced by societal and organizational influences outside of social work. These include the legislation establishing worker councils; the nationalized structure of labor unions, whose collective actions depersonalize labor disagreements on the local level; societal acceptance of the advanced welfare state model; greater governmental involvement in business regulation; and most importantly, a progressive approach to human resources management in many enterprises based on the belief in a common interest and the mutual loyalty of management and workers.

Within large enterprises in the Netherlands, ISW has achieved substantial inter- and intraorganizational integration. Its goals are supported by government legislation and societal values regarding work. But, like the United States, Dutch industrial social workers are facing difficult issues arising from the introduction of new technology, fiscal constraints, and the organizational and economic effects of increased competition.

COMPARISON OF EUROPEAN AND AMERICAN PRACTICE

European industrial and American occupational social work not only have different practice bases but developed out of distinct traditions. For the European countries earlier development of social welfare legislation and the economic and social devastation of World War II gave rise to industrial social work. In America, alcohol and drug problems provided a focus and laid the groundwork for occupational social work. Nevertheless, a number of developmental stages have occurred in both European and American practice that indicate a common evolutionary progression. Not too dissimilar from Ozawa's (1980) hypothesized stages, these developments move practice from a micro to a macro level and from a peripheral to an integrated component of the organization.

Although it is difficult to neatly categorize similarities and differences within a tight framework, the cursory examination of European ISW does allow some comparisons with practice in America, particularly with focus on the issue of integration.

Organizational Integration

One of the more significant yet least appreciated dimensions of OSW is the degree of integration of the program within the corporate or union structure. Integration can best be defined as the linking of the OSW function with the needs, goals, and values of the work organization. The process of development involves an increasing degree of integration between the social work function and the organization's needs.

The range of ISW programs analyzed in the European settings highlighted this dimension by the marked contrast between ISW practice in the four countries. There seems to be a strong relationship between program impact and effectiveness and the degree of integration of the social work program into the organization. Those programs that had become integrated were better known, more utilized, and involved with organizational change to a much more significant degree than those programs that were on the periphery of the organization.

This principle of integration has yet to be tested empirically, and no clearly conceived strategies and planning stages have been developed for achieving integration. Nevertheless, several behavioral outcomes can be observed for those programs which seem to be integrated.

Knowledge and understanding of the program was universal. Obviously for a program to be successful it has to be known and understood. In Holland, for example, employees and managers knew there were industrial social workers in their organization and understood their role and function in great detail. A district manager of a large service organization there expounded at length about where he thought social workers could be more effective in the area of organizational change. This discussion revealed an intimate understanding of ISW practice and its potential to the organization. In contrast, the social worker visited in a large multinational company in France was found in a small office far removed from the corporate staff headquarters. Her interaction with anyone but clients seeking individual assistance was quite limited.

The program was utilized by the company for more than individual problems. The involvement with macro problems seems to be a reliable measure of acceptance and integration. The complexity and political sensitivity of larger corporate problems are not lightly entrusted to outside or fringe members of an organization. In Germany, for example, the director of social work of a large electronics company was entrusted with the development of a corporate-wide alcoholism policy and program in a country and culture where the problem of alcoholism in industry has not been addressed and where little precedent exists.

The agenda of the industrial social worker is proactive and organization wide. A final indication of this level of integration appears in the program goals and objectives. In the countries and companies where integration seemed high, the social workers had a full menu of projects, programs, and issues extending well beyond traditional social work activities and involving considerable integration with the company and its problems. Consequently, these social workers were addressing issues of technological innovation and participating in organizational and intraorganizational consulting and problem solving as well as performing the traditional counseling roles. This contrasted with less integrated programs wherein the primary function of the social worker was to minister to the counseling needs of individuals or to run programs such as recreational summer camps for employees.

Ozawa's (1980) stages of development can be utilized to contrast the degree of integration between the two continents. For example, Ozawa's "Stage II" encompasses a more comprehensive program that integrates a variety of services. In Holland this has been the designation of external and internal functions, whereas in the United States the development of the broad brush EAP marked the second stage. "Stage III," according to Ozawa, involves organizational intervention requiring macro-systems approaches. In Holland, and to a degree in France and Germany, this is evidenced by the development of social teams, influence in personnel policies, and review of the social work agenda by the workers' councils. Occupational social work in the United States is just beginning to address integrating organizational approaches, primarily through informal systems. The fourth stage involves a community organization approach that promotes industrial democracy. Occupational social work in the United States has not realized the degree of fourth stage activity that has been observed in Europe, particularly in Holland. This is in part due to a more democratic workplace climate and more successful integration of ISW in Europe. The trend in European ISW is towards a more macro practice that reflects an integrated role for social work in human resource policy development. The apparent difference was the relative importance of the human resource issues being addressed to the maintenance and success of the organization. Partially responsible for this was the legal mandate for the role of ISW in France and the more historically and culturally bound practice in Germany.

The lack of program designation (such as EAP) serves to allow industrial social workers to view their actions more ecologically, relating micro issues to macro policy concerns more readily. The ability to solve problems in this manner is closely related to the capacity to gain influence within the organization. The ways in which ISW has gained organizational influence in Europe vary from effective informal relations in the Netherlands and France to more formal organizational influence in Germany. Legislation mandating functions of industrial social workers in France also act to solidify social work positions, but may limit their flexibility as well.

The cause of a program's degree of integration into the organization is not easily determined, but several factors that contribute to the integration are worth noting.

1. *Integration is a developmental process.* Programs are generally initiated through a single mandate or function. As occupational social workers move into the mainstream of the organization, what they do, who they are, and how their knowledge and skills can contribute to the organization become better known. Consequently the maturing process of occupational social work is a broadening process by which the needs of the organization and the expertise of the social workers and their functions become better known and utilized.

2. *The process of integration has to be purposeful.* If a social worker is hired by an organization to counsel employees on personal problems, there is little to prevent that role from changing. If integration into the mainstream is to occur, a purposeful strategy and plan need to be adopted. This proactive position conceptualizes the client to be the organization, thus its needs to exist on macro and micro levels, with the social worker playing the critical role of identifying, analyzing, and working with the organization to solve its problems. Unless this broad conceptualization of the client system is held and a purposeful strategy is developed, the social worker will tend to relate to a narrow (although important) function and risk being tangential to the organization.

3. *The process of becoming integrated is essentially political.* Whereas occupational social work is generally discussed within a progressional, functional, or technical framework, in order for it to become meaningfully integrated into the organization it must assume a political role. This role is necessitated by the very nature and functions of organizational behavior. All organizational players compete for scarce resources, vie for influence and power, and seek to secure their positions and value to the organization. If social workers desire to move toward the core of the organization and become valued and integrated throughout the organization, they have to master these dynamics. Acceptance and, therefore, integration come through fighting "turf battles," surviving power struggles, forming organizational alliances and gaining status. Real political savvy is needed to plot a strategy, build alliances, and gain the credibility needed to achieve the goal of integration.

Integration also manifests itself within social work education, which differed considerably among the European countries. In Switzerland, where ISW is least developed, social work education serves as a training ground for people entering personnel occupations. In the Netherlands several social work academies have instituted four-year programs designed specifically for ISW training. France, in addition to its designated ISW program, offers an advanced degree in ISW. In Germany ISW has not become a full specialization but is covered in the curriculum of some social work fachhochschules.

In the final analysis, integration is a sign of a matured and effective occupational social work program. The historical development of European ISW confirms the potential that integration can achieve. It also illustrates the limitations that exist for those programs that have remained in a more narrowly functional role that is less central to the operation and life of the organization.

LESSONS FOR AMERICAN OSW: THE DANGER OF EAP FORECLOSURE

The analysis of ISW practice in Europe lends itself to the design of an evolutionary developmental model and suggests this as a useful method to critically observe OSW practice within the cultural context of the United States. The commonalities of both micro and macro issues in American and European occupational social work are not surprising. The significance of the cultural context of practice and the differing methods of occupational social work education are, however, important to note. In the United States, OSW is now rapidly maturing to the point where it will be moving from the fluid state characterizing the early stages of development to one of institutionalization, tighter professional standards, and more rigid program boundaries. It is all the more important during this period to reflect on the European experience, particularly within this developmental perspective, and draw from relevant and appropriate principles to guide the maturing process of OSW.

European ISW has had the advantage (or disadvantage, depending on one's perspective) of not having a psychiatric practice model. Consequently their practice is free from the treatment environment and treatment industry that shape most American OSW. This allows a practice that addresses a broader range of employee and employer needs, even though in some countries practice has focused on basic needs of housing, recreation, etc.

For American occupational social workers, the EAP has become the major program vehicle. Although the EAP has made significant contributions particularly in the chemical dependency area, too much concentration on this area may inadvertently limit the scope of a broader, more fully developed approach to OSW. In our culture, which understands an individual orientation toward problems, there is the possibility that the social work function could remain locked into a narrow EAP focus. Individually oriented helping tasks are only one part, and perhaps only one small part, of a broad spectrum of involvement and interventions in the life of an organization and the lives of its people.

The companies and practices observed in Europe can serve as a caution to American practice, particularly with regard to the danger of marrying OSW with the EAP and foreclosing other needs and opportunities within the workplace. The wide range of practice that was observed in European companies provides a glimpse of what occupational social workers can contribute and the diverse roles they can play. Since they have not tied themselves into a particular treatment program, such as an EAP, they are more free to identify emerging human needs and respond appropriately.

The comparison of European and American social work in work organizations provides an opportunity not only to compare common elements of practice, but also to examine present and predicted directions of American OSW in light of a more mature European model. While cultural and social factors cannot be discounted, it is clear that the evolutionary development of discrete stages and programs has occurred and will continue to occur in both settings. It is also apparent that the social work function has the potential of becoming increasingly integrated into the organization through both formal and informal systems. Although this integration has the advantages of realizing more organizational and structural change, as demonstrated in some of the European practices, it raises questions of vision and values for American occupational social workers. Thus a dilemma of broadening program directions and integration versus allowing too narrow a focus, as through EAP foreclosure will create the underlying tension that will need to be addressed by the next generation of occupational social work practice.

CHAPTER TEN
EDUCATING PRACTITIONERS FOR THE WORKPLACE

INTRODUCTION

The training and education of social work practitioners for operating within work organizations raises several basic questions.

Do practitioners need special knowledge and skills?
What specific knowledge and skills do they need?
How do they receive such training?
What should a graduate curriculum contain?
How are experiential-based learning projects structured?
What are the ramifications for schools of social work?

As occupational social work develops as a field, increased specialization, sophisticated program models, and new practice roles will emerge. All of these developments will necessitate an educational process and program to prepare practitioners to operate effectively within the limitations of the workplace and to provide a foundation on which to build professional legitimacy and identification.

Over the past decade, rapid development of EAPs, wellness programs, employee fitness programs, and health promotion and prevention programs has occurred with only minimal development in professional education. Social work has been the only profession that has begun to develop some consistent specialization and educational programs on a national level. That situation, however, is quickly changing; a number of credentialing and certification programs are being proposed and developed, particularly in the EAP and health fitness fields. (ALMACAN, 1985).

In the early stages of industrial social work, practitioners relied primarily on their generic training and specialized their skills through on-the-job training. As the field of practice developed, there emerged a greater awareness of the serious knowledge and skill deficiencies that existed for social workers who were practicing within work environments. In a 1981 survey of practitioners in Washington state, 70 percent reported specific areas of post graduate course work they had taken to supplement their generic master of social work (MSW) training (Vinet and Jones, 1981). The areas included general business principles, service specialization techniques, and analyses of labor and economic issues.

The current challenge for social work education is to keep pace with, and where possible anticipate, the rapidly changing work environment where expanded programs and service components require specialized educational preparation. The traditional OSW educational programs have offered (and must continue to offer) an educational core that introduces students to work, work organizations, and social work roles and functions within this environment. As specialization increases within the occupational arena, and as social workers break new ground, educational programs will have to respond to these developments.

For example, counseling within an EAP will require specialized knowledge and skills particularly in the areas of substance abuse, disciplinary processes, and supervisory roles. Operating within a human resource department will also require specialized knowledge, specifically in the areas of benefits, corporate policies and procedures, and labor–management contracts or agreements. While each of these requires specialized knowledge, all require a basic understanding of work organizations and their roles, functions, and dynamics. Consequently, the context of practice comprises a complex environment that challenges social work education to blend core knowledge with increasing practice specialization.

THE CURRENT STATUS OF EDUCATIONAL ACTIVITIES

A decade ago training for practitioners in the workplace was practically nonexistent. With the exception of a few schools in New York and Boston, schools of social work had not yet discovered this area of practice, and curricula materials had not yet been developed. Since that time the social work schools have been a catalyst for occupational program development and have taken the lead in responding to the dramatic growth of human service opportunities within work organizations. The 1978–79 Council on Social

Work Education, a project funded by the National Association of Social Workers (NASW), reported that 26 out of 82 graduate schools had 117 field placements in 48 industry and union settings (a significant percentage of these were located in just three schools). A 1982 study of graduate schools of social work reported: thirty-one schools have an industrial social work course; seventeen schools have an industrial social work concentration; fifty schools have industrial social work field placements; twenty-two schools have plans to develop industrial social work concentrations in the near future (Gould and Holosko, 1982).

All of this data reflects growth within a relatively short time span. Most graduate programs either currently have courses in industrial social work or are in the process of developing them. Bachelor of Social Work (BSW) programs are increasingly becoming interested or involved in this area, although there is some question concerning the appropriateness of BSW students, who are generally considerably younger, working within work organizations. Much of what has emerged as OSW education has developed through networking, World of Work concentrations or programs, individual focus areas such as EAPs, labor programs, social services to consumers, or other specialized areas. The University of Pittsburg has conceptualized three educational-programming models that recognize the broad range of practice and cut across macro and micro methods.

Although there is a wide diversity of educational programs, a standardized program is increasingly emerging that can best be discussed under the two traditional components of social work education: class-based education, and field education.

Knowledge and Skills—Class-Based Learning

Occupational social work has rapidly expanded from a primarily counseling and rehabilitation role to a practice that reflects numerous roles and involves considerable differences in knowledge and task requirements. Initially created as a vehicle to assist alcoholic workers, OSW now includes practitioners in such diverse areas as developing child care programs, assisting banks in servicing trust accounts, working with dislocated auto workers, and consulting with management personnel to solve organizational crises. These diverse roles, program models, and emerging trends in human services at the workplace raise many questions regarding the education and training of social workers.

What blend of educational and experiential background is most useful to workplace practitioners?

What curriculum design is best suited to preparing practitioners for the workplace?

What specific knowledge areas should be included in a curriculum?

What skills are essential to effective functioning within the workplace?

What education should be delivered at the master's level and what should be left to continuing education programs?

Because this field of practice is so new, few definitive answers exist to these questions at this time. Nevertheless, schools are gradually evolving curricula that attempt to meet the needs of the workplace. These educational needs can generally be categorized into skills and knowledge areas.

Skills The skill base of practitioners in the workplace is conceptually so broad as to preclude any realistic and practical curriculum. Because most practitioners wear multiple hats— clinical, consulting, administrative, evaluative, etc.—the concomitant skills required for each of these roles are too numerous to master. For example, in the Vinet and Jones (1981) study of social services and work, practitioners illustrated their competence by listing their primary use of traditional social work methods according to the following example (pp. 19–20).

CASEWORK

diagnosis, motivational interviewing, assessment
brief therapy
crisis intervention
information and referral
case management

GROUPWORK

task-oriented groups
training seminars in specific areas (e.g., stress management, time management, health promotion, and behavior modification)
training in communication for new supervisors
on-the-job training, orientating new employees, and basic adult education courses for handicapped or non-English-speaking workers

COMMUNITY ORGANIZATION

resource development through community directories for information and referral
building informal and formal support systems and networks within unions and industries
planning and administering programs (e.g., record keeping, budgeting, staffing)
policy development both for specific programs and general organization-wide human resource management
needs assessment and evaluation

The skills required in these three areas are obviously extensive, and it would be unrealistic to expect individual practitioners to acquire such a broad range of skills. Nevertheless, these examples do reflect the reality of practice at this stage. Specializations have not developed into subspecialities or tracks within either OSW practice or education, and most practitioners are operating alone or with one other colleague. The result in too many cases is a broadly based practice that makes unrealistic demands concerning skill acquisition.

A second example of skill requirements is found in a survey of EAP professionals in the Minneapolis–St. Paul area (Birkland, 1983). Respondents were asked to rate twenty skills on a 5-point Likert Scale (5 = most important) according to how important they perceived each of these three levels. The results are shown in Table 10.1.

TABLE 10.1

a)   *Important for EAP staff to possess*

Question: How important do you think it is for an EAP to have staff who possess the following skills or knowledge?

Categories rated most important:	Mean Scores
. Ability to assess chemical dependency	4.8
. Familiarity with several service agencies and health care delivery systems	4.8
. Ability to conduct crisis counseling	4.8
. Knowledge of professional ethics and legal liabilities	4.7

b)   *Important for the Respondent to Personally Improve*

Question: How important is it for you to personally improve the following skill or knowledge area in the future?

Categories rated most important	Mean Scores
. Ability to carry out EAP promotion within the organization	3.6
. Ability to assess mental health or coping skills	3.5
. Personal time management skills	3.5
. Familiarity with social service agencies and health care delivery systems	3.5
. Ability to conduct program evaluation	3.5

c)   *Important for Entry Level EAP Professional to Possess*

Question: How important do you regard the following skill or knowledge for people just entering the EAP field? (Use your position as a frame of reference.)

Categories rated most important:	Mean Scores
. Knowledge of professional ethics and legal liabilities	4.2
. Ability to conduct short-term counseling	4.1
. Ability to conduct crisis counseling	4.1
. Familiarity with social service agencies and health care delivery systems	4.1
. Ability to assess chemical dependency	4.4

These specific skills related to EAPs reflect again the wide range of clinical administration, organizational, and consultative skills utilized despite the inability of one person to acquire them. For occupational social workers engaged in roles other than the EAPs, the skill requirements become even more diffuse.

Knowledge The knowledge component of the curriculum addresses those areas of theory information (descriptive or analytic) or research that enable practitioners to function effectively in the workplace. At present no coherent curriculum design has been developed that has been universally accepted. Instead, a more amorphous curriculum has emerged consisting of independent modules on which there seems to be some general agreement. Below are a number of knowledge areas (not ordered by priority) that any occupational social worker would be expected to know. This is knowledge distinct from general social work education that represents elements of an occupational social work curriculum. It is divided into two sections: knowledge pertinent to work and work organizations and knowledge pertinent to the practice and programs of occupational social work.

ELEMENTS OF THE CURRICULUM RELATED TO WORK AND WORK ORGANIZATIONS

Work and work organizations. For most social workers work and work organizations are unknown and often alien areas and environments. Consequently any curriculum must contain essential information and theories on the nature and function of work; work culture; types of work organizations; the dynamics and boundaries of work environments; and the meaning of work from psychological, sociological, and cultural perspectives.

Economics. Underlying the work dimension economic forces operate that influence work, workers, and work organization. While it is expected that all social workers would have some economic theory in their education, it is especially important for those who have chosen to practice in work organizations to get a solid grounding in micro economics and political economics.

Labor–Management. At the heart of the American capitalist system is a labor–management system that functions in most work organizations. This will differ within each organization, with some having strongly entrenched unions and others having only the most informal vestiges of labor organization. However, the dynamic of the employee–employer relationship is complex and yet crucial to understanding the very nature of work organizations.

Unionization and collective bargaining. Related to the labor–management issue is the formalized institution of unions. Although less than a quarter of the work force currently belongs to a union, unions do represent a major force. Students should have at least a rudimentary understanding of unions—their history, organization, and major roles and functions in the workplace—and of the collective bargaining process.

Organizational theory and analysis. Social workers are generally situated within work organizations under the sponsorship and legitimacy of an existing organizational unit, such as the personnel, human resource, employee relations, or medical department. The location and position of this suborganizational unit and its power, history, function, status, and image within the larger organization affect all activities and programs conducted by the occupational social worker. The organization is essentially the context in which social workers will practice. Understanding its complexity requires knowledge of organizational structure, theory, and function as well as a framework and set of tools for being able to analyze the organization.

Values. No curriculum could be established without a major core on values, ethics, and confidentiality. For most social workers these are central issues as they move into work organizations. On the other hand, these same issues are defined, perceived, and acted on quite differently by different work organizations.

Corporate social responsibility and community relations. These two areas are becoming increasingly important both for corporations and social workers. Companies are becoming more aware of the symbiotic relationship that exists between themselves and the larger communities in which they operate and to which they relate. Social workers are in a position to assist companies in these areas both by reason of their training and by their interests and values. In the curriculum the growing body of literature in these areas should be at least exposed to students.

ELEMENTS OF THE CURRICULUM
RELATED TO OCCUPATIONAL
SOCIAL WORK

Occupational social welfare. This body of knowledge underlies all practice of human service within work settings. Both the historical and conceptual literature, while sparse, provide the student with an understanding of occupational welfare systems that exist within the corporation setting and parallel and supplement the public social welfare system. OSW practice will in most instances be directly related to this system.

Program types and roles. A growing body of information is building related to the human service programs and staff roles within work organizations. In addition to counseling and EAPs, more recently developed programs and roles concerning health promotion, preretirement, affirmative action fitness and social corporate responsibility programs should be described.

Alcohol and drugs. Inclusion of coursework on substance abuse is virtually mandatory in the occupational social work curriculum. This is particularly true for those students who are interested in EAPs. There has been considerable (and largely justified) criticism of social workers who have gone into EAPs without any or adequate substance abuse training.

Program development. The stages of program development have become important knowledge. Unlike social service agencies in which this function is handled by administrators, most social workers in companies or unions will have program development as well as planning and administrative responsibilities. The knowledge and skills involved in designing, marketing, implementing, and evolving programs will be essential for responding to client system needs.

Special employee populations. Social workers in work organizations are increasingly asked to work with special employee populations. These include alcoholics, the disabled, the handicapped, the stressed and preretirees. In addition, the more recent emergence of issues concerning women and minorities comprise legitimate areas of study. Education regarding the general characteristics and needs of these populations should be integrated into the curriculum.

The above are some of the major curriculum components for preparing social workers for the workplace. Obviously they do not constitute a totally comprehensive and integrated curriculum but are merely a collection of knowledge and skill areas that those who have pioneered work-based practice cite as essential background. No two-year program can begin to cover all these areas in depth, but the curriculum should attempt to acquaint the student with each to some degree.

This knowledge can be transmitted through a number of vehicles. Separate and specialized courses will be needed in some situations to adequately cover the material. Some material, however, can be integrated into already existing courses that are part of the general curriculum. A few schools have utilized mini courses, in which material can be covered in an intense one-, two-, or three-day course. Other schools have developed non-credit seminars for those students placed in work settings. These seminars serve to enhance on-the-job learning. The structural vehicles through which this knowledge content is delivered vary from school to school, but this knowledge is necessary to provide the adequate background students need to operate competently, professionally, and effectively to meet the challenges and problems of the workplace.

Field Internship and Curriculum—
Experiential Learning

For most social work students, field placements constitute the major, if not the most important, component of their graduate education. This is particularly true for those students who have chosen to practice in the workplace. The work environment is a relatively unknown surrounding for most social workers, and the practice of social work in these areas still represents a new phenomenon. Consequently the opportunity of experiential-based learning offered by field placement becomes a central part of the educational process.

In most instances the internship takes place within the business industry or union, under the supervision of a trained social worker. The focus of the learning is developed around concrete activities on the micro and/or macro level. The student spends a significant amount of time (usually two or three days a week) in the internship throughout the year. Although the type of internship can differ by role and function, the educational experience has several basic components. Many of these parallel classroom-based learning.

Essential knowledge of the work environment Each student should be expected to understand the particular work environment within which his or her internship takes place. This is no easy task since all work environments are complex and the student is an outsider in a time-limited situation. However, understanding the work environment is imperative. Even though the student may be more concerned with being able to counsel the employee or conduct the need assessment for the EAP, the nature and dynamics of the environment form the essential context that should be incorporated into the student's understanding of work-based practice.

This knowledge is admittedly complex and, given the brief duration of the internship, difficult to assimilate. A series of questions help to indicate the parameters and guide the learning process.

What is the history of the corporation (union)?
How is it organizationally arranged?
What are its goals?
How do the major components relate to one another?
What is the corporate culture?
What issues are presently of primary concern to the organization?
What are the formal arrangements for employees to represent their issues?
How good are labor–management relations?
How do the human service functions relate to the organization?
What is the state of the art in human resources or personnel in this organization?
Does the company have a strategic plan, and if so what are future plans?

This is just a sampling of questions that indicate the knowledge areas useful for social workers to better understand their work environment. How to assimilate this knowledge is the challenge for both the student and the teaching supervisor.

There will exist few written aids, and the formal and informal channels and structures are not easily identified. In order to overcome these natural barriers, structured activities can be built into the internship. Examples of these are: attendance at a series of meetings with department representatives as well as at open employee meetings; regular visits and informal discussions with employees in the cafeteria; tours of company operations. All of these activities are attempts to provide a better understanding of the environment to the student. Each situation is different, and the supervisor has to create the structure and the opportunities while the student tests her or his ability to negotiate the environment to meet his or her own end—a better comprehension of the work organization.

Access to mainstream activities   If internships are going to be developed in work settings, they should be associated with the mainstream activities and not relegated to some incidental project. Interns need to be given sufficient responsibilities to test their skills and abilities. Because most field placements are taking place in settings where social work and human service activities are new, there is often a tendency to become overly concerned with the student status and consequently to design the internship so as not to jeopardize the larger program. This should not be done to the detriment of the student's learning. If tomorrow's practitioners are going to be ready for the challenges of this field, they need to be trained in as close to "battlefield" conditions as is feasible.

How is this translated to the workplace? There are several guidelines. First, interactions with the principal "actors" should be arranged. This doesn't mean the student will hold a meeting with the vice president of human resources during the first week of the internship. Such a meeting might be arranged, however, after the intern has adequate understanding of the company, has been briefed on the issue, and has successfully held meetings with others in the company. Second, the supervisor can make a point to include the intern in a project in which the supervisor is involved. This will allow a certain amount of modeling for the student as well as provide an actual opportunity for the student to participate in a project with the supervisor as a cushion. A final device is to include in the internship the expectation that a product will be delivered. This can take the form of a report, a study, an evaluation, a handbook, a proposal, a training package, or similar projects. This product orientation insures completion of a significant project for which the student has primary responsibility. It also allows a contribution to be made to the workplace for which the student and the program can take credit and on which a critical evaluation of the student's skills can be made. For this reason a presentation to significant people in the organization should be scheduled. In addition to giving the intern valuable experience in presentation and testing written and verbal communication skills, it highlights the important contribution of the student's project to the organization.

These projects are not as easily devised for strictly clinical students, but should be encouraged in all settings. The more responsibility and individual autonomy granted to the intern, the better the learning situation will be, and the more parallel the learning experience will be to the future practitioner's desired role.

Supervision Supervising social work students is a component of the field internship that in most instances determines the overall effectiveness and quality of the educational experience. The major challenges to the supervisor include structuring the learning process, choosing meaningful tasks, fitting students with appropriate tasks according to their personal educational goals and needs, and insuring constant monitoring and feedback.

Integrating this component into the internship is not always as easy as it is in general social work settings. Because there are relatively few social workers who are employed in work organizations, finding available supervision can present a problem. In the early stages faculty sometime served this function. In 1974 one of the authors spent three years supervising interns at five work organizations selected by the school of social work as training sites. Since the organizations had no social workers, he acted as a "circuit judge," spending one half-day at each place to work with the students as well as translating the social work role to others in each organization to insure regular student supervision.

Building adequate supervision is primarily the responsibility of the school. Because of its centrality to the learning process, it deserves careful attention both in selecting the supervisor and in choosing the task and the learning environment. In many instances other non-social workers can be drawn into the educational plan, yielding their social expertise and knowledge. Although social work education sometimes seems parochial and rigid with regard to insisting that MSW trained social workers provide the supervision, it does not exclude the rich talent that exists in all work organizations. The social work supervisor establishes professional standards to guarantee a level of proficiency and growth and in some instances to be used as a "weeding-out" process.

Evaluation and feedback   The final component comprises feedback and evaluation. A mechanism needs to be established and a process agreed on and developed by which evaluative information can be shared with the student. It is important to remember that the students placed in work settings are primarily there for an educational experience. The tendency to use them as another working hand has to be tempered by their need to experience their growth and development within an educational environment. This learning can come about primarily by carefully structured situations that are then processed and evaluated by supervisor and student. A regularly scheduled supervisor–student session will best provide this learning. If such teaching sessions are left only to available time, chances are that weeks will go by while valuable learning opportunities are lost to the pragmatic realities of too many tasks and too little time.

Once again this component should not be relegated exclusively to the social work domain. If the student is interacting with others within the work environment, the supervisor should tap these resources as part of the feedback and evaluation process. In addition mechanisms such as daily logs can be used to assess the student's approach, interactions, analytical skills, and use of self. A set of learning goals mutually agreed on in the early stages of the internship will help structure activities to meet these goals and provide a format for evaluation.

The above components constitute a minimum set of criteria by which internships in the workplace should be evaluated. It is particularly important in this practice arena to examine these components since the allure of the work setting can overshadow educational objective. Clearly a student can learn a tremendous amount by "hanging out," observing, and talking to individuals within a work organization. To maximize learning, however, a more structured internship should be developed. This will insure an educational experience that appropriately challenges the learner while insuring that the basic knowledge and skills necessary for practicing in the work environment are included.

Developing Field Placements

Choosing the site for field placement can depend either on the traditional social work method of locating a qualified social work supervisor or on finding a potential work environment in which social work students can be trained. If the social work supervisor is available, the need for developing the educational experience is minimized, and the particular task(s) is the object of concern. If such a person is not available, however, considerable work is required to insure a good learning experience.

The school of social work will assume primary responsibility for developing the field placement either through its field education department of through a faculty member involved with OSW. Generally some type of contract is negotiated between the school and the work site. This contract specifies in some detail the student assignments, the supervision arrangements, and any financial agreements. The latter two points deserve some further elaboration.

Social work supervision, as discussed earlier, is of paramount importance. However, the absence of such a person in a work organization need not prevent the presence of an internship. Much of the learning can be acquired through non-social workers, whose knowledge, experience, and skills are invaluable to the learning process. Several alternative arrangements exist for social work supervision. In some cases the site will provide financial resources that will allow supervision to be purchased. In other situations social workers from community-based agencies volunteer as a way to get experience in the workplace and to strategically position themselves within a work environment. This role can be invaluable for an agency that is attempting to expand its services to the work world.

Remuneration for students is another point for consideration. Since the majority of work-based placements exist within the private profit-making sector, paid placements or stipends should be the norm. When the contract is negotiated with the corporation, a set stipend should be established as part of the internship. Very little, if anything, is provided for free within work organizations, and many would contend that cultural values would support the adage "you get what you pay for." Considering the amount of time the student will spend in the organization and the services provided, it is not unreasonable to build in a stipend. It is considerably easier to do this before the placement is established than while it is in operation: existing patterns are harder to break. There may be cases in which the company or union will not agree to such an arrangement, and a decision will have to be made whether to keep the placement. There are no absolutes in this matter, and numerous variables will influence the final decision.

The actual process of developing field placements requires assessment, negotiations, and careful contracting between the school and the site. Before meeting with an representatives of the company or union, several factors have to be assessed. Who is the appropriate individual to first approach? Who is the individual(s) who can make the decision regarding the internship? What has been the history of the organization in the development of OSW? Are there specific opportunities for social work students? All of these sample questions indicate the type of information that should be gathered during the assessment phase. This is an important step in the development process because it minimizes unnecessary and time-consuming visits while insuring a workplace. A complex and changing work environment will challenge the profession of social work not just in creating new EAPs but more fundamentally in understanding the range of old and new problems which exist in work organizations. Responses to these problems will require an updated image of social workers as skilled professionals, grounded in knowledge of work organizations and culture and skilled in a variety of interventions.

Concerted action and strategic decisions by the social work profession during the next decade will determine whether OSW becomes just another practice area or whether it develops into a widely recognized profession. On one side of the equation the need for human service or occupational health professionals is increasingly evident. What only a few years ago was a reluctant opening of a few industry's doors to the treatment of alcoholism has now grown into a much broader range of program and interventions from stress management to physical fitness. Much of this expansion can be traced to a redefined concept of human resources combined with a higher valuing of employees and the relationship between employee health, motivation, and morale.

In spite of the opportunity for social work to address a new world of individual and institutional human needs at work, there remains inherent dangers.

Social work is not alone in addressing human needs in the workplace. There are large numbers of non-credentialed EAP practitioners; an Academy of Corporate Health and Fitness Professionals has been established. Many counselors, psychologists, and public health professionals are addressing well-planned, professional first meetings that will favorably impress the organization.

The negotiation phase involves terms of the contract, conditions of the field placement, and specific concerns such as supervision, stipends, and physical space and resources for the student. Often, many of these details are overlooked only to emerge at a later date when negotiating may be more difficult. Other items, such as space, represent a scarce commodity within most organizations and have to be bargained for up front. The symbolism of an item such as space is as important as the necessity of obtaining it in order to operate. Status is important in the negotiating process; the OSW placement cannot afford to be relegated within the organization to a place where client services will be negatively impacted. For example, locating a counseling office in the basement with difficult access gives a message throughout the organization about its lack of value.

Just as negotiating is a critical skill in guaranteeing the integrity of the placement, an awareness of the linkage between the school and the site is also necessary. The relationship between the two exists on many levels, including political and operational. The field placement often limits the relationship and necessitates careful contracting and communication to enhance the linkage. This linkage can also be seen as a vehicle by which the school can increasingly develop the nature and quality of the relationship over time. This perspective allows the school to look for and act on opportunities within the workplace. A school–workplace relationship that starts with an internship in a counseling program can often be developed into a resource for other activities concerning such issues as retirement, disabilities, and health promotion research.

The Nature of Field Assignments and Placements

Much of what occurs within work-based field placements is found in any social work placement. Nevertheless, there are some unique characteristics of work environments that influence the field placement. For one thing, most placements, particularly the macro placements, tend to be more unstructured than structured. Assignments will often lead into uncharted areas, and the visible supports and structures of the community social service agency are not present within the work organization. Consequently such placements may not be a good fit for those students who need a great deal of structure. The unstructured situation demands self-starters, requiring both the type of student who is comfortable without step-by-step direction and the kind of supervisor who can create the structure necessary to achieve program goals.

The nature of the experience is limited by the student's own limits and the supervisor's creativity. Some students have entered into counseling roles and operated no differently than an office-bound therapist. Others, with the assistance of their supervisor, have immersed themselves in the employee population, made efforts to know the work organization and culture, and begun to identify specific needs. For most educational experiences the assignment is the deciding factor. Some examples of student assignments in Boston provide a sample:

A preliminary study of a telephone company's human resource functions that resulted in a council where coordination and communications among units could be realized

The formation and administration of a therapy group of recently divorced male managers

A study of child care needs within a large computer company

A study of health care costs containment

The development and implementation of supervisors' training program

Exploration of preretirement needs and the formulation of proposed policy

Development of a staff of plant managers to advise the allocation of corporate funds to community managers' needs

These examples give an idea of the possibilities that exist for student responsibility and potential learning. The careful selection of learning assignments can be used by the work organization to address areas of need while providing a learning opportunity. Students represent an invaluable resource whose skills, knowledge, and time can be channelled into areas for which program staff do not have the time or to which the student brings a particular interest, enthusiasm, and talent. In any event, both the student and the site benefit from imaginatively conceived and carefully structured assignments.

THE ROLE OF SOCIAL WORK EDUCATION IN OCCUPATIONAL SOCIAL WORK

Any process of curriculum building is as much a political as a rational one. Building specialized content in any area requires the identification of a curriculum that is compatable with the general curriculum, but is sufficiently distinct to provide the content necessary for educating the student in a particular area. Thus, creating a program of specialization in occupational social work requires a careful welding of the specialized content with the general curriculum. It is important to safeguard the completeness of general curriculum since it provides the knowledge base for the professional social worker. Regardless of any specialized training in work and organizations, the most valued aspect to the workplace of a social worker is his or her basic social work training. To weaken this training in order to produce specialists would risk loosing that which work organizations most value—the skilled and knowledgeable social worker who is able to assist them in solving their human problems and create a healthy environment.

The development of a curriculum which prepares social workers for the workplace has just begun to emerge. Interestingly, social work education has been responsible for both the initiation of programs and for the development of this field. At the same time social work faculty remain the field's most severe critics. Despite the genuine value dilemmas discussed in this book, schools of social work are still the center of activities and exert a powerful force in shaping and directing the future of this field.

The roles that schools of social work continute to play in shaping the learning process occur in four primary areas: school-based education; profession-based education; research; and national organization.

School-Based Education

The bulk of this chapter has described and discussed the education and training for social workers who practice in work settings. Schools will continue to develop curriculum and import the resources needed to prepare future practitioners. This task is far from completed. There are no agreed-on prerequisites yet established. As more social workers become immersed in work programs, the schools will need to conduct more studies and research that will act as a catalyst encouraging experienced practitioners to filter and assess their roles and functions, thereby articulating the content and framework for curriculum. The field, such as it is, is too new and idiosyncratic to manifest a well-developed curriculum, and the wisdom and learning of current practitioners can be most useful if tapped for future development.

Within the school environment, basic conflict remains between traditional and occupational social work. The very notion of social workers operating with and for corporations is a source of considerable consternation among many social work professors and practitioners. The perceived value conflicts between this field of practice and the mandates of the profession constitute a major barrier for this field. Many have seen the rapid rise of the field as a "sellout" in hard economic times, other have seen the new field of practice as a poor allocation of resources in meeting society's problems. In any event, the uneasy relationship between traditional and occupational social work remains an obstacle to the comprehensive integration of this specialization into the generic curriculum alongside other specializations.

A final aspect of the school-based education concerns the insulation of the education itself. As social work interfaces and interacts with work organizations, much needs to be learned by social workers from the work organizations. Currently most school curricula rely almost exclusively on social work faculty and visiting social work practitioners. However, to enhance the learning process through a full range of resources, schools will have to overcome this provincialism and bring personnel from work organizations into the process. To accomplish this, schools can enlist as guest lecturers school of management faculty and key operatives in labor and management, and can engage exchange or visiting work personnel to spend a semester or year helping the school strengthen its curriculum and program. This exchange will in part reduce a growing chauvinism among social workers in work organizations that serves only to draw boundaries around a growing profession preventing collaboration necessary to generate a superior education.

Profession-Based Education

As OSW practitioners become more immersed in their roles, the need for continuing education increases. Ninety percent of the respondents in the Vinet and Jones (1981) study expressed the need for more educational seminars in particular areas of business as well as general education forums to stimulate an exchange of ideas. Extending the learning process beyond the MSW training will be necessary if the field is to develop professionally and the practitioners are to maintain their credibility. The range of needs is endless given the dynamic and complex nature of workers and work organizations. The MSW curriculum can only provide a base or core knowledge. Although experience is a great teacher, the developing theory, research, and program models need to be communicated to those practitioners whose busy schedules often isolate them from these developments. While national meetings can aid this process, well-designed courses will be needed to help fulfill this educational objective.

Research

Virtually no research has been conducted or is currently being conducted by social workers in the area of work-based human services. Despite the huge gaps in understanding the role, function, and effectiveness of these programs, little effort has been made to provide answers and begin putting together a respectable body of research data. There are several factors that can explain this deficiency, including the newness of the field; the difficulty of gaining access to work organizations to conduct research; and the poor "track record" of the social work profession in conducting research. Despite these factors, the social work profession must include in its learning process substantial and continuing research and evaluation in order to lay claim to a field of practice and a role in which professional expertise is demonstrated. This will require ongoing research projects based in both the school and work environments and often in partnership.

National Organization

While learning and educational activities occur on a local level, there also exist national issues. As the presence of social workers has continued in work organizations, a number of educational and practice issues have emerged. On one level social workers, by possessing a professional degree, are perceived as a threat by noncredentialed staff members, such as alcoholism counselors within the EAPs.

A second national issue lies within the social work profession itself. As occupational social work becomes mainlined into professional practice the need for leadership and national organization emerges. To date the Council on Social Work Education (CSWE), NASW, and several schools of social work have taken the lead and organized conferences. The first, in 1978, brought together 100 social workers who were practicing in work settings to discuss and pull together their practice experience. A second more specialized conference took place at the Wingspread Conference Center of the Johnson Foundation in Racine, Wisconsin, in which twenty-six practitioners, educators, union, and management representatives reacted to several presentations by renowned social work educators. In 1985, NASW organized a national symposium that more than 1,300 social workers attended.

National organization becomes increasingly important as OSW expands. Social workers and social work educators are in a unique position to assume leadership in developing program models, proposing practice standards, and continuing the expansion of work-based programs. The growing body of knowledge and the traditional social work skills are well-suited to the development and implementation of human service programs at work. As the profession assumes a leading role, it will enable a better trained and educated group of professionals to institutionalize these programs and services.

CHAPTER ELEVEN
OCCUPATIONAL SOCIAL WORK
Future Scenarios

INTRODUCTION

Foretelling the future is at best a risky business. Forecasts are often colored by the hopes and fears of the augurer. More scientific methods like the Delphi method and factor analysis are subject to the aberrations of unexpected events or developments. Therefore, wishing not to predict on the basis of our own prejudices and "giving a note" to the unexpected possibilities of the next couple of decades, we will examine the future of occupational social works (OSW) within the context of three driving forces:

> social work education
> the demands of the workplace
> social work practitioners

As these forces bump and rub against one another— mitigating this, reinforcing and exaggerating that—the future of occupational social work will evolve. We will suggest three plausible scenarios, but first a brief glimpse at these driving forces.

SOCIAL WORK EDUCATION

Historically social work schools constituted the main force in the evolution and development of OSW. While the practice arena has strengthened considerably and the National Association of Social Work (NASW) has taken a more active role in recognizing and promoting OSW, the schools will continue to shape programs, provide leadership, and be on the "cutting edge" of this young field.

Within our social work schools, a major issue will be the continuing tension between a primarily clinical orientation and a more generic approach that incorporates elements of casework, groupwork, and community organization management and planning. More traditional faculties will respond with some ambivalence to student demand for workplace preparation by offering a few courses aimed at treatment in the workplace. Others will approach OSW as a new client, assessing needs, context, and resources to proactively establish curriculum that will give students the best possible preparation for practice in the work setting. Such schools will allocate resources and support faculty members who have decided to lead, to learn, and to provide curriculum for occupational practice that reflects a long-term commitment to the field. Though the tension between clinical practice and generic practice in the work setting is active in both NASW and the Council on Social Work Education (CSWE), both organizations have now legitimized and sanctioned occupational social work practice. This in itself is an important development in the evolution of curriculum development. However, and this is a critical caveat, *time* is an element currently being ignored as a factor in curriculum development. While factions argue over *what* constitutes appropriate curriculum, time marches implacably on. Students come and go, entering the workplace in varying stages of preparation. Schools both at the master of social work(MSW) and bachelor of social work (BSW) level will increasingly offer OSW training, but the levels of competency and comprehensiveness will greatly vary. Nevertheless, the education at all levels will continue to act as the catalyst, the promoter, and the focus for OSW.

THE DEMANDS OF THE WORKPLACE

While the profession argues, defines, and shapes the practice of OSW, work institutions are experiencing their own changes. The future of OSW is inextricably tied to the future of work, which is in great flux and transition and is increasingly interdependent on its environment. The future of work is dependent on the dynamics of a global economy, the demands and changes of the workforce, and the directions and needs of individual companies. Since the energy crisis of the 1970s and the increase in foreign competition, the American work complex has contracted, trembled, changed, and grown in aberrant and often unpredictable ways. Leaders and followers of the American work scene have tried and experienced "excellence," participation, labor–management collaborations, lean–mean management, automation, education, obsolescence, and invention in the span of a decade. Simply coping with this kaleidoscopic turbulence is a life-stretching exercise for all involved, and the one constant is the continuance of this fluid state. The planet is shrinking; the world economy is being altered; the global work force has a myriad of needs and expectations. Neither left nor right politics seem adequate to the complexities of the late 20th century. These macro factors are accompanied by other events: changing demographics that place more women in workplaces; automation with its implications for job redesign and retraining; and the increased responsibility corporations and unions are assuming for health promotion, prevention, and treatment. Both the macro and micro factors are changing the workplace and the work force and ultimately demanding new responses.

SOCIAL WORK PRACTITIONERS

Social work practitioners constitute three subgroups: student practitioners, experienced mainstream practitioners, and practicing occupational social workers. The needs and demands of these three subgroups interacting with the dynamics of social work education and the work environment will form the outline of the future of occupational social work.

The social work student of 1985 is profoundly different from the student of 1965. Post-Viet Nam, post-War on Poverty, even post "flower power," these students have grown up in a different historical context; have had different role models; are more likely to be dissimilar in politics, experience, expectations, and desires; and may well have different aspirations from past generations of social work students. Today's student has grown up, not in the turbulence of war and a fight for racial equality and social justice, but in the turbulence of layoffs, cutbacks, Reagan prosperity, and isolationism. Their world view is affected by this "worldwind" of events.

Practicing, mainstream social workers have watched status and opportunity decline as the issues on the American work scene "heated up" and Reaganomics tried its "fixatives." Government cutbacks and changing notions of "help" have caused many social workers to seek opportunity in other fields, reassess their roles, or continue doggedly in the face of heightened problems and shortened resources.

Occupational social workers, some of whom represent the new social work student and some of whom represent attempts by traditional social work to respond to new new world needs, are divided between those who practice from the outside of the work–worker–workplace complex (contractors and providers) and those who practice from within (employees/members of the work organization). The two paradigms evolved from these two groups are that of the "arms-length," task-oriented practitioner and that of the "roll-up-the-sleeves," process-oriented practitioner. In all likelihood both models are important, but the question remains: What is the future of occupational social work?

At least three potential scenarios exist to answer that question: In an attempt to utilize a strategic planning tool, a best case, midcase, and worst case is suggested (Table 11.1) based on a scanning of environmental factors, projections, and the driving forces discussed above. Each of these scenarios encompasses a complex set of variables and while the ability to predict the future is always limited, they do suggest potential based on present knowledge.

Scenario I: Best Case

It is 1995. Though Reagan has been out of the political arena for some time, his imprint on the land lingers. The privatization of social services has leveled off to a relatively stable public–private partnership that shows signs

TABLE 11.1   Scenario Variables: The Outlook for OSW

	Best	Middle	Worst
Social Work Education	Strong core curriculum on work offered in 30-40% of U.S. social work schools with specialties in policy and practice	Social work schools institutionalize introductory courses on work and make continued attempts to improve clinical curriculum	Ambivalence continues to reign with no commitment either to substantive curriculum or decision to get out of occupational social work and concentrate efforts elsewhere
Work World	Continually sophisticated attention given to human beings and human systems in the context of work	Both humanist and rationalist actions and policies are active	Reactionary response to turbulence of the times is such that human relations abandoned, lean and mean self-reliance prevails
Practitioners	Practitioners feel increasingly free to apply core social work teachings to all manner of human needs, in the heart of the workplace	Both the contracting movement and the employee OSW movement continue to effect the shape of the work complex	Seeking job opportunity more fervently than equal partnership in defining the future of work, practitioners move towards contracting and farther from "work-centered practice"

of lasting into the 21st century. Now, more comfortable in supporting the public–private spectrum, 40 percent of all social work schools in the United States offer a curriculum on OSW that includes core courses on work, worker, and workplace; policy and practice courses in clinical practice; human resources; systems; and organizational work. Faculty members have enriched themselves by spending sabbaticals in the workplace and in schools of management and industrial relations. Workplace experts are frequently found in the halls and classrooms of schools of social work that also still host community organizers, labor organizers, clinicians, and family therapists.

Social work schools are now contributing substantially to the research literature on work and have a credible voice in the policy arena and among postindustrial policy makers. A few schools are contemplating creating a doctorate in OSW and accreditation now includes a review of OSW competencies.

American industry, now experiencing competition from the Pacific Basin and Third World countries, is increasingly aware that employees are both precious assets and highly variable humans. Aware that a cavalier treatment of employees has long-term costs—chasing cheap labor around the world is in itself costly—industry leaders now pay at least as much attention to the "care and feeding" of their employees as they do their factories. Employees, for their part better educated and more independent, articulate their needs with an expectation that they can have a say in how those needs will be met. Less victimized and more autonomous, they participate in setting agendas and priorities and in allotting resources.

Practitioners, less timid, less apologetic, and less disaccordant about serving the workplace as well as the ghetto have "rolled up their sleeves" and "planted both feet" in the work system. Contracting as a means of providing service is on the decline, and social workers, better educated and more aware of the needs of both worker and workplace, have become legitimate change agents and service providers in the macrocosm of work and society.

Scenario II: Worst Case

It is 1995 and we are in the second term of another conservative president. Watching resources and funding continue to dwindle, social work administrators and faculty still cling tenaciously to whatever is left and hopelessly watch others eat into their share of school budgets. Unable to resolve faculty ambivalence regarding occupational social work and unwilling to take the lead by setting curriculum standards, schools have adopted a laiśsez faire attitude toward OSW. A few hit or miss courses exist that are the result of tireless lobbying on the part of a few true believers. While keeping the movement visible, the courses do little to truly prepare students to enter the workplace as practitioners.

The workplace, tired of the rapid pace of change and the chaos of the 1980s, has abandoned the attention to culture and human resources so prevalent in that era and is now in another period of rationalism. Control, separation of work and personal life, self-reliance, and achievement are the new values. Nevertheless, students and seasoned practitioners alike continue to gravitate toward the workplace. Innumerable enterprising provider agencies compete to provide "treatment" to troubled employees. However, with no educational standards, philosophic principles, or "quality control" processes, workers/consumers are now subject to the vagaries of an undisciplined practice and have no guarantee of professional social work service.

Scenario III: Middle Case

Somewhere between cockeyed optimism and hysterical despair, OSW in 1995 will exist. However, the extremes are not to be dismissed quickly as they represent leanings and drifts of spirit or interest. So what's the amalgam of the extremes, what's a third, more likely scenario?

Again it is 1995. Classical social workers have made a fragile truce with occupational social workers. Time and dollars are now allotted to OSW curriculum with less ambivalence, but the emphasis is on clinical OSW practice, which has become the mainstay of practice in most workplaces. Other applications of social work knowledge in the workplace are still considered "fringe" activities—slightly suspect cousins who are corrupting the core values of social work. Some excellent research has been done that contributes to a person-centered understanding of work, yet funds are still limited for the macro perspective.

Slowly American businesses are adapting to the complexities of both a global economy and the multiple needs and expectations of the late twentieth century worker. Having come to appreciate the need for expertise in psychosocial understanding, but wishing to maintain some distance from it, providers' contracts are now a routine budget consideration. Only a handful of unique companies continue to maintain and expand their internal OSW departments; human resource personnel remain the primary referral agents to outside practitioners.

Practitioners, discouraged and frustrated in attempts to "break in" to specific businesses as full-fledged member professionals, increasingly band together to offer consulting services, special contracts, and training activities. These groups have little influence on the workplace policy or practice but do provide important, though limited, intervention.

FUTURE DIRECTIONS

Obviously no one has a special reading on the future of occupational social work. The above scenarios depict alternative outcomes, some more desirable than others. Although external events are of significant influence, the challenge to social work of shaping OSW remains clear. As usual the choice facing the professor and the individual social worker is whether to lead or follow, act or react.

To fully understand the future of OSW, we return to the indicators discussed in chapter one. OSW is a movement within a larger context in which the economy, the privatization of social services, changing demographics, and issues of productivity are all factors influencing the human dimensions of work, workers, and workplaces. Not only can the profession not ignore these realities, but it must become more informed to meet the common human needs of the health promotion and prevention issues. For OSW to continue its growth, it must identify its unique contribution and training in such a way as to secure its niche and legitimize its presence.

OSW has yet to "carve out" its territory. As other groups and professions, such as those mentioned above, enter the workplace, OSW will have to intensify its claim making by defining territory and expertise and proving its effectiveness in operating within the occupational role. While this seems excessively parochial and reflects all of the negative aspects of professionalism, it is of absolute necessity if the profession is to be a credible force in work organizations. The political facts of life dictate such behavior; and social work, which has occasionally recognized its self-interest (i.e., licensing and third-party reimbursement), needs to make organizational efforts not yet evident. The NASW, both nationally and on the local chapter level, will need to become more aggressive to compete with other organized groups.

A final danger is a general "rush to treatment" too often found in social work practice. The ease of establishing EAPs and providing clinical services is only facilitated by social work training, culture, and the mechanisms set up by insurance companies to provide reimbursement for service. If OSW lapses into this format it will abandon the opportunity to recognize and deal with all of the other human problems and issues that are not of a narrowly defined clinical nature. Given the power of insurance mechanisms and the predeliction towards clinical services within the profession, this remains a constant threat to a broadened notion of OSW.

Thus the OSW described in this book faces a new world of great opportunity for working with the problems and potentials of an underserved and largely ignored population—workers. In terms of development, OSW is still very much in its infancy. In comparison to European industrial social work it has many stages of growth ahead. Its future, while not totally predictable, is filled with promise and excitement. All of this is tempered by a number of threats or dangers, not the least of which is the movement of other professions to capitalize on the strengths and progress of OSW. To what extent the profession, through its schools, national organizations, and individual practitioners, conceptualizes and claims this field is the challenge that faces the next decade. For the sake of employees, employers, and work organizations—all of whom daily confront and struggle with the human dimension—we can only hope that the field's potential becomes actualized.

BIBLIOGRAPHY

ADAMS, G., ROMAN, P., GREEN, G., *State-based Occupational Alcoholism Programming: The 1976 Survey*. Tulane Center for Monitoring of Occupational Alcoholism Programming. New Orleans, 1977.

AKABAS, S.H., KURZMAN, P. *Work, Workers and Work Organizations: A View from Social Work*. Englewood Cliffs, N.J.: Prentice-Hall, Inc., 1981.

AKABAS, S., KURZMAN, P., & KILBER, N. *Labor and Industrial Sites for Social Work Practice*. New York: CSWE, 1978.

ALLAN, D.F. *Benefit Wages or Social Obligation*. Ithaca, N.Y.: Cornell University Press, 1968.

ANDERSON, R.E., & CARTER, I.E. *Human Behavior in the Social Environment*. Chicago: Aldine Publishers, 1974.

ASMA, F.E., EGGERT, R.L., & HILKER, R.R. "Long Term Experience With Rehabilitation of Alcohol Employees," *Journal of Occupational Medicine*, 13(12) (1971), pp. 581–585.

ASMA, F., et al. "Twenty Five Years of Rehabilitation of Employees and Drinking Problems," *Journal of Occupational Medicine*, 22(4) (1980), pp. 241–244.

BARRIEK, et al. "Mental Distress as a Problem for Industry," in *Mental Wellness Programs for Employees*, eds. Richard Egdal and D. Walsh. New York: Springer-Verlag, 1980.

BARTELL, T., "The Human Relations Ideology: An Analysis of the Social Origins of a Belief System," *Human Relations*, 8(29) (1976), pp. 737–749.

BEAUCHAMP, D., "Exploring New Ethics of Public Health," *The Journal of Health, Politics, Policy and Law*, 1(1976), pp. 338–354.

———, *Beyond Alcoholism: Alcohol and Public Policy*. Philadelphia: Temple University Press, 1980.

BILIK, S., "Industrial Alcoholism Program Movement in Germany," (unpublished, 1984), 32 pp.

BIRKLAND, E., "Occupational Social Work Practice in Minnesota," (unpublished, 1983).

BLUE, F., "Compensation in Cases of Mentally Impaired Employees," *Benefits Quarterly*, 8(1980), pp. 190–198.

BRANDEIS, S.D., *American Welfare Capitalism 1880-1940*. Chicago: University of Illinois Press, 1976.

BRAYBROOKE, D., & LINDBLOOM, C.E. *A Strategy of Decision: Policy Evaluation as a Social Process*. New York: The Free Press, 1963.

CAHALAN, D., *Problem Drinkers: A National Survey*. San Francisco: Jossey-Bass, 1970.

CASE, J.B., "Integrating EAPS with Health Education Efforts," in *The Human Resources Management Handbook: Principles and Practice of Employee Assistance Programs*, eds. S. Klarreich, J.L. Francek, E.C. Moore. New York: Praeger, 1985.

COX, F.M., "Alternative Conceptions of Community Conceptions: Implications for Community Organization Practice," in *Strategies of Community Organization*, eds. F.M. Cox, J.L. Erlich, J. Rothman, J.E. Tropman. Itasca, IL: F.E. Peacock, 1979.

DEAL, T.E., & KENNEDY, A.A. *Corporate Cultures: The Rite and Rituals of Corporate Life*. Reading, MA.: Addison-Wesley, 1982.

DENTLER, R., & ERICKSON, K. "The Function of Deviance Groups," *Social Problems*, Fall, 1959, pp. 98–107.

EGDAHL, R.H., & WALSH, D. *Mental Wellness Programs for Employees*. New York: Springer-Verlag, 1980.

EMANET, B., & JEVCK, J. *Catalogues and Counters: A History of Sears Roebuck and Co.* Chicago: University of Chicago Press, 1950.

ERFURT, J.C., & FOOTE, A. *Occupational Employee Assistance Programs for Substance Abuse and Mental Health Problems*. University of Michigan Institute of Labor and Industrial Relations. Ann Arbor, MI, 1977.

ERICKSON, E., *The Life Cycle Completed*. New York: Norton, 1982.

ETCHEN, L., & ROMAN, P.M. *Models of Supervisory Training for the Implementation of Employee Alcoholism Programs*. Tulane Center for Monitoring of Occupational Alcoholism Programs. New Orleans, 1977.

FINE, M., AKABAS, S., & BELLINGER, S. "Cultures of Drinking: A Work Site Perspective," *Social Work*, 27(1982), pp. 411–436.

FLEMING, C.W. "Does Social Work Have a Future in Industry?" *Social Work*, 23(May, 1979), pp. 183–185.

FOOTE, A., ERFURT, J.C., STRAUCH, P.A., & GUSSARDO, T.L. *Cost-effectiveness of Occupational Employee Assistance Programs: Test of an Evaluation Method*. Institute of Labor and Industrial Relations, University of Michigan-Wayne State University. Ann Arbor, MI, 1978.

FOSSEN, P. "Occupational Programming for Alcoholism: The Consortium," *Labor Management Alcoholism Journal*, 11(6) (1975), pp. 1–13.

FRANKEL, G. "Alcoholism Treatment in the Patient Hospital or Day Program," *Alcoholism, Health and Research World*, pp. 32–36.

FROST, R. *The Death of the Hired Man. A Tribute to the Source: Poems by Robert Frost*. New York: Holt, Rinehart and Winston, 1979.

GITLOW, S.E., & PEYSER, H.S. *Alcoholism: A Practical Treatment Guide*. New York: Grune and Stratton, 1980.

GOOGINS, B. "Employee Assistance Programs," *Social Work*, 20(6) (1975), pp. 464–476.

——, "The Use and Implementation of Occupational Alcoholism Programs by Supervisors: An Analysis of Barriers," Ph.D. Dissertation, Florence Heller Graduate School of Advanced Studies in Social Welfare, Brandeis University, 1978.

——, "Avoidance of the Alcoholic Client," *Social Work*, 29(2) (1984), pp. 161–166.

GOOGINS, B., & COLLIER, A. "Day Treatment in the Work Place," *EAP Digest* (May/June, 1984), pp. 19–26.

GOOGINS, B., & KURTZ, N.R. "Factors Inhibiting Supervisory Referrals to Occupational Alcoholism Intervention Programs," *Journal of Studies on Alcohol*, 40(11) (1980), pp. 1196–1205.

——, "Discriminating Participating and Non-participating Supervisors in Occupational Alcoholism Programs," *Journal of Drug Issues*, 11(2) (1981), pp. 199–216.

——, "The Role of Supervisors in Occupational Alcoholism Intervention," *EAP Digest*, 1(3) (1981), pp. 14–19.

GOULD, G.M., & HOLOSKO, M.J. "Marketing and Selling Industrial Social Work Graduate Field Placements," (unpublished, 1982).

HASENFIELD, Y. "Program Development," in *Strategies of Community Organization*, eds. F.M. Cox, J.L. Erlich, J.L. Rothman, and J.E. Torpman. Itasca, IL: F.E. Peacock, 1979.

HAYWARD, B.J., SCHLENGER, E.W., & HALLEN, J.B. *Occupational Programming: A Review of the Literature*. Raleigh, N.C.: The Human Ecology Institute, 1975.

HENDERSON, R.M., & BACON, S.D. "Problem Drinking: The Yale Plan for Business and Industry," *Quarterly Journal of Studies on Alcohol*, 14(2) (1953), pp. 247–262.

HEYMAN, M.M. "Referral to Alcoholism Programs in Industry: Coercion, Confrontation and Choice," *Journal of Studies of Alcohol*, 37(7) (1976), pp. 900–907.

JOHNSON, H.R., & TROPMAN, J.E. "The Settings of Community Organization Practice," in *Strategies of Community Organization*, eds. F.M. Cox, J.L. Erlich, J. Rothman, J.E. Tropman. Itasca, IL: F.E. Peacock, 1979.

KANTER, R.M. *Men and Women of the Corporation*. New York: Basic Books, 1977.

———, *Work and Family in the United States: A Critical Review and Agenda for Research Policy*. New York: Russell Sage Foundation, 1977.

KAPLAN, D. "Introduction to the Disorders of Change," *Social Work*, 27(5) (September, 1982), pp. 404–410.

KIEFHABER, A., & GOLDBECK, W.B. "Industry's Response: A Survey of Employee Assistance Programs," in *Mental Wellness Programs for Employees*, eds. R. Egdahl and D.C. Walsh. New York: Springer-Verlag, 1980.

KURTZ, N.R., *Identification and Referral in Work Organizations: The Role of Supervisors in Occupational Programs*. Bethesda, MD: U.S. Development of Health and Human Services, 1981.

KURTZ, N.R., & GOOGINS, B. "Managing the Alcoholic Employee: Toward a Model for Supervisory Interventions," *Industrial Management*, 21(3) (1979), pp. 15–21.

KURTZ, N.R., GOOGINS, B. & WILLIAMS, C. "Clients' Views of an Alcoholism Program," *Labor Management Alcoholism Journal*, 10(3) (1980), pp. 107–113.

———, "Supervisors' Views of an Occupational Alcoholism Program," *Alcohol Health and Research Work*, 4(1980), pp. 44–49.

KURZMAN, P., & AKABAS, S.H. "Industrial Social Work as an Arena for Practice," *Social Work*, Jan., 1981, pp. 52–60.

LEE, P. "The Future of Professional Social Work," in *Social Work as Cause and Function*, New York: NASW, 1937.

LIEBOW, E. *Tally's Corner: A Study of Negro Streetcorner Men*. Boston: Little, Brown and Company, 1967.

MANELLO, T.A., PADDOCK, H., WAIH, W. & SEAMAN, F.J. *Problem Drinking Among Railroad Workers: Extent, Impact and Solutions*. Washington, DC: University Research Corporation, 1979.

MAXWELL, M.A. "A Study of Absenteeism, Accidents and Sickness Payments in Problem Drinkers in One Industry," *Quarterly Journal of Studies on Alcohol*, 20(1959), pp. 203–312.

———, "Early Identification of Problem Drinkers in Industry," *Quarterly Journal of Studies on Alcohol*, 21(4) (1960), pp. 655–687.

MCCRADY, B.S., PAOLINO, T.J., LONGABAUGH, R.L. & ROSSI, J. "Effects on Treatment Outcome of Joint Admission and Spouse Involvement in Treatment of Hospitalized Alcoholics," *Addictive Behaviors*, 4(1979), pp. 155–165.

MILLER, F., & COGHILL, J. "Sex and the Personnel Manager," *Industrial and Labor Relations Review*, 18(Oct., 1964), pp. 18–28.

NIAAA, *Alcohol and Health, 2nd Report to the Congress*. Washington, DC: U.S. Government Printing Office, 1974.

NIAAA, *Alcohol and Health, 4th Report to the Congress*, Washington, DC: U.S. Government Printing Office, 1980.

NORRIS, J.L. "Alcoholism in Industry," *Quarterly Journal of Studies on Alcohol*, 11(4)(1950).

———, *Alcoholism in Industry: Archives of Environmental Health*, 17(3) (1968), pp. 436–445.

O'TOOLE, J., ed. *Work and the Quality of Life*. Cambridge: MIT Press, 1974.

———, *Making America Work*. New York: Continuum Press, 1981.

OZAWA, M., "Development of Social Services in Industry: Why and How?" *Social Work*, 25(6) (1980), pp. 464–470.

PELL, S., D'ALANZO, C.A. "Sickness Absenteeism of Alcoholics," *Journal of Occupational Medicine*, 12(6) (1970), pp. 198–210.

PERLIS, L. "Unionism and Alcoholism: The Issues," in *Alcoholism and its Treatment in Industry*, ed. C.J. Schramm. Baltimore: Johns Hopkins University Press, 1977.

PEROW, C. *Complex Organizations*. Glenview, IL: Scott Foresman, 1972.

PRESNALL, L.F. "Folklore and Facts about Employees with Alcoholism," *Journal of Occupational Medicine*, 9(4) (1967), pp. 187–192.

PRESNALL, L.V. "Basic Principles of Behavioral Problems Control." (Paper presented at the Seminar on Alcohol and Drug Dependencies in Business and Industry, Workman's Compensation Board of British Columbia, Vancouver, B.C., 1972.)

Report of Special Task Force to the Secretary of Health, Education and Welfare, *Work in America*, MIT Press, 1973.

ROGER, D.T. *The Work Ethic in Industrial America*. Chicago: University of Chicago Press, 1978.

ROMAN, P.M. "From Employee Alcoholism to Employee Assistance," *Journal of Studies on Alcohol*, 42(3) (1981), pp. 244–272.

———, "Secondary Prevention of Alcoholism: Problems and Prospects in Occupational Programming," *Journal of Drug Issues*, 11(1977), pp. 327–343.

ROMAN, P.M., & BLUM, T. "Core Technology," *The ALMACAN*, 15(3) (1985), pp. 8, 9, 16, 18, 19.

ROMAN, P.M., & TRICE, H. "Alcohol Abuse and Work Organizations," in *The Biology of Alcoholism*, eds. B. Kissin, and H. Begleiter, 4. New York: Plenum Press, 1976.

ROMANUSHYN, J.M., *Social Welfare: Charity to Justice*. New York: Random House, 1971.

SCHENGER, W.E., HALLAN, J.B., & HAYWARD, B.J. *Characteristics of Selected Occupational Programs*. Raleigh, NC: The Human Ecology Institute, 1976.

SHAIN, M., & BERNARD, B. "Towards Coordination of Employee Health Promotion and Assistance Programs," in *The Human Resources Management Handbook: Principles and Practice of Employee Assistance Programs*, eds. S. Klarreich, J. Francek, D.C. Moore. New York: Praeger Publishers, 1985.

SHAIN, M., & GROENEVELD, J. *Employee-assistance Programs: Philosophy, Theory, and Practice*. Lexington, MA: D.C. Heath, 1980.

SHEEHY, G. *Passages: Predictable Crises of Adult Life*. New York: Bantam Books, 1977.

SINCLAIR, A. *Prohibition: The Era of Excess*. Boston: Little, Brown and Company, 1962.

SKIDMORE, R., BALSAM, D., & JONES, O. "Social Work Practice in Industry," *Social Work*, 19, May, 1974, pp. 280–286.

SLOAN, A. *Personnel: Managing Human Resources*. Englewood Cliffs, NJ: Prentice-Hall, 1983.

STRAUS, R., & BACON, S.D. "Alcoholism and Social Stability: A Study of Occupational Integration in 2,023 Male Clinic Patients," *Quarterly Journal of Studies on Alcohol*, 1951, Vol. 11, pp. 231–260.

TAYLOR, F. *Principles of Scientific Management*. New York: Harper and Row, 1911.

The President's Commission on Mental Health, *Report to the President*, Vol. 1, 2, 3. Washington, DC: U.S. Government Printing Office, 1978.

TITMUSS, R.M. *Commitment to Welfare*. New York: Pantheon Books, 1968.

TRICE, H., "Identifying the Problem Drinker on the Job," *Personnel*, 34(1957), pp. 527–533.

———, *Alcoholism in Industry: Modern Procedures*. New York: Christopher D. Smithers Foundation, 1962.

———, "The Job Behavior of Problem Drinkers," in *Society, Culture, and Drinking Patterns*, eds. D.J. Pitman, and C.R. Snyder. Carbondale, IL: Southern Illinois University Press, 1962.

———, "Applied Research Studies: Job-based Alcoholism and Employee Assistance Programs," *Alcohol Health and Research World*, Spring, 1980, pp. 4–16.

TRICE, H., & BELASCO, J.Z. "The Alcoholic and his Steward: Union Problem," *Journal of Occupational Medicine*, 4(3) (1966), pp. 481–487.

TRICE, H., & BEYER, J. *Work Related Outcomes of the Constructive-confrontation Strategy in a Job-based Alcoholism Program*, (unpublished manuscript, 1983)

———, "Employee Assistance Programs: Blending Performance Oriented and Humanitarian Ideologies to Assist Emotionally Disturbed Employees," *Research in Community and Mental Health*, 4(1984), pp. 245–297.

TRICE, H., BEYER, J., AND COPPESS, C. "Rites and Ceremonials on Organizational Cultures." *Perspectives on Organization Sociology: Theory and Research*, forthcoming, JAI Press.

TRICE, H., & ROMAN, P. *Spirits and Demons at Work*. Ithaca, NY: New York State School of Industrial and Labor Relations, Cornell University, 1972.

TRICE, H., & SCHONBRUNN, M. "A History of Job-based Alcoholism Programs: 1900-1955," *Journal of Drug Issues*, 11(2) (1981), pp. 171–198.

TUCKER, J. "A Worker-oriented Alcoholism Troubled Employee Program: A Union Approach," *Industrial Gerontology*, 11(4) (1974), pp. 20–24.

U.S. Bureau of Labor Statistics, *Welfare Work for Employees In Industrial Establishments in the United States*, Bulletin No. 250, 1919.

VINET, M., & JONES, C. *Social Service Work: Initiation of Social Workers into Labor and Industry Settings: Procedures and Professional Identification Issues*. Silver Springs, MD: NASW, 1981.

WALSH, D.C. "Employee Assistance Programs," *Health and Society*, 60(3) (Summer, 1982), pp. 492–517.

WALSH, D.C., & EGDAHL, R.H. *Mental Wellness Programs for Employees*. New York: Springer-Verlag, 1980.

WEINBURG, A. "Managing Medical Costs Through EAPs," *Pension World*, December, 1983, pp. 49–53.

WEINTER, H.J., AKABAS, S.H., SOMMER, J.H., & KREMEN, E. *The World of Work and Social Policy*. New York: Columbia University School of Social Work, 1971.

WRICH, J.J *The Employee Assistance Program*. Center City, MN: Hazelden, 1974.

YANKELOVICH, D. *New Rules: Searching for Self-fulfillment in a World Turned Upside Down*. New York: Random House, 1981.

——, "The Meaning of Work," in *The Worker and the Job*, ed. J.M. Rosow. Englewood Cliffs, NJ: Prentice-Hall, 1974.

——, "The New Psychological Contracts at Work," *Psychology Today*, May, 1978, pp. 46–50.

INDEX

A

Academy of the Lynx-eyed
  and Galileo, 48
Adam, Edgar
  and welfare work, 21
Addams, Jane, 21, 64
Addictions Research Foundation
  survey of, 115–116
Affirmative Action officers
  functions of, 88–90
Affirmative Action specialist, 88–90
Affirmative Action
  and social and community change, 7–8
  corporate, 89
  social work roles, 7–8
Agencies
  specialized alcoholism, 153–54
Akabas, 15
Alcoholics Anonymous, 134, 151, 152, 153,
  154
  and OAP's, 148
  tenet of, 140
  Occupational Alcoholism Programs, 135
Alcoholic Employee
  and confrontation, 145–147
  management and treatment of, 142–149

Alcoholic Treatment
  barriers to, 149–54
Alcoholism
  and avoidance, 154
  and confrontation, 152
  and cultural attitudes, 140–41
  and denial, 144, 152–53
  and fear of confrontation, 152
  and intervention, 138
  and job performance, 139, 143
  and operational definition, 140
  and social work, 154
  and the disease model, 152
  and welfare system, 19
  and worker's compensation, 105
  as an illness, 151, 152
  confrontation, 147, 149
  difficulties in treatment, 145
  etiology of, 142
  identification of, 138–139, 142
  ideology of, 111–12
  illness versus symptom, 151–52
  impact on employee performance, 138
  in the workplace, 133–145
  linkage to the workplace, 142
  myths surrounding, 150–51
  referral stage, 148

Alcoholism (*cont.*)
rehabilitation process, 147
successful treatment of, 152
symptom versus cause, 151–52
treatment and reintegration, 148–49
Alcohol
problem of, 132
Allan, Donna
Benefits Wages or Social Obligation, 28
Allis Chalmers
and alcohol programs, 134
ALMACA, 24, 41–42, 137
Al-Anon, 153
American Medical Association
on alcoholism, 151
American welfare capitalism
historical perspective, 18–19
Anthropology
and social work, 56
and work, 55–56
Asma, et al.
on study of Illinois Telephone Co., 107
on industrial accidents and alcoholism, 105
Assessing program need
flaws in approach, 163
Automation
and work, 59
Avoidance
and alcoholism, 154

B

Barriers to treatment
and denial, 152–53
and fear of confrontation, 152
and therapeutic nihilism, 151
and myths, 150–51
and specialized alcoholism agencies, 153
Barrie, et al.
on employer responsibility, 104
Bartell
on human relations movement, 22–23
Beauchamp
on myths about alcoholism, 151
Benefits and services
supplemental, 33–34
Benefits
childcare, 34
educational, 34
employee services, 34
expanded health,
fringe, 27–28
importance of, 29
profit sharing, 34
sabbaticals, 34
supplemental unemployment income, 34

of Occupational Welfare System, 33
Beyer (Germany)
ISW program at, 172–173
Bilick
on Industrial Social Work in Germany, 172
Birkland, 190
Blue
on worker's compensation, 105
Boston University
Center for Industry and Health Care, 114
Brandeis, 20, 21
on American welfarae capitalism, 24
on employee housing, 25
on industrial responsibility, 26
Brawn, 22
Braybrooke and Lundbloom
on program development, 156

C

Cahalan
on national survey findings, 106
Calvin, 45, 47–48
Carter and Anderson
on culture, 71
Case
on EAPs, 114
Changes
demographic, 15
Change
and social work, 59
within thet work world, 15
Chaplin, Charlie
and *Modern Times*, 52
Citroen Automobile Co. (France)
ISW program at, 174–76
Civilization and its Discontetnts
Sigmund Freud, 51
Civil rights, 15
Client system
and EAPs, 157, 158
concept of, 156–157
Communities
as stakeholders, 81
Community relations
with corporations, 8–9
Community
and workplace, 39–40
Concept
of client system, 156–157
Conference
Mental Wellness Programs for Employees, 114
Social Work Practice in Labor and Industrial Settings, 6
Confrontation method